Contributions to Management Science

More information about this series at http://www.springer.com/series/1505

Inga Minelgaite • Svala Guðmundsdóttir •
Árelía E. Guðmundsdóttir • Olga Stangej

Demystifying Leadership in Iceland

An Inquiry into Cultural, Societal, and Entrepreneurial Uniqueness

 Springer

Inga Minelgaite
University of Iceland
Reykjavik, Iceland

Svala Guðmundsdóttir
University of Iceland
Reykjavik, Iceland

Árelía E. Guðmundsdóttir
University of Iceland
Reykjavik, Iceland

Olga Stangej
Institute of Quality Management and Business
Administration (IQB-FHS)
FHS St. Gallen, University of Applied Sciences
St. Gallen, Switzerland

ISSN 1431-1941   ISSN 2197-716X   (electronic)
Contributions to Management Science
ISBN 978-3-319-96043-2   ISBN 978-3-319-96044-9   (eBook)
https://doi.org/10.1007/978-3-319-96044-9

Library of Congress Control Number: 2018950440

This Springer imprint is published by the registered company Springer Nature Switzerland AG
The registered company address is: Gewerbestrasse 11, 6330 Cham, Switzerland

Acknowledgment

This book is the brainchild of four women, leadership researchers and practitioners, who came together to investigate and reflect on Icelandic leadership, attempting to demystify, unveil, and introduce leadership in Iceland to the reader through, first and foremost, cultural and societal uniqueness. It would not exist without the invaluable contribution of a number of incredible personalities who supported us during this process: research participants, reviewers, colleagues, family members and friends, publishers, and inspirers.

Our sincerest *Thank you* goes to all the participants in the research, which has been carried out over the course of writing this book: interviewees, focus group members, respondents in the survey, women and men board members, sports coaches and sportsmen, middle-level managers, and entrepreneurs. A great number of them took part in the research and helped us in answering the questions about different facades of leadership.

We were honored to collaborate with reviewers, who encouraged us to take an extra step in our quest for answers, believed in us, and were as enthusiastic about the idea of the book as we were. Their extensive feedback, compelling competence, and remarkable work ethic inspired us to the greatest extent. Therefore, our most sincere thanks go to Dr. Christopher Leupold, the Isabella Cannon Professor of Leadership at the Elon University (USA), and Prof. Dr. Vlad Vaiman at the California Lutheran University (USA).

We are grateful to our colleagues at the University of Iceland, School of Business, for providing feedback, helping with organizational aspects, and supporting with encouraging words when it was needed. We are also grateful for our colleagues' cooperation who also contributed to parts of this book.

We are very thankful to our families and friends, who encouraged us with their love, support, and understanding; who lent their ear when we needed to be listened to and embraced during the critical moments and reminded what a deep trust they have in us and in the success of an endeavor we have taken upon us; and not the least, who showed enormous patience to our busy schedules and postponed meetings over coffee or dinner!

We want to express our gratitude to Springer Publishing and all the team for their guidance, advice, and support, as well as flexibility when it was needed. Thank you!

Last but not least, we would like to thank all the great leaders—teachers, writers, and researchers—who inspired us during our lifetime and who continue to inspire and motivate us to ask questions, search for answers, and share our knowledge with others. We want to thank great leaders, men and women, whose actions changed and are still changing the world for the better. Your words and actions motivate us to be the change we want to see in the world.

Contents

About the Authors

Inga Minelgaite is an Assistant Professor at the School of Business, University of Iceland. Her main research field is (cross-cultural) leadership and gender. Inga is also interested in emerging fields of leadership such as neuroscience of leadership and followership. Inga has fifteen years of experience working in senior and top management positions in various sectors of business and in multiple countries. Inga is a North-East-Central Europe Area Manager for the Global Preferred Leadership and Cultural Values and a member of a number of other research networks.

Svala Guðmundsdóttir is an Associate Professor and currently serves as the Vice Head of faculty and Acting Chairman for the Business Research Institute and the MBA program at the School of Business, University of Iceland. She also serves as a board member at the National Ballet School of Iceland. Her research field is within cross-cultural studies along with human resources. For the past nine years Svala has been teaching change management, human resources and international management.

Árelía E. Guðmundsdóttir is an Associate Professor at the School of Business within the University of Iceland, where she teaches an elective course on Future of work and Leadership. Her research areas are leadership, gender equality, and career development. Árelía has published books and articles on leadership, gender equality, employment relations, career, and self-development. Árelía has worked as a consultant for major Icelandic organizations for over 20 years and has participated in public debate in both Icelandic and UK media on her field of expertise.

Olga Stangej is a Visiting Researcher at the Institute of Quality Management and Business Administration (IQB-FHS) at the FHS St. Gallen University of Applied Sciences, Switzerland. She is also a founder of the Baltic Institute of Family Business. Olga has been simultaneously engaged in academic research, business and management teaching, consulting, and practice. Her research, educational activities, and projects lie in the field of management with a particular focus on leadership and family business.

Part I
Leadership and Culture

Chapter 1
Introduction

Keyword Icelandic leadership

From the southwest to the northeast, the rift of the Mid-Atlantic Ridge crosses Iceland. As this rift divides the Eurasian and the North American tectonic plates, one can stand on different continents at the same time. Rather metaphorically, the roots of Icelandic culture and leadership stem from both Northern America and the neighboring Nordic countries. An island geographically, and a small nation statistically, in the several last decades, Iceland has piqued genuine curiosity around the world regarding a multitude of factors, including leading positions in gender equality, sports championships, or effective recovery from the crisis. The question "How did you manage to attain these results?" is often cloaked as in mystery.

As we publish this book in 2018, Iceland has a reason to celebrate—10 years have passed since 2008 when a relatively small island had the unwanted attention of the whole world as it was the first to be severely hit by the financial crisis. The magnitude of this collapse was so large that it could have been associated with either a survival or a fall of the whole nation. What could have easily turned into a catastrophe, however, became a successful case and a significant part of the economic history of the country. As a result, a long trail of research and discussions surrounding the crisis, its antecedents and consequences among the scholars, practitioners, policymakers, and society, chased the country. While a large part of this discussion has been nested within economics and politics, some blank spots now have formed in regard to other domains, such as leadership.

This book focuses not on the crisis of 2008 but on a bigger picture of cultural, societal, and entrepreneurial transformations where leadership has a central role. When survival of Iceland is considered, resilience, which often generally comes at play, is just a tip of an iceberg. In discourse on survival of Iceland with regard to successful recovery from the crisis, leadership emerges as an overlooked factor that contributed to the survival of the country. On a deeper level of analysis, resilience indeed appears as not only an outcome but also an antecedent to leadership. The purpose of this book is to explore beyond the tip of an iceberg and unpack the leadership phenomenon in Iceland—that is, in a way demystify the Icelandic leadership through cultural, social, and entrepreneurial uniqueness.

© Springer International Publishing AG, part of Springer Nature 2018
I. Minelgaite et al., *Demystifying Leadership in Iceland*, Contributions to
Management Science, https://doi.org/10.1007/978-3-319-96044-9_1

While writing this book, we were many times asked if it is a book on leadership in Iceland or a book on Icelandic leadership. As the chapters of this book disclose, leadership in Iceland can be characterized through the lenses of adaptive and situational leadership, accompanied with follower-centrism and gender equality. At the same time, if there is a type of leadership that would be called "reinventing," it perhaps could be associated with Icelandic leadership.

Leadership development in Iceland resembles the logic of sagas, where certain leadership emergence and establishment manifests through a series of arduous actions that trigger a social transformation. By definition, leadership in Iceland evolves through a set of challenging natural, humanitarian, or economic events, be it a volcanic eruption or a collapse of the economy. The continuous fate of facing the challenges that emerge beyond individual control, from the outer environment, has been a leitmotif of Icelandic history, with geographical isolation, active volcanoes, breaking glaciers, and other examples. Nevertheless, as Fóstbrœðra saga, one of the Icelandic sagas from the thirteenth century, tells, "If a man's time has not come, something will save him." It could be suggested that Icelanders live in sagas to this day: when one could see the ramification over the horizon, at the very last moment, they often develop a solution.

For example, the hot springs in Iceland's Blue Lagoon, admired by tourists, mark the Iceland's leadership in renewable energy, through glaciers and rivers that were employed to generate the electricity through geothermal fields and hydropower, and geothermal water supplies delivered to the most Icelandic homes. What is often unknown is that harnessing geothermal energy to a great level was evoked by the oil crisis in the 1980s. After the crisis, many countries returned to the oil-dependent energy, while Iceland continued to develop renewable, geothermal energy, what soon substantially contributed to the country's transformation from one of the economically weakest, to one of the most developed countries in the world. This story of economic leadership, which was later hampered by the economic collapse in 2008 and restored again, may have its roots deeper in the cultural and social uniqueness.

Indeed, if one could frame the leadership in Iceland, it could perhaps be coined as a phrase "what shakes you, shapes you." As a reflection on icebergs, for example, from the time of the settlement of Icelanders to the eighteenth century, they exposed a greater knowledge and experience of glaciers than most nations (Björnsson 2017). In direct terms, Icelanders have had extensive experiential learning with regard to uncontrollable events, such as breaking of glaciers that expose one to risky consequences. Such an experience is an example of the continuous struggle for survival in an inhospitable country and the "Vikings" or settlement heritage (Loftsdóttir 2010).

In fact, it was not until the great smog hit the country when Icelanders developed the idea of harnessing geothermal power that eventually contributed to their economic leadership. It was not until the economic crisis of 2008, which strongly hit the economy but suddenly, due to decreased prices, contributed to the growth of the tourism sector that was often considered irrelevant before. Icelanders have learned how to harness the crisis to a degree that the widely adopted Icelandic phrase "þetta reddast," meaning, "it will turn out ok," is often considered as a national motto.

Certainly, leadership development through external challenges also relies on the intrinsic potential, which can be illustrated through the examples of such a small nation as Icelanders making their way to the top in, for example, handball at the Olympic Games in Beijing in 2008 or reaching the quarter-finals stage at the UEFA European Championship in 2016, and FIFA World Cup in 2018. It seems that certain geographical isolation and the necessity to adapt to uncontrollable events, once again shapes a particular leadership mentality. Hence, living on an island per se requires developing a strong internal locus of control and being able to enact multiple roles. For example, for the majority of post-war years, it was very common for individuals to engage in multiple occupations (Guðmundsdóttir 2002). Similarly, most professional sportsmen in Iceland have a different primary profession with the former head coach of the football team, for example, firstly running his dental practice. Such a combination of multiple roles and activities calls for and promotes versatility and diversity among individuals, all relating to situational and adaptive leadership. In this vein, individuals continuously reinvent themselves and rediscover their leadership potential.

Leadership as a phenomenon in Iceland can be best understood through its advancement. Therefore, this book firstly unravels the cultural, societal, and entrepreneurial specifics of Iceland that result in contextually unique leadership. Secondly, the following chapters present a contextually sensitive grip on leadership vis-à-vis the prominent events that have triggered its development. The book is respectively organized in four parts. The Part I discloses the leadership in relation to Icelandic culture by providing a summary of historical development of the societal culture and leadership, the current organizational culture, and the expected leader profiles through the followers' perspective. The Part II of the book is dedicated to an exploration how leadership in Iceland is transforming, including the Icelandic business environment before and after the financial crisis of 2008, the entrepreneurial intents among Icelanders, and the investigation into the future of the tourism industry that currently is one of the key domains where entrepreneurial leadership is developing. A special focus in Part III is dedicated to the topic of gender equality which strongly correlates with the role of transforming societal values in shaping leadership behavior. The chapters in this part provide evidence on how generally praised gender equality, for which Iceland is always distinguished, transcends leadership and flips traditional perceptions of roles, albeit equivocally. The final, Part IV of this book presents four specific cases of leadership in action that are uniquely tied with the context of Iceland. These cases stem from a number of different fields that have recently deserved international interest and attention: entrepreneurship in pharmaceutical and fishing industries, public sector and politics, and sports. Being a first academic book on leadership in Iceland, it was written with an aim to serve as a basis for further research on contextually specific leadership, leadership education, and policy-making.

References

Björnsson H (2017) Iceland. In: The glaciers of Iceland. Springer, pp 103–127
Guðmundsdóttir ÁE (2002) Íslenskur vinnumarkaður á umbreytingartímum: Sveigjanleiki skipulagsheilda, stjórnun og endurskipulagning efnahagslífsins. Háskólinn í Reykjavík, Reykjavík
Loftsdóttir K (2010) The loss of innocence: the Icelandic fnancial crisis and colonial past (Respond to this article at http://www. therai. org. uk/at/debate). Anthropol Today 26(6):9–13

Chapter 2
Societal Culture in Iceland: From the Past to the Present

Who dares wins
The Saga of Hrafnkel Freysgothi, c.9

Abstract The societal culture of a nation is embedded in its history. The Saga Age or Söguöld represents the first century of modern-day Iceland's history and through narratives captures the determination, strong-mindedness, adaptability, and the inclination to explore new horizons and resources. These societal characteristics, along the line of continuous, challenging events, shape the core of leadership in Iceland and are further summarized in this chapter.

Keywords Societal culture · History of Iceland

2.1 Historical Profile

According to existing sources, Iceland was settled in about 800 A.D., when Irish monks came to the island (Nordal and Kristinsson 1975). Old Icelandic sources say that the Gaelic monks left Iceland when the Norse colonization began. It is generally assumed that Ingólfur Arnarson arrived in Iceland with his family around 874 A.D. and settled near Reykjavik, where Iceland's capital is located today. The Icelandic Landnámsbók, or the Book of Settlements, was written in the twelfth and thirteenth centuries and provides a comprehensive overview of the 400 first settlers, their origin, and the locations where they settled. It is believed that most of the initial settlers came from Scandinavia or had Celtic roots. The early sources indicate that many of the first settlers arrived in Iceland while they were escaping the tyranny of King Harald Fairhair who had unified Norway and later extended his power to the Orkneys. At that time, most natives were heathens with the chieftain—priests, the Goðar, but at the end of the tenth century, Christianity was adopted. The influence of the Icelandic church then became essential for cultural life with many of the priests coming from prominent families.

© Springer International Publishing AG, part of Springer Nature 2018
I. Minelgaite et al., *Demystifying Leadership in Iceland*, Contributions to
Management Science, https://doi.org/10.1007/978-3-319-96044-9_2

As the population increased, the need for a more formal societal structure became urgent. In 930 A.D., the first General Assembly or Althingi met on the plains of Thingvellir, which is situated approximately 45 km to the east of the present-day Reykjavik. At that time, a common law was adopted for the country. This code of law and the procedures were derived from the body of Norwegian law and adapted to meet the specific Icelandic conditions at the time. The Constitution represents the highest national legal authority, and Iceland received its first Constitution in 1874 and the current one in 1944. Iceland became a free and sovereign state on 1 December 1918 and is seen as an important turning point in Iceland's campaign for self-determination. Today, Althingi, the Icelandic parliament, is based upon the principle of representative democracy where the power originates with the people who in turn delegate this power to their elected representatives.

The first century of modern-day Iceland's history occurred in 930–1030 and is referred to as the Saga Age or Söguöld, during which the major body of sagas, representing medieval Icelandic literature, were recorded. The sagas are narratives that depict Iceland's settler families and their descendants and hence capture the stories of men's quarrels, their exploits at home and abroad, as well as love stories. During this time, men were eager to explore their surroundings in hopes of expanding their territory and acquiring more resources. A particularly notable accomplishment of Icelandic voyages was their discovery of Greenland in 982. Continuing their travels westward from Greenland, Icelandic expeditioners discovered the North American continent in 1000. Although Icelanders did not settle in North America, it is believed that one of their own was the European descendent born there by the name of Snorri, the son of Thorfinn Karlsefni. The Sagas also tell a story of brave women who encouraged rivalry and encouraged their men to vengeance. They were often described as women of wisdom, determination, and strong-mindedness but also greedy and of vengeful nature (Nordal and Kristinsson 1975).

The next period, or around 1030–1118, is referred to as the Age of Peace or Friðöld. During this period, the country became increasingly settled which necessitated a new form of social order. Christianity played an important role in this transition, as its tenets taught men (and women) to adopt new attitudes and behave in gentler ways. It was during this time that the Icelandic scholars of the day wrote the first book in their native language, and Icelandic literary rapidly gained momentum for the following 150 years. During the fourteenth and fifteenth centuries, a substantial part of the nation's great literature was written such as *Njáls Saga*, *Laxdæla Saga*, and *Gunnlaugs Saga Ormstungu*.

The next period, around 1230–1262, is referred to as the Age of the Sturlungs or Sturlungaöld. During this time, power was highly centralized and in the hands of a select few. This delicate balance of power was often disrupted, however, when a member of the same leading family acquired authority over entire districts or quarters of the country. The increasing influence and demands of the Church became more intransigent in this period, influenced by more forceful political policies that were promoted. In 1262, Icelanders swore alliance to the Norwegian king Hakon IV and made a treaty with the monarchy to secure peace and a more lawful government in the country. This act in 1264 was named *Gamli Sáttmáli*, which in Icelandic means the *Ancient Pact*, and established a union between Iceland and Norway. However, in 1380, the Danish and Norwegian monarchies were united, and Iceland was transferred to the Danish monarchy. During that time and for the next two centuries, Iceland experienced volcanic eruptions and Black Death that resulted in worse economic conditions along with shortages of labor. The sixteenth century reflected a time of radical changes. With the advent of the Protestant Reformation in Europe, new attitudes were born not only toward religion but also in social, political, and intellectual matters as well. Iceland was not left unaffected by these new idea trends, although it did not experience the same progress and economic development as did the other nations. This actually marked somewhat of an age of repression and decline in Iceland. With an increase in Danish royal power and subjugation to harsh economic policy, Iceland was seen as merely a source of income for the Danish Crown. As a result, Iceland was left behind in the general economic advances that the rest of Europe enjoyed for almost 200 years.

In 1703, a detailed census of Iceland's population was taken, which numbered just over 50,000. During this time, Danish authorities had begun to manifest a greater interest in Icelandic society, particularly in its school system. The ability to read was soon widespread among the people in Iceland. However, the early sixteenth century brought new difficulties for Icelanders as a result of the war between England and Denmark. The emphasis for the independence was led by Jón Sigurðsson who was born on 17 June 1811. In 1851, the struggle for the independence reached its momentum when representatives of the Danish Crown made an effort to pass a new legislation which ignored the requests made by the Icelanders. Jón Sigurðsson spoke out against the representatives of the Crown and said the well-known words "Vér mótmælum allir" or "We all protest." In honor of his legacy, his birthday was chosen as Iceland's National Day. In 1874, Iceland was granted its first Constitution. Althing, the parliament of Iceland, was given a shared legislative power with the Crown, local government autonomy, and control over its own national finances. As Iceland began to enjoy greater independence in its affairs, World War II brought new challenges. When Denmark was occupied by Germany in 1940, the British invaded Iceland, and in 1941, Great Britain and the United States agreed that US forces would occupy the island. In the summer of 1941, Althing came to an agreement with the United States for the defense of the country. Following World War II, the Icelandic people turned out in vast numbers and formally voted by an overwhelming majority to dissolve the union with Denmark and to reestablish a republic. This was formally and ceremoniously accomplished at a gathering on the ancient assembly place of the nation, Thingvellir, where Althing is located. On 17 June 1944, Iceland was officially declared as a republic. After the war, the United States continued to operate an air base at Keflavik Airport. In a step to Iceland's solidifying an allied relationship as it growing interest in foreign policy, in 1946 the two nations came to an agreement that allowed the United States to continue its use of Keflavik Airport. In addition, Iceland became a founding member of NATO, which further solidified the nation's presence and involvement in world affairs. The historical development of Iceland marks several unique highlights reflected in the next sections.

2.2   Economic Profile

Iceland is 103,000 square kilometers (or 64,000 square miles) in geographic size, which is about the same size as the US state Maryland. The current population is around 350,000 with an estimated 10% of its inhabitants of foreign-born nationality. Most Icelanders are members of the Lutheran State Church. Reykjavik is the capital with a population of around 127,000, and the main religion in Iceland is Evangelical Lutheran. The climate is cold temperate oceanic, highly changeable, and heavily influenced by the warm Gulf Stream and Arctic currents. With only three inhabitants per square kilometer, Iceland is one of the least densely populated countries in Europe.

Iceland is mountainous and of volcanic origin with several glaciers, one of them, Vatnajökull, the largest glacier mass in Europe. Iceland harnesses both hydroelectric power and geothermal energy, and these make Iceland one of the greenest environments in Europe. Iceland is a world leader in the application of renewable geothermal energy for both domestic and industrial purposes with nearly 90% of Icelandic homes relying on geothermal energy as their heating source (Orkustofnun 2010). With geothermal energy and glacial rivers and access to clean water, these conditions enable Iceland to produce unpolluted products and to open new possibilities including in bio and health technology where purity and sustainability are essential.

Today Iceland is a modern state that provides its citizens access to universal health care, education, and social security. Life expectancy for females is 84 years and for males 81 years. Citizens earn the right to vote when they are 18 years of age, and the voter turnout was 79% during recent elections (OECD 2017). Remarkable economic progress has led to companies actively serving the global market. With current unemployment rate of 2.7% across all sectors, Iceland presents the third smallest unemployment rate across the countries of the Organization for Economic Co-operation and Development, commonly referred to as the OECD countries (OECD 2018). Fisheries remain one of the strongest pillars of the Icelandic economy. Despite its relatively small size and population, Iceland is considered to be one of the world's leaders in total fisheries. The monetary unit is Króna, and gross domestic product (GDP) in 2015 was 12 billion euros. Export of goods and services was 53% of GDP in 2015, and imports of goods and services were 46%. The GDP per capita was 22.66 thousand euros in 2015, with the lowest poverty rate in the OECD (2017). According to the Central Bank of Iceland (2016), the spending on health, education, social security, welfare, and other social affairs amounted to 25.7% of GDP in 2014. The standard of education is considered high, with compulsory schooling between the ages of 6 and 16. In Iceland, as in most OECD countries, university enrolment of those pursuing secondary education has increased substantially in recent years. In 2015, 39% of the Icelandic adult population held a university degree (The Central Bank of Iceland 2016).

Historically, Icelandic economy has been built on marine and energy resources, with investment and services being the primary drivers of growth. During the years just before the financial crisis of 2008, the financial services and construction sectors were the primary drivers of economic growth; as such, the contraction following the financial crisis was most pounced within those sectors. After GDP growth resumed in 2010, the contribution from the services sector has been driven by the recovery of domestic demand and growth in tourism-related services (Kjartansson et al. 2002).

Fish and other marine products have traditionally been the mainstay of goods exports, although they have been declining as a share of total exports since the early 1990s. In 2015, fish and other marine products accounted for 42% of goods exports and 22% of total exports, down from 63% and 41%, respectively, in 2000. Exports of manufactured goods have been expanding tremendously in importance. Tourism has been among the fastest-growing industries in Iceland in recent years and has established itself as the third leading pillar of the Icelandic economy. In the past few years, tourism has contributed over 50% of the growth during the post-crisis period (The Central Bank of Iceland 2016).

2.3 Cultural Profile and the Antecedents for Leadership

Albeit being a small country, some turning points in the history of Iceland have indirectly paved the way for the development of a particular societal culture and mentality that exists today. For example, as indicated previously, Athingi was founded in 930 and, as a result, is one of the oldest parliaments in the world. Every 4 years, the electors choose 63 representatives to sit in the parliament. The President of the Republic of Iceland is elected for a term of 4 years. Iceland has had six presidents, with Ólafur Ragnar Grímsson as the longest-serving president of Iceland (1996–2016). An educator and a politician, he has been renowned for advocating environmental issues. Among the presidents was Vigdís Finnbogadóttir, the fourth president and the first democratically directly elected female president. At the time of her appointment in 1980, she was divorced and a single mother. She served for 16 years and that is the longest-serving of elected female head of any country to date. During her presidency Iceland hosted the meeting between the US president Ronald Reagan and Soviet leader Mikhail Gorbachev in 1986.

Another example is the Icelandic language, which is an Indo-European language belonging to the subgroup of North Germanic language. The primary comparative evidence shows that the modern languages to which Icelandic is linguistically most closely related are Faroese and Norwegian, but traces of Celtic influence can be found. The Icelandic language is considered to be one of the cornerstones of the Icelandic culture, as well as the source of pride and identity. Although Icelandic was under threat from Danish influence during the occupancy, Icelandic has retained its roots as it generally does not adopt foreign words, instead opting to form new words or to give new meaning to old words by way of maintaining the purity of the language (Nordal and Kristinsson 1996).

According to Ronen and Shenkar (1985), countries can be clustered by their culture. Ideas, values, beliefs, and norms are embedded in a country's culture and, as a result, affect the leadership, behavior, and goals of individuals and organizations. In the GLOBE research conducted by House et al. (2004), European societies, for example, were grouped into five different clusters: Nordic Europe, Anglo, Latin Europe, Germanic Europe, and Eastern Europe. Studies, based on factors such as language, history, religion, and technological development, indicated that Denmark, Finland, Iceland, Norway, and Sweden belonged to the Nordic group (Eyjolfsdottir and Smith 1996; Hofstede 1980; House et al. 2004; Ronen and Shenkar 1985). The term *Nordic* established as a reference to five Scandinavian countries (Denmark, Finland, Iceland, Norway, and Sweden) exclusively, with their model of the welfare state, shared history, culture, religion, and similar languages. Hofstede's work of drawing a world cultural map is one of the most comprehensive and cited research (McSweeney 2002; Shi and Wang 2011). In his original framework, Hofstede introduced four dimensions: power distance (PDI), individualism-collectivism (IDV), masculinity-femininity (MAS), and uncertainty avoidance (UAI) (Hofstede 2001). Hofstede and Bond (1988) later added the fifth dimension to the framework called confucian dynamism, subsequently it was renamed as a long-term orientation (LTO) (Hofstede and Minkov 2010; Hofstede 2001). When looking at these values for Iceland, it can be seen that Iceland scores low on this dimension or similar to the other Nordic nations representing equality among members of the society and equal rights, the willingness of subordinates to disagree with superiors and social welfare with the education provided along with free healthcare.

The low score on power distance suggests that the hierarchy in Iceland is a mean of convenience, suggesting the accessibility of the leaders and the continuous exchange of information and consulting between the managers and the employees (Hofstede Insights 2018). Relatedly, Iceland has been found to score very high on individualism along with nations like the United States, Canada, and the United Kingdom (Guðmundsdóttir et al. 2015). Representing individualist culture where children grow up learning to distinguish themselves as "I" instead of "we" and learn that someday they will have to make it in society on their own merits (Hofstede 1991, 2001). In regard to the masculinity dimension, Iceland scores very low or similar to the Nordic counties (Guðmundsdóttir et al. 2015). This represents itself in the behavior of, for example, Nordic leadership style that emphasizes the need for personal relationships, quality of life, caring for the elderly, and to show concern for the environment. Also, this represents itself in women participating in the workforce, but Iceland had been ranked on top of the Global Gender Gap Report for the past 8 years (World Economic Forum 2017; Hofstede 1991, 2001).

Iceland has been found to score a little higher than the other Nordic countries on the uncertainty avoidance dimension representing the degree to which people prefer to experience structured over the unstructured situation (Guðmundsdóttir et al. 2015). It declares how the rules for behavior are clear for any given situation. The rules may be expressed, or they may be unwritten and merely a matter of custom or tradition. Hofstede (2001) has argued that societies with a tendency to score higher on the UAI have a scheme for situations and feel that what is different is dangerous, while countries with low UAI do not experience differences as a threat. Finally, the LTO dimensions are concerned with the Confucian idea and refer to values such as persistence and thrift, past and present orientation, respect for tradition, and fulfilling social obligations. Iceland has been found to score higher than the other Nordic countries on this dimension (Guðmundsdóttir et al. 2015).

2.4 Concluding Remarks

When comparing the five Hofstede's dimensions to the other nations, the results indicate that although the Nordic countries share a similar background in relation to origin, legislation, and cultures for more than 1200 years, there is a considerable difference between Iceland and the other Nordic countries when it comes to national cultures (Guðmundsdóttir et al. 2015). This difference is especially pronounced in the individualism dimension, but Matthíasdóttir (2004) argues that the Icelandic nation in the twentieth century, after seven centuries of foreign rule, bears most of the characteristics of more individualistic Western societies. She further argues that there was such a great need to escape the foreign oppression and discussed in the old sagas or the stories told of Norwegian lords fleeing the dominations of King Harald the "fair-haired" who wanted to minimize their power and bring Norway under his rule. Matthíasdóttir (2004) further argues that these displaced heroes from Norway had settled in Iceland to establish a nation of freedom and independence. Further, the idea of individualism can be seen in the writing among poets and academics until Iceland got its independence in 1944. Moreover, the discussion continues today about joining the European Union. While Denmark, Finland, and Sweden have joined it, Norway and Iceland have decided not to join. However, the debate still continues about eventually becoming a member. While Iceland is similar to the other Nordic countries, it still considerably mirrors many of the elements of the Anglo cluster as categorized by both Hofstede (2001) and House et al. (2004), which includes Canada, New Zealand, the United Kingdom, Australia, and the United States.

While the history of modern Iceland is based on the sagas that depict heroic stories of the settlers, the development of organizational leadership in Iceland continues to follow this strand. The constant need to adapt to the changing conditions and situations, while initiating structure, preserving the identity, and engaging in follower-centric approach that is required to lead, is pronounced even stronger in the contemporary leadership in Iceland. These contextual characteristics of the national leadership and the events that have strongly affected it are further discussed in the next chapters.

References

Economy of Iceland (2016) The Central Bank of Iceland, Reykjavík

Eyjolfsdottir HM, Smith PB (1996) Icelandic business and management culture. Int Stud Manag Organ 26(3):61–72

Guðmundsdóttir S, Guðlaugsson Þ, Aðalsteinsson GD (2015) Icelandic national culture compared to national cultures of 25 OECD member states using VSM94. Stjórnmál & Stjórnsýsla 11(1):19

Hofstede G (1980) Motivation, leadership, and organization: do American theories apply abroad? Organ Dyn 9(1):42–63

Hofstede G (1991) Cultures and organizations. Intercultural cooperation and its importance for survival. Software of the mind. McGraw-Hill, London

Hofstede G (2001) Culture's recent consequences: using dimension scores in theory and research. Int J Cross Cult Manage 1(1):11–17

Hofstede G, Bond MH (1988) The confucius connection: from cultural roots to economic growth. Organ Dyn 16(4):5–21

Hofstede Insights. (2018) What about Iceland? Available via https://www.hofstede-insights.com/country/iceland/. Accessed 29 Apr 2018

Hofstede G, Minkov M (2010) Long-versus short-term orientation: new perspectives. Asia Pac Bus Rev 16(4):493–504

House RJ, Hanges PJ, Javidan M, Dorfman PW, Gupta V (2004) Culture, leadership, and organizations: the GLOBE study of 62 societies. Sage, Thousand Oaks, CA

Kjartansson HS, Jónsson G, Friðriksson G, Karlsson G, Jónsson JB, Stefánsdóttir K (2002) Ísland á 20. öld. Sögufélag

Matthíasdóttir S (2004) Hinn sanni Íslendingur: þjóðerni, kyngervi og vald á Íslandi 1900–1930. Háskólaútgáfan, Reykjavík

McSweeney B (2002) Hofstede's model of national cultural differences and their consequences: a triumph of faith-a failure of analysis. Hum Relat 55(1):89–118

Nordal J, Kristinsson V (1975) Iceland 874–1974, The Central Bank of Iceland. Ísafoldaprentmsiðja hf, Reykjavik

Nordal J, Kristinsson V (1996) Iceland, The Republic: handbook. Central Bank of Iceland,

OECD (2017) Better life index. OECD. Accessed 29 April 2018

OECD (2018) Unemployment rate (indicator). Accessed 29 April 2018

Orkustofnun (2010) Geothermal development and research in Iceland. Reykjavik

Ronen S, Shenkar O (1985) Clustering countries on attitudinal dimensions: a review and synthesis. Acad Manage Rev:435–454

Shi X, Wang J (2011) Interpreting hofstede model and globe model: which way to go for cross-cultural research? Int J Bus Manage 6(5):93

World Economic Forum (2017) Global gender gap report.

Chapter 3
Leadership in Iceland: A Historical Context

*A person should not agree today to what they'll regret
tomorrow.*
Bandamanna Saga, c.10

Abstract The purpose of this chapter is to frame the circumstances that affected the development of leadership in Iceland. Leadership is a result of different societal and economic processes, whereas in the case of Iceland, it is a relatively young phenomenon and it is strongly associated with the economic development of the country. Throughout the nineteenth century and in the 1900s, the quality of socioeconomic conditions in Iceland was among the lowest in Europe. This chapter recollects the development of organizational leadership traditions in Iceland.

Keywords Leadership in Iceland · Icelandic leadership · Historical context

3.1 The Bigger Picture

Organizational structures and management often reflect the nuances and differences of national cultures (Chen 2004; Cheng 1995; Hofstede 1991; Lok and Crawford 2004; Trompenaars and Hampden-Turner 1998). Hence, the changes in management and leadership practices may similarly reflect the structure and values of organizations and societies. Therefore, a complete analysis of leadership should involve consideration of the economic environment, management styles prevailing in the country, financial markets, political system, and other cultural features.

Traditional organizational forms (Weber 1968) reflect the concepts of differentiation, rationalization, and specialization and are characterized by the hierarchy, division of labor, and managerial control. Traditional structures set clear boundaries for employees and allow social environments to be easily controlled through the departmentalization and the rational acceptance of leaders and followers. In short,

© Springer International Publishing AG, part of Springer Nature 2018
I. Minelgaite et al., *Demystifying Leadership in Iceland*, Contributions to
Management Science, https://doi.org/10.1007/978-3-319-96044-9_3

these structures make it easy for people to understand their roles and how they are expected to behave in organizational settings (Yukl et al. 2002).

In contrast, more modern organizational forms, emerging in response to the fast-changing nature of today's business environments, are defined as having organically oriented structures and operations (Palmer and Dunford 1997; Morgan 1997). These structures and operations are designed to create a more fluid relationship between the organization and its environment. This, in turn, is supposed to improve the organization's operational flexibility and thus the ability to deal with internal changes as well as to react to activities in the external environment (Volberda 1999). Advancements in technology have further increased the need for a different leadership style that would involve sharing knowledge and information; these are essential in today's business world. Thus, most modern organizations are knowledge-driven, and technology is used both to gain deeper understanding and to increase efficiency. Leaders within such organizations are dependent on those who have the resources and knowledge within technology, and most leaders need to work with both people who are of another generation than they are, as well as from other cultures. Thus, the need for empathy, compassion, and companionship has increased, as the key aspect of effective leadership is helping employees and organizational members to navigate through the environment which can appear as ever-changing and often ambiguous (Guðmundsdóttir 2002), in line with a concept of an organization as an open system (Katz and Kahn 1978a). Hence, the role of flexible and adaptive leaders, who diagnose the situations and accordingly adjust the behavior, has increased (Yukl and Mahsud 2010).

More significantly, these changes have led to the widespread adoption of empowerment strategies. Such a shift is natural since if one flattens an organization's structure, there is little choice but to empower the employees at the lower level of the hierarchy with broader decision-making. As a result, the traditional "limits to power" are set as boundaries to hierarchy, and intellectual authority is also diminishing. In short, empowerment deactivates traditional power relationships that are based on vertical forms of differentiation (Clegg 1990). In turn, empowerment leads to greater autonomy among employees (Spreitzer 1995), which is needed to be adaptive and reactive to the environment, especially in the light of fast changes within society.

3.2   Icelandic Leadership in the Landscape of Traditions

The emergence of Icelandic organizational leadership can be better understood by comparing it to central characteristics of traditions in other countries. Two such traditions are identified here: the Anglo-Saxon tradition of Great Britain, the United States, and Australia and the North-European tradition of Scandinavian countries and Germany (Marginson and Sisson 1994; Lane 1989; Murakami 2000). Table 3.1 summarizes the main differences between the two traditions.

Table 3.1 Comparisons between the Anglo-Saxon and North-European traditions, and factors that influence management style

	Anglo-Saxon tradition	North-European tradition
Management-employee relations	Uncooperative	Cooperative
Ownership	Share ownership	Family ownership
Financial markets	Developed	Less developed
Planning	Short-term	Long-term
Influence of supervisory boards	Strong	Strong
Human resource management	Individualistic	Collective
Collective bargaining	Low cooperation	Corporatist agreement
Worker participation in decision-making	Low	High

Financial markets in Anglo-Saxon countries have been more developed, enabling business leaders to be more focused on short-term financial goals in order to increase the market share of their profit-driven organizations. In turn, this has affected human resource management such as relationships with employees which are often viewed as financial investments by the managers. Usually, the labor markets are decentralized, and the trade unions have traditionally been weak in these countries, and formal inclusion of employees in decision-making was not a part of the collective bargaining system (Guðmundsdóttir 2016). The North-European tradition of Scandinavia and Germany are generally different. For example, more companies are family-owned, and their financial markets have not been as developed as in the Anglo-Saxon model. Management and labor relations have been more cooperative. Collective bargaining has been based on a corporatist mode, where trade unions, employee federations, and the state negotiate on the most important issues regarding the labor market. Participation of employees is thus integrated into the system (Gustavsen 2011).

Moving from practice to theory, the majority of leadership literature is based on the Anglo-Saxon definitions and practices. For example, this general orientation is especially evident in the following sampling of leadership definitions:

- Leadership is the influential increment over and above mechanical compliance with the routine directives of the organization (Katz and Kahn 1978b).
- Leadership is the process of influencing the behavior of an organized group toward goals (Rauch and Behling 1984).
- Leadership is influencing processes affecting the interpretations of events for followers, the choice of goals for the group or organization, the organization of work activities to accomplish the goals, the motivation of followers to achieve the goals, the maintenance of cooperative relationships and teamwork, and the enlistment of support and cooperation from people outside the organization (Yukl 1998).
- Leadership is a process of social influence, whereby a leader steers members of a group toward an objective (Bryman 1992).
- Leadership is the ability of an individual to motivate others to forgo self-interest in the interest of a collective vision and to contribute to the attainment of that

vision and the collective by making significant personal self-sacrifices over and
above the call of duty, willingly (House and Shamir 1993).
– Leadership is a process where both positive and highly developed organizations
  motivate self-knowledge and development with discipline in a positive way for
  both leaders and followers (Avolio et al. 2009).

The underpinnings of the Anglo-Saxon traditions are clearly embedded in these
and other widely adopted leadership definitions. Virtually they are all developed in
the United States. Central to these theories is the understanding of power and the
ways of influencing people. In the model of power by J. R. French and B. H. Raven,
proposed in 1959, six bases of social power were identified: reward, coercion,
legitimacy, expertise, reference, and information, all based on an Anglo-Saxon
tradition (Raven 1992). According to them, power can be gained through different
ways of influencing people.

The European leadership model is more diverse as the countries are more
culturally heterogeneous. In a comprehensive study on the relationship between
culture and leadership concepts in Europe which focused on cross-cultural differences in leadership, six European cultural clusters were identified (Brodbeck et al.
2000) in addition to the Anglo-Saxon tradition:

1. The Nordic cluster, including Denmark, Finland, Norway, and Sweden
2. The Germanic cluster, including Austria, Western Germany, and Switzerland
3. The Latin cluster, including Belgium, Italy, Spain, Portugal, and France
4. The Middle East cluster, including Greece and Turkey
5. The Central European cluster, including countries such as Poland and Slovenia

The concepts of leadership vary across European countries. However, the unify-
ing idea behind all of them is to move beyond a formal role in influencing others, one
must first be perceived as a leader. This is different from French and Raven's model
that suggests ways of leaders influencing others but does not take into account the
approval of a leader by the followers. In respect to culturally endorsed leadership
concepts, it is expected that the less these concepts overlap in cross-cultural leader-
follower relations, the less likely it is that the leader will be accepted. In turn, it is less
likely that interpersonal relationships between the leader and the follower will be
characterized by trust, motivation, and other qualities that ultimately lead to high
performance (Brodbeck et al. 2000). Compared to the models of Southern and
Eastern Europe, the Nordic model of leadership relies more on the leaders who are
inspirational and relationship-oriented. More specifically, individuals in these cultures are much more prone to strongly endorse leaders who promote team integration
and team collaboration. Nordic managers have been consistently characterized as
individualistic but also more "feminine" and employee-oriented than those further to
the South (Smith et al. 2003). This combination of individualism and orientation
toward relationships is unique to Nordic culture that values self-sufficiency but also
tasks leaders with helping people achieve it through inspiring and empowering the
leader-follower exchange.

3.2.1 The Early Basis for Leadership in Iceland

The Icelandic model could be categorized as fully embracing neither the North-European nor the Anglo-Saxon tradition. Even though Iceland gained independence in 1918, it was under the sovereignty of the Danish crown until 1944; as such, the Icelandic model of leadership certainly is rooted in the Nordic tradition. For example, most of the public and labor market institutions in Iceland were based initially on the Danish model. However, the development of the Icelandic labor market has been different throughout the last century. In the post-World War II period, Iceland enjoyed a high standard of living similar to the other Nordic countries. Modern Icelandic economic history spans just over one century. In the early years of industrialization, the economy was fundamentally based on fisheries and agriculture. In recent decades, the economy has diversified into export-oriented manufacturing and processing industries and range of services for both export and domestic consumption (Guðmundsdóttir 2002). The country evolved into a typical modern state in the last decades of the twentieth century, and at the time, significant changes took place in fishing, food processing, and marketing. Before the 1990s, the Icelandic model was very different from both models and could not be categorized as a part of the North-European or the Anglo-Saxon tradition, as it is captured in Table 3.2.

As depicted in Table 3.2, the Icelandic tradition was very different from the two traditions before the 1990s. Financial markets were underdeveloped, and companies were usually family-owned, labor relations were uncooperative, and the strike rate in Iceland was the highest in Europe (Guðmundsdóttir 2002).

3.2.2 Leadership Development in Iceland After 1990s

At the turn of the twentieth century, Iceland's organizations have not had the infrastructure yet to foster optimal professional management and leadership (Guðmundsdóttir 2002). Leadership is heavily associated with long-term planning (House and Shamir 1993; Yukl 1998), which was also nearly impossible for a long time in Iceland due to fluctuations in the national economy. This can be explained by the fact that after Iceland's economy gained its strength, the country had the highest strike rate in Europe and inflation was often very high before the 1990s (Kristinsson et al. 1992). Icelandic business environment remained underdeveloped and was marked by the lack of entrepreneurial and corporate experience. In the 1990s, the Icelandic leadership model went through a major transformation in response to the restructuring that was taking place in the country as a whole. Iceland joined the European Economic Area in 1996 and as a consequence was forced to change its restricted economic system to one that increasingly became more open. Changes in law and regulations made it possible for banks and other financial institutions to develop and grow more rapidly. Ownership became more diversified, cooperation in

Table 3.2 Comparisons between Iceland before the 1990s and the Anglo-Saxon and North-European traditions

	Anglo-Saxon tradition	North-European tradition	Icelandic tradition
Management-employee relations	Uncooperative	Cooperative	Uncooperative
Ownership	Share ownership	Family ownership	Family/individual ownership
Financial markets	Developed	Less developed	Undeveloped
Planning	Short-term	Long-term	Short-term
Influence of supervisory boards	Strong	Strong	Weak
Human resource management	Individualistic	Collective	Individualistic
Collective bargaining	Low cooperation	Corporatist agreement	Low cooperation
Worker participation in decision-making	Low	High	Low

the labor market increased, and corporatist relations were established as trust increased. This shift paved the way for a vibrant entrepreneurial environment that fosters socioeconomic development. However, this environment changed again after the financial collapse of the banking system in 2008 (see Líndal 1995, for an overview of pre-existing industrial relationships). These changes are summarized in Table 3.3.

The recession of the early 1990s dramatically affected the changing Icelandic model, enhancing the role of trust in employment relations that refers to both better cooperation between actors and increased participation of employees within individual organizations. Stability in employment relations meant that for the first time in Iceland's post-war history, the inflation reached a similar level as in the other western countries, and the strike rate decreased dramatically. Thus, long-term planning became possible for managers and leaders for the first time in Icelandic business environment. Accordingly, the emergence of professional management became apparent, followed by leadership as an integral part of it.

As it is often noted throughout this book, Iceland was hit hard during the 2008 global financial crisis when its three major banks collapsed. Immediately prior to this, from 2002 to 2008, the banking sector had undergone rapid changes where they became both large and global. Today, the export economy is based on three major pillars: fisheries, heavy industries (mainly aluminum production), and tourism. Since the financial crisis, tourism has grown rapidly; in particular, it has witnessed almost an exponential growth in inbound tourism. In 2017, approximately 2.5 million guests visited the country, in comparison to roughly 490,000 in 2009 and a similar figure in 2010 (Gil-Alana and Huijbens 2018). The living standard in Iceland is among the highest in the world, and the country was rated first in 2017 based on Human Development index among nations (http://hdr.undp.org/). The development

Table 3.3 Comparison between Iceland after 1990 and the Anglo-Saxon and North-European tradition

	Anglo-Saxon tradition	North-European tradition	Icelandic tradition
Management-employee relations	Uncooperative	Cooperative	Uncooperative
Ownership	Share ownership	Family ownership	More share ownership
Financial markets	Developed	Less developed	Undeveloped
Planning	Short-term	Long-term	Short-term
Influence of supervisory boards	Strong	Strong	Weak
Human resource management	Individualistic	Collective	Individualistic
Collective bargaining	Low cooperation	Corporatist agreement	Corporatist
Worker participation in decision-making	Low	High	Higher

of leadership in Iceland after the 1990s has been researched from multiple perspectives.

One of the main conclusions of the research on the restructuring of Iceland's economic system in the 1990s is that Icelandic leaders are better at coping with the crisis than economic boom times (Guðmundsdóttir 2002). Such a pattern is partly explained by the flexible Icelandic labor market where demand for the workforce at times exceeds the supply and the culture of combined individualism and collectivism. Thus, for the majority of post-war years, it was very common for individuals to have two jobs, such as working as a teacher as a first position and taking a side-job of a driver (Guðmundsdóttir 2002). When financial crisis hit companies in 2008, they relied on a legal framework and the culture of acceptance when laying people off. Even when the banks fell the same year and 20% of their employees were laid off due to downsizing, these former employees felt better than those who stayed, and the social stigma associated with being laid off was not high (Snorradóttir et al. 2015). The tendency to believe that "we will find a way" combined with a flexible and multi-skilled workforce to a certain extent turned the crisis into a project that called for proper leadership and management. Such a mentality might have been shaped by the living conditions in a country that is shaken by volcanic eruptions, earthquakes, avalanches, and extreme weather conditions on a daily basis and calls for an immediate action to survive. A similar pattern in Icelandic leaders' behavior was observed in the case of the financial crisis that caused a flood of bankruptcies. The flexibility of the labor market system and the fast reaction coupled with adaptive and situational leadership set the basis for the newest "Icelandic miracle" as many foreign correspondents titled the rapid turnover of the economy in recent years (see, e.g., Washington Post 2015).

3.3   Leadership in Iceland Today

Icelandic leaders today continue to build on the tradition of nimbleness, responsiveness, and quick decision-making. One of the factors that likely contributed to these adaptations was the cumulative experience from the past events, such as the economic situation before the 1990s, when long-term planning was not possible due to fluctuations in the environment caused by inflation, employee strikes, and other related factors (Guðmundsdóttir and Guðjónsson 2013). In a research that analyzed the responses of leaders and managers to the crisis when the external forces required them to downsize, the flexibility of companies, that is, how adaptive and quick they were to respond to the changing situation, was key to their performance (Guðmundsdóttir and Guðjónsson 2013). The research on reaction of managers to the financial crisis of 2008 covered two time periods: 8 months after the collapse and 8–20 months after the collapse. The results indicated strong flexibility in both the private and the public sectors. Although the public sector showed a delayed response to the economic situation, it increasingly and vigorously adopted nontraditional and hard methods as time elapsed from the collapse (Einarsdóttir et al. 2011). However, as it was noted earlier, long-term planning and the "professionalization" of business in Iceland were still relatively new concepts. In a study of explanatory factors regarding the financial crisis, one specific factor that emerged was a weak business culture in the Icelandic society that enabled conditions conducive to corruption and questionable business practices. It was previously suggested by Vaiman et al. (2010) that the weak business culture should be considered as a different kind of corruption falling beyond the traditional definition. This weak business culture can be identified as the lack of tradition and consideration toward the set of explicit and implicit rules that facilitate business interactions in a society. In the case of Iceland, it was compounded by the lack of diversity and tight personal networks in managerial relationships and ownership which were a significant characteristic of Icelandic business (Ólafsson and Pétursson 2010; Vaiman et al. 2011). These conclusions are in line with Snaebjornsson's research (2016), which highlights the followers' perspective on business leadership in Iceland and suggests that the followers in Icelandic business companies assign extreme importance to the competence of the leader when identifying the central characteristics of a leader. Thus, the factors that explain why Icelandic leaders can be better at handling crises than boom periods are also likely to be the ones that are of hindrance. The ability to adapt quickly and be flexible might not give the leaders skill sets for shaping traditions that support a strong culture.

3.4   Concluding Remarks

As described in the different historical periods above, organizational leadership in Iceland is both relatively young and fragile. It still retains some underlying assumptions from the several last centuries and has been especially impacted by the notable developments over the last three decades. The evolution of leadership in Iceland suggests that it is strongly shaped not only by the needs of the followers but also by the broader environment or the context at a given point of time (Kristjánsson and Guðmundsdóttir 2010). Despite Iceland being a small and tightly knit society, the organizational leadership, as we discuss it today, primarily relates to the business environment. At the same time, there are indicators that leadership in public organizations is slightly different and in some cases shows more long-term planning and service toward the followers (Guðjónsson and Gunnarsdóttir 2014). Nevertheless, significant lessons learned by the society in the face of the crisis of 2008 have played a major catalyst role in a societal culture. The changes toward strengthening the social responsibility, along with a match and borrowing from both Anglo-Saxon and Northern-European tradition, open up the way for Iceland's own, unique type of leadership.

References

Avolio BJ, Walumbwa FO, Weber TJ (2009) Leadership: current theories, research, and future directions. Annu Rev Psychol 60:421–449

Brodbeck FC, Frese M, Akerblom S, Audia G, Bakacsi G, Bendova H, Bodega D, Bodur M, Booth S, Brenk K (2000) Cultural variation of leadership prototypes across 22 European countries. J Occup Organ Psychol 73(1):1–29

Bryman A (1992) Charisma and leadership in organizations. Sage, London

Chen M (2004) Asian management systems: Chinese, Japanese and Korean styles of business. Cengage Learning EMEA, Hampshire

Cheng B-S (1995) Hierarchical structure and Chinese organizational behavior. Indigenous Psychol Res Chin Soc 3:142–219

Clegg S (1990) Modern organizations: organization studies in the postmodern world, Sage, London

Einarsdóttir A, Ólafsdóttir K, Arnardóttir AA (2011) Frá mjúkum yfir í harðar samdráttaraðgerðir á vinnumarkaði. Sveigjanleiki fyrirtækja og stofnana í kjölfar hruns. Stjórnmál stjórnsýsla 2 (7):333–352

Gil-Alana LA, Huijbens EH (2018) Tourism in Iceland: persistence and seasonality. Ann Tour Res 68:20–29

Guðjónsson GI, Gunnarsdóttir S (2014) Þjónandi forysta og starfsánægja í Háskóla Íslands. Icel Rev Polit Admin 10(2):497–520

Guðmundsdóttir ÁE (2002) Íslenskur vinnumarkaður á umbreytingartímum: Sveigjanleiki skipulagsheilda, stjórnun og endurskipulagning efnahagslífsins. Háskólinn í Reykjavík, Reykjavík

Guðmundsdóttir ÁE (2016) Jón Gnarr: the joker that became a leader. Icel Rev Polit Admin 12 (1):151–170

Guðmundsdóttir ÁE, Guðjónsson J (2013) Skapandi sveigjanleiki

Gustavsen B (2011) The Nordic model of work organization. J Knowl Econ 2(4):463–480

Hofstede G (1991) Cultures and organizations. Intercultural cooperation and its importance for survival. Software of the mind. McGraw-Hill, London

House RJ, Shamir B (1993) Toward the integration of transformational, charismatic, and visionary theories. In: Chemers MM, Ayman R (eds) Leadership theory and research: perspectives and directions. Academic, San Diego, pp 88–107

Katz D, Kahn RL (1978a) Organizations and the system concept. In: Classics of organization theory, pp 161–172

Katz D, Kahn RL (1978b) The social psychology of organizations, vol 2. Wiley, New York

Kristinsson GH, Sveinsdóttir HÞ, Jónsson H (1992) Atvinnustefna á Íslandi 1959–1991. Reykjavík Félagsvísindastofnun Háskóla Íslands

Kristjánsson JS, Guðmundsdóttir ÁE (2010) Leiðtogi í góðæri, skúrkur í kreppu? Áhrif tíðaranda á ímynd leiðtoga. Þjóðarspegillinn 103–113

Lane C (1989) Management and labour in Europe: the industrial enterprise in Germany, Britain, and France. Edward Elgar, Aldershot

Líndal S (1995) Labour legislation and industrial relationships in Iceland. Int J Comp Labour Law Ind Relat 25(2):112–132

Lok P, Crawford J (2004) The effect of organisational culture and leadership style on job satisfaction and organisational commitment: a cross-national comparison. J Manage Dev 23 (4):321–338

Marginson P, Sisson K (1994) The structure of transnational capital in Europe: the emerging Euro-company and its implications for industrial relations. In: New Front Eur Ind Relat, pp 15–51

Morgan G (1997) Images of organization, 2nd edn. Auflage, Thousand Oaks

Murakami T (2000) Trade union strategy and teamwork: the British and German car industry. Labor Stud J 24(4):35–52

Ólafsson TT, Pétursson TG (2010) Weathering the final storm. The importance of fundamentals and flexibility. School of Business, Arhus University

Palmer I, Dunford R (1997) Organising for hyper-competition: new organisational forms for a new age. N Z Strat Manage 2(4):38–45

Rauch CF, Behling O (1984) Functionalism: basis for an alternate approach to the study of leadership. In: Leaders and managers. Elsevier, pp 45–62

Raven BH (1992) A power/interaction model of interpersonal influence: French and Raven thirty years later. J Soc Behav Pers 7(2):217–244

Smith PB, Andersen JA, Ekelund B, Graversen G, Ropo A (2003) In search of Nordic management styles. Scand J Manage 19(4):491–507

Snaebjornsson IM (2016) Leadership in Iceland and Lithuania: a followercentric perspective. University of Iceland, Reykjavik

Snorradóttir Á, Tómasson K, Vilhjálmsson R, Rafnsdóttir GL (2015) The health and well-being of bankers following downsizing: a comparison of stayers and leavers. Work Employ Soc 29 (5):738–756

Spreitzer GM (1995) Psychological empowerment in the workplace: dimensions, measurement, and validation. Acad Manage J 38(5):1442–1465

Trompenaars F, Hampden-Turner C (1998) Riding the waves of culture. McGrawHill, New York, p 162

Vaiman V, Davídsson PÁ, Sigurjonsson TO (2010) Revising a concept of corruption as a result of the global economic crisis–the case of Iceland. In: Organizational immunity to corruption: building theoretical and research foundations, p 363

Vaiman V, Sigurjonsson TO, Davidsson PA (2011) Weak business culture as an antecedent of economic crisis: the case of Iceland. J Bus Ethics 98(2):259–272

Volberda HW (1999) Building the flexible firm: how to remain competitive. Oxford University Press, New York

Washington Post (2015) The miraculous story of Iceland. https://www.washingtonpost.com/news/wonk/wp/2015/06/17/the-miraculous-story-of-iceland/?utm_term=.b73a5a4031e9. Accessed 29 Apr 2018

Weber M (1968) Economy and society: an outline of interpretative sociology. Bedminster, NewYork

Yukl G (1998) Leadership in organizations, 4th edn. Prentice-Hall, Englewood Cliffs

Yukl G, Mahsud R (2010) Why flexible and adaptive leadership is essential. Consult Psychol J Pract Res 62(2):81

Yukl G, Gordon A, Taber T (2002) A hierarchical taxonomy of leadership behavior: integrating a half century of behavior research. J Leadersh Org Stud 9(1):15–32

Chapter 4
Organizational Culture in Iceland: Welcoming the Uncertainty

Wisdom is welcome wherever it comes from.
Bandamanna Saga, c.10

Abstract Icelandic organizational culture is considered to be very young compared to other European countries. Iceland went from being a relatively poor agricultural to an advanced, sophisticated economy within only a 100 years. It is believed that organizational culture reflects the fundamental values of the national culture. This chapter provides a brief summary of organizational culture in Iceland as a portrait of leadership context, including its key cultural values—such as equality, high work ethic, positive attitude, and varied degree of uncertainty in the face of major societal changes, e.g., the financial crisis of 2008.

Keywords Organizational culture · Iceland · Work ethic · Individualism · Equality

4.1 The Bigger Picture

As Schein (2010) contends, both leadership and organizational culture have become complicated topics in their own right and are, in fact, two sides of the same coin. When one considers the potentially profound influence that the leader, and often the founder, has on organizational culture development, this statement appears quite obvious. The concept of organizational culture gained momentum around the 1980s when scholars and practitioners alike, including Ouchi, Pascale and Athos, Deal and Kennedy, Peters and Waterman, and Kanter, explored the underlying values of organizations, how those values affect the performance, and what implications do they have for managers (Calori and Sarnin 1991; Petty et al. 1995). It has been argued that organizational culture forms an identity for the members of the organization, facilitates their commitment to the organization and each other, and shapes their work and nonwork-related behavior (Peter and Waterman 1982; Siehl and

Martin 1981). From a broader perspective, a number of scholars have investigated national culture and discovered the links between it and corporate culture, unemployment, population growth, political stability, and management style (Casimir and Keats 1996; Harrison and Huntington 2000). Over the past decades, organizational culture has been investigated and developed by the researchers in multiple social science fields including anthropology, social and cognitive psychology, and sociology (Schein 2010). Still, many scholars find the organizational culture difficult to define, as it remains invisible, it is only perceived through feelings, as well as it is largely based on habits and shared meanings among its organizational members. Nevertheless, Schein (2010) argues that some of this confusion arises due to not differentiating the levels of the culture, which range from the surface level where tangible and overt manifestations can be directly observed and experienced to the deeper level that Schein labels "the essence of culture," which are deeply embedded, unconscious, basic assumptions. What is embedded in between these layers are the "various espoused beliefs, values, norms, and rules of behavior that members of the culture use as a way of depicting the culture to themselves and others" (Schein 2010, p. 25). In this strand, Schein (2010) identifies three levels of organizational culture: artifacts, espoused beliefs and values, and basic underlying assumptions. Espoused beliefs and values and basic underlying assumptions are at the basis of the culture and hence can be the primary perspectives for understanding organizational culture, while artifacts alone are difficult to decipher (Schein 2010). Therefore, in an attempt to unpack the Icelandic organizational culture, the chapter will further tackle these specific levels of cultural analysis in line with Schein's (2010) conception of basic underlying assumptions as the deepest level of analysis. However, the chapter opens with a tribute to artifacts, reflected in perceptions by the observers—the guests from abroad who had a chance to experience the Icelandic organizational culture.

4.2 Artifacts and Observer Perceptions

Ísleifsdóttir and Guðmundsdóttir (2015) employed a somewhat different approach in their study of Icelandic organizational culture. Instead of interviewing native Icelanders who were "born into" the nation's culture, the authors interviewed 12 international expatriates who had been working for Icelandic companies and had resided in Iceland for more than a year. The participants were from Germany, Ireland, Guatemala, Brazil, Scotland, the United States, Canada, the Netherlands, South Africa, Denmark, and Britain. As "outsiders" in a sense, these respondents shared their experiences in Iceland and their observations of the culture and its main characteristics. James from the United States and William from Canada found Icelandic culture to be midway between European and American cultures. James had this to say "From the places that I have been now in Western Europe... I feel like Iceland is kind of like this halfway point between American culture and European culture." While participants varied somewhat on certain perceptions, there was a good degree of consistency on this point. This overarching perception perhaps summarizes several reflections concerning two artifacts—organizational climate and structure—outlined further.

4.2.1   Organizational Climate

Organizational or group climate is one of the cultural artifacts that can be observed relatively easily (Schein 2010). With regard to organizational climate in Iceland, one of the most common impressions shared by respondents was that Icelandic culture was relaxed or laid-back. William from Canada contended:

> It's a very laid-back culture. People tend to take things as they come and they are not necessarily planning a lot...It's both professionally and in daily life. So it's very different, especially professionally because in Canada nobody acts that professionally.

Although most respondents in the study appreciated how relaxed Iceland's workplace climate was, some also pointed at its drawbacks. Chloe from Ireland, for example, noted:

> I think people are a lot more laid-back here. They just think we will worry about that tomorrow, it will sort itself out. Whereas in the UK that is definitely not the case—people sort things ahead of them happening or you have meeting to predict the bad things that are gonna happen instead of being just reactive to them when they do. That took a bit of getting used to, very frustrating at the start.

Although it may seem paradoxical that one would "struggle" in an environment characterized as relaxed and flexible, it was nonetheless the case for Chloe and others coming from cultures where planning and structure were valued and practiced more than flexibility. Max from the Netherlands also mentioned that much more relaxed approach of Iceland affected the meetings; people were frequently too late and were often discussing things that had nothing to do with the topic. Still, such an informal work style was successfully applied in order to achieve high performance and work ethic.

This relaxed atmosphere extends even to more personal aspects of life, including openness to employees' private life. Gabriel from Brazil mentioned a big difference in the attitude of people toward children in Iceland and in the United Kingdom, where he had been living for years. As he described, in Iceland he could see small children running all over the place and playing, and that people could pretty much take their children anywhere they wanted. For him, this was quite a contrast from what he experienced in the United Kingdom, which is considered to be more restrictive.

It is important to note that this notion of "relaxed" or more "open" environment should not be confused with not having high standards or commitment in order to achieve them. In other words, flexible as they may be, Icelanders still value hard work. As an extension to organizational structure, Ólafsson (2003) notes that Icelanders possess high work ethics. To support his claim, he points out that the work week in Iceland is one of longest ones found in the Western world.

Additionally, Icelanders define a large part of their personal worth and achievement through their work. In the study by Ísleifsdóttir and Guðmundsdóttir (2015), one of the respondents, Max from the Netherlands, thought that Icelanders were generally very loyal to their workplaces and worked hard. However, James from the United States and Simon from Denmark both felt that Icelanders were sometimes too casual at work and got away with it easily. On the other hand, Alexander from Germany, William from Canada, and Gabriel from Brazil agreed with James from the United States. They all felt that working hours were much more flexible in Iceland than they were accustomed to it. Gabriel said that in Brazil it was an unwritten rule that employees never go home before the boss. He said he much preferred Iceland's working hours to Brazil's:

> The company basically trusts you to know that you have done your job. . .correctly and that
> you can take the liberties in terms of arriving later or going sooner as long as you make sure
> that you are doing your job, which I think is a great thing, it empowers employees.

When communication is concerned, some guests from abroad find the Icelandic people to be withdrawn, even cold, distant, and reserved. Several respondents in this study noticed that Icelanders did not use facial expressions to show their feelings as much as people did in their home countries. Thomas from the United Kingdom agreed and told a story about giving the first presentation to his colleagues:

> The first time I did a presentation. . . that was a little funny because there was a big screen and
> I was standing there talking about it and there was a group full of Icelandic people and I
> remember half way through the presentation. . . I am thinking I don't know if this is terrible
> or brilliant, I have no idea by their faces, I can't read their faces. At the end of it they. . . just
> said this is good, we like where this is going this is good. . .sometimes it took a little bit to get
> used to the Icelandic faces not being as expressive, it is a generalization of course, you'll
> meet some with very expressive faces but if there is an average then they are showing less
> with their face.

In line with these impressions, William from Canada also concluded that Icelanders, based on their neutral facial expressions, were rather quiet and appeared somewhat cold. Max from the United States agreed and said this was specifically applicable to many Icelandic men; it was often impossible to read from their faces whether they were happy or sad—their expression was always the same.

4.2.2 Organizational Structure

Similarly, the management of employees in Iceland, in connection to the surrounding Nordic culture, is often decentralized and democratic, where organization charts are flat and the hierarchical gaps among individuals are very small (Tixier 1996). For example, in organizational settings, Icelanders tend to use titles and surnames less and less and rely on the first names instead when addressing each other (Andersen 2005). Gabriel, from Brazil, had this to say:

> ...I think there is something that is very distinct about Iceland which makes the society flat in general, which is everybody refers to each other by their first names, there is no Mr. and Mrs. even though there is somebody that you should treat differently, like an older gentleman or something, you are not ever going to call him Mr. last name, which I find very, very interesting... You could probably bump into the president and call him by his first name.

Many respondents in the study felt that the company they worked for was characterized by a flat hierarchy. Thomas from the United Kingdom concluded that due to the reason there was less of a difference among social classes as he was used to in the United Kingdom, there seemed to be far less of a differentiation made among professions and job levels.

For example, whereas elsewhere people might make a distinction between engineers and the specialists, they are treated the same in Iceland. More than just interesting, Thomas found this to be beneficial for the company. Richard from South Africa appreciated the opportunities to speak to the CEO of the company in the same manner as to a middle-level manager while answering the phone. However, some of the respondents would not share such a positive view of this egalitarian communication style. Simon from Denmark felt that the communication in his Icelandic workplace was too informal, too friendly, and not professional enough. Nevertheless, in general, the respondents were very pleased with their workplace and felt that they generally had more privileges in Iceland than they were accustomed to. In addition, James from the United States was very happy with the duration of the summer holidays. When he was working in the United States, he would not be eligible to take summer vacation during the first year of employment and would only get 1 week of paid vacation during the second year. He said that if he were to have a similar job in the United States, he would probably be getting 2 weeks off during the summer, while in Iceland he gets almost double of that or 6 weeks.

The flat organizational hierarchy is also prominent with regard to gender equality, a characteristic that often leaves the guests from other countries surprised. In a study by Ísleifsdóttir and Guðmundsdóttir (2015), most respondents felt that gender equality was more pronounced in Iceland than they were commonly accustomed to. They confirmed that the participation of women in the labor force was greater and better recognized. Richard from South Africa said that his supervisor was a female and his fellow Icelandic colleagues thought that this was a very natural thing. In his previous workplaces, female supervisors were often poorly received. He found it very positive how gender equality prevailed in Iceland.

In sum, the external observers of Icelandic culture highlight the relaxed and laid-back organizational culture, flat hierarchy, and informal communication styles. At the same time, the culture is characterized by little or even no outwardly expressed emotions. These observations refer to the cultural artifacts that can be easily traced. In order to gain deeper understanding, one needs to unveil the espoused believes and values, discussed in the next section.

4.3 Espoused Beliefs and Values in Icelandic Culture

In Schein's (2010) perspective, espoused beliefs and values are the conscious elements of an organizational culture. It has been argued that many of the Icelandic values overlap with other Nordic countries, although certainly some differences are present.

One of the cultural artifacts that immediately captures new observers is Iceland's relaxed and laid-back organizational climate in Iceland. Among cultural values that are likely to determine such climate as the interrelation of two cultural dimensions, individualism and collectivism, that both of which coexist to extent in Icelandic culture. Icelanders have been known to exercise high individualism in social and work situations but also tend to show signs of collectivism. This finding was discovered in a comparative study of Icelandic and Nordic companies. On the one hand, Icelanders rely heavily on their own experience and training. In this vein, individualism in Iceland is considered to be a positive characteristic, as it relates to taking up risks and thinking outside the box. On the other hand, they differ from other European participants to the extent that they also rely heavily on their colleagues (Eyjolfsdottir and Smith 1996; Kristjánsdóttir and Martin 2009). Individualistic countries are characterized by prevalent for employees to show initiative at work. Individuals seek for more challenges and motivation, while reward is also more individualized (Aðalsteinsson et al. 2011). Snaebjornsson (2016) compared Iceland with nine other homogenous samples using Hofstede's seven-dimensional Values Survey Module 08 (VSM08; see http://geerthofstede.eu/) and collected within the framework of Centre for Cross-Cultural Comparisons (CCCC) led by professor Romie F. Littrell. Snaebjornsson (2016) indicated that Iceland scored similarly—average—in individualism dimension compared with other countries within the CCCC VSM08 samples. Above-described fluctuations indicate temporary shifts in culture in the light of major events that shocked society, namely, the financial crisis of 2008.

The next dimension which may in part influence the relaxed climate in Icelandic culture relates to uncertainty. Iceland is generally characterized as low uncertainty country and can be easily observed by the facades of social life indicating low uncertainty as described by Hofstede (1984). These include emotional need for formal rules. As observed in Iceland, these rules will be a matter for convenience, in line with Eyjolfsdottir and Smith (1996) research, describing people in Iceland feeling comfortable in situations with few rules, resulting in pragmatic opportunism —preference for indulging one's freedom. Furthermore, other indicators, such as formalization, standardization, and ritualization of organizations, implicit models of organizations, and types of planning, are used. The meaning of time, appeal of precision and punctuality, the showing or hiding of emotions, and tolerance for deviant ideas and behavior can be observed with little difficulty in Iceland and indicate low uncertainty. The low uncertainty has also been confirmed by Snaebjornsson (2016) where she collected sample of business people in Iceland. Furthermore, Snaebjornsson (2016) compared Iceland scores of societal values with nine more countries and found out that Iceland was least uncertainty avoidant of all and provided extensive contextualization for these results. However, interesting findings were discovered in a study by Aðalsteinsson et al. (2011), shortly after financial crises, where Iceland scored high on the uncertainty avoidance dimension, and it is assumed that individuals in countries scoring high on this dimension often show more anxiety when threatened with change and express a greater need for stability in general. Individuals are less likely to take risks but instead are more likely to adhere to deeply rooted values and uphold as well as engage in traditions. In general, high uncertainty people are more likely to perceive changes as negative; from a work perspective, this means that they are less likely to change jobs. Aðalsteinsson et al. (2011) also believe that uncertainty avoidance has increased in Iceland due to the economic collapse of 2008 that shook the society. Similarly, the restrained communication in terms of expressions is best understood when specific assumptions are considered. All of these basic assumptions that underlie Icelandic culture will be outlined in the next section.

Looking at organizational structure, observers often mark the flat hierarchy and little to no hierarchical barriers in communication. These customs are related to societal values stemming from egalitarianism as a critical cultural dimension. According to Hofstede et al. (2010), egalitarianism is generally associated with equal opportunities, low-power distance, individualism, and femininity. The results of the study by Aðalsteinsson et al. (2011) indicate that this constellation accurately matches Icelandic culture. According to the study, Icelandic national culture is characterized by low-power distance, femininity, and high individualism. According to Ólafsson (2003), Icelanders put a strong emphasis on equality in all forms, both in relation to gender equality and the rights of any individual to have the same opportunities and quality of life as the rest of the population in Iceland. Ólafsson (2003) points out that Icelanders' respect for superiors within companies is moderate. Iceland has also been found to score low on masculinity. In Iceland, it is more common that women work outside home and occupy management positions than in other countries where strong masculinity prevails.

It is complicated task to describe Icelandic organizational culture and to determine whether it was influenced more by American culture or merely followed the pattern of normal modernization of the Western world (Hannesson 1964). Furthermore, Icelandic organizational culture differs from Scandinavian, and even though it is leaning more toward an American way of managing (Davidsdottir 2006), it does not fully resemble US business culture either; hence organizational culture in Iceland appears to be unique as contested by Snaebjornsson (2016).

4.4   Basic Underlying Assumptions in Icelandic Organizational Culture

As Schein (2010) contends, when implementation of certain beliefs and values results in repeated success, a set of basic underlying assumptions is formed. Over time, these assumptions are generally taken for granted by organization members and result in little variation in a social unit (Schein 2010). The first basic underlying assumption is related to nearly all observations highlighted by the observers— relaxed atmosphere, flat hierarchies, and ease with which people can communicate across titular boundaries and levels. Organizational culture and management style in the Nordic countries and Iceland in particular are considered to be fueled by a widespread idea that business needs to be managed and employees need to be treated in a socially responsible way (Brewster 2007; Smith et al. 2003). Accessibility and accountability toward employees are often a requirement for the managers (Smith et al. 2003). Furthermore, in countries where the power distance is low, such as Iceland, supervisors tend to see their subordinates as their equals and even consult with them often (Hofstede 1980). The findings by Snaebjornsson (2016) on pre-ferred leader behavior in Iceland extend these reflections. The employees in Iceland expect the ideal managerial leader to maintain a close-knit organization and resolve conflicts within the organization.

The relaxed and laid-back atmosphere is in fact deeply rooted in Icelandic culture. Eyjolfsdottir and Smith (1996) say that the tendency to respond positively to uncertainty is a very strong characteristic of Icelandic culture. Eyjolfsdottir and Smith (1996) connect this to the hunters' community in the country, as hunters need to be prepared for anything because environmental conditions can change at any moment. Icelandic people need to be more tolerant than many other nations due to rapidly changing weather conditions, earthquakes, volcanic eruptions, and other natural disasters. This need to be able to respond and adapt to changes in the natural world affects the corporate culture as well. However, Icelanders are considered to be very flexible and to have a generally positive attitude toward the changes in the workplace. Such an attitude can be associated with the leader's approach to communication with the followers that relies on exchanging of information, sharing knowledge, and consulting with each other. In fact, sometimes they are so positive toward these changes that they can even become careless. When Icelanders face difficulties, the phrase "We'll manage" is the common mantra. Although after the collapse of economy in 2008, when Icelanders became less tolerant for uncertainty, this constructive and positive attitude can, in fact, be the element that enabled the country to recover at considerably rapid pace.

When observing Icelandic communication styles, foreigners often find it to be dull in emotions and facial expressions, often leaving individuals from other countries puzzled. In fact, such an impression is often confused with the well-tempered attitude of Icelanders and individuals from the Nordic regions: they simply avoid small talks and are less willing to speak without a purpose (Jungner and Skytt 1987; Lawrence and Spybey 2018; Lindkvist 1988). Similarly, Nordic managers tend to express their disagreement through silence rather than raised voice. It is also believed that managers tend to avoid conflict and the atmosphere is somewhat "sterile." In spite of this moderate and peaceful attitude in general communication, the managerial leaders in Iceland are expected to maintain an active voice, when necessary. As the study by Snaebjornsson (2016) illustrates, the leader is expected to be a representative figure, including representation of the group and speaking on its behalf, and in doing so, be persuasive in his argumentation and convincing.

4.5 A Special Note on the Cultural Shift

Some cultural nuances of Iceland had a contradictory influence, combining both positive and adverse effects on the society and economy preceding the economic crisis of 2008, and eventually resulted in a certain cultural shift. While direct communication is generally considered to be a positive characteristic, Vaiman et al. (2011) identified how a lack of diversity and tight personal networks in managerial relationships along with the ownership hampered Icelandic culture. On a similar note, a study by Mixa and Vaiman (2015) focused on the saving ratio of Icelanders in the years prior to 2008, where overall positive tolerance for uncertainty and presence of individualism made them more vulnerable during the economic downturn. Mixa and Vaiman (2015) argue that Icelanders were much more risk-seeking during the prelude of the crisis. According to them, "nations with a high degree of individualism may be more apt to financial disasters when liberalizing their financial system" as "they may be more likely to accept success stories that often occur during the first years following liberalization and continue on a reckless financial path" (Mixa and Vaiman 2015, p. 370). They consider this tendency as one of the possible explanations why Iceland was hit so much worse than the other Nordic countries. In their article they compare individualism scores and savings ratio among the Nordic nations and find a correlation between the two. As the rise in Icelandic stock market prices indicated, prior to the bust in 2008, there was a perceived sense of national success due to the increased growth in the banking and financial sector. The public believed that Icelandic bankers were among the best in the world, despite the fact that modernized banking in Iceland was only a few years old. From a perspective by Þorvaldsson (2009), a CEO of an Icelandic bank that had a subsidiary in London described his journey toward becoming a CEO as he had only learned the basics of banking investment in a relatively short time. In the study by Ísleifsdóttir and Guðmundsdóttir (2015), respondents mention nepotism as one of the characteristics of the Icelandic business world and society in general. For example, James had a similar story to tell about nepotism and how it became a big part of Icelandic culture:

> In America there is a lot of red tape and there is a process to everything. You fill out a form and you wait in the line. You always have to follow the rules and there is no short cuts or anything but here it was like, "OK, fill out that paperwork and now I'm going to call my cousin who works in that office and now it's done"... That does not happen in the States.

After the collapse of the financial system and economy in 2008, discussions on the Icelandic business culture determined that it was apparent and it was not sufficiently open or transparent (European Commission 2010; Sibert 2009; Wade 2009). In their deep research, supported by ten expert interviews and conducted within the period of 6 months in 2009, Vaiman et al. (2011) argue that the collapse of the financial sector and the economic crisis in Iceland in 2008 was caused mainly by the country's weak business culture. As mentioned previously, in 2008, the Icelandic banking sector was larger than the entire Icelandic economy at the time; as such, its collapse had an overwhelming effect on Icelandic society. The authors further argued that the weak business culture could be identified as the lack of tradition and adherence to a set of explicit and implicit rules that governs business interactions in society. As Hofstede et al. (2010) point out, increasing individualism two decades before has been one of the forces leading to deregulation in the Western world. This idea fits well with Olafsson's (2003) description of the main characteristics of Icelanders—having a strong sense of individualism and independence and resenting central authority. In 1995 Iceland experienced dramatic transformation with its borders opening up and moving toward greater liberalization that resulted in many of the state's assets being sold, including the three main banks.

Following the economic depression in 2008, hidden corruption in the Icelandic business community was revealed, and nepotism was found to play a big part in the Icelandic business industry. These are two of the main reasons for unethical traditions and corruption in Icelandic society. Before the economic crisis, Iceland was found to be one of the least corrupt countries in the world. The Corruption Perception Index (CPI), developed by Transparency International (TI), showed that in 2005, Iceland was on the top of the list and ranked as the least corrupt nation in the world (Transparency International 2005). However, in 2009, it fell to the eighth place and in 2010 to eleventh. This downward trend continued, as in 2017 report Iceland slipped further to 13th (Transparency International 2017), considered on the list of approximately 180 countries. All these events have urged Icelanders to revisit their organizational culture and anticipate particular changes, discussed in the next chapters.

4.6   Concluding Remarks

Icelandic organizational culture is tightly connected with the national culture and is marked by relaxed and laid-back organizational climate, supported by flat organizational structures, and direct communication. All these characteristics that are noted by observers are deeply rooted in cultural value dimensions, including interplay between individualism and collectivism, tolerance for uncertainty, low-power distance, and low masculinity. In turn, these cultural values stem from basic underlying beliefs. Taken together, all of these elements of Icelandic organizational culture tend to produce positive outcomes that are appreciated by the outsiders. However, when certain elements, such as immediate networking to a degree of nepotism, and moderate individualism, reached high manifestation, they contributed to the economic crisis of 2008. Eventually, a cultural shift occurred, evoking major changes in the business environment and society in general, and that will be discussed in the next chapters.

References

Aðalsteinsson GD, Guðmundsdóttir S, Guðlaugsson ÞÖ (2011) Íslensk Þjóðmenning í ljósi menningarvídda Hofstede [Icelandic National Culture in the light of Hofestede´s dimensions]. Icel Rev Polit Admin 2(7):347–362

Andersen E (2005) Icelandic names. Skipping Stones 17(5):17

Brewster C (2007) Comparative HRM: European views and perspectives. Int J Hum Resour Manage 18(5):769–787

Calori R, Sarnin P (1991) Corporate culture and economic performance: a French study. Organ Stud 12(1):049–074

Casimir G, Keats D (1996) The effects of work environment and in-group membership on the leadership preferences of Anglo-Australians and Chinese Australians. J Cross Cult Psychol 27 (4):436–457

Davidsdottir S (2006) Icelandic companies in Scandinavia: methods and reputation. Trade Council of Iceland, Reykjavík

European Commission (2010) Commission opinion on Iceland's application for membership of the European Union

Eyjolfsdottir HM, Smith PB (1996) Icelandic business and management culture. Int Stud Manage Organ 26(3):61–72

Hannesson JS (1964) The American impact in Iceland. In: Åhnebrink L (ed) Amerika och Norden. Nordic Association for American Studies, Stockholm, pp 59–74

Harrison LE, Huntington SP (2000) Culture matters: how values shape human progress. Basic Books, New York

Hofstede G (1980) Culture's consequences. Sage, Beverly Hills

Hofstede G (1984) Culture's consequences: international differences in work-related values. Sage, London

Hofstede G, Hofstede GJ, Minkov M (2010) Culture and organizations, software of the mind, intercultural cooperation and its importance for survival. McGraw Hill, New York

Ísleifsdóttir AI, Guðmundsdóttir S (2015) Expatriates in Iceland: culture, the workplace and communication with Icelanders. Int J Bus Res 15(3):61–77

Jungner T, Skytt C (1987) A study in cross-cultural management of Swedish subsidiaries in France. Stockholm School of Economics, Stockholm

Kristjánsdóttir ES, Martin JN (2009) Why can't you speak up? Intercultural communication between Icelandic and Spanish employees. Rannsóknir Í Félagsvísindum 9:159

Lawrence P, Spybey T (2018) Management and society in Sweden. Routledge/Kegan Paul, London

Lindkvist LG (1988) A passionate search for Nordic management. Institut for Organisation og arbejdssociologi, Handelshøjskolen i København

Mixa M, Vaiman V (2015) Individualistic vikings: culture, economics and Iceland. Stjórnmál Stjórnsýsla 11(2):355

Ólafsson S (2003) Contemporary Icelanders: Scandinavian or American. Scand Rev 91(1):6–14

Peter TJ, Waterman RH (1982) In search of excellence: lessons from America's best-run companies. Warner Book, New York

Petty MM, Beadles NA, Lowery CM, Chapman DF, Connell DW (1995) Relationships between organizational culture and organizational performance. Psychol Rep 76:483–492

Schein EH (2010) Organizational culture and leadership, vol 2. Wiley, New York

Sibert A (2009) Could Greenland be the new Iceland? http://www.voxeu.org/index.php?q=node/3857. Accessed 29 Apr 2018

Siehl C, Martin J (1981) Learning organizational culture. Working Paper. Graduate School of Business, Stanford University

Smith PB, Andersen JA, Ekelund B, Graversen G, Ropo A (2003) In search of Nordic management styles. Scand J Manage 19(4):491–507

Snaebjornsson IM (2016) Leadership in Iceland and Lithuania: a followercentric perspective. University of Iceland, Iceland

Þorvaldsson A (2009) Ævintýraeyjan: Uppgangur og endalok fjá rmá laveldis [Frozen assets: how i lived Iceland's boom and bust]. Bókafélagið, Reykjavik

Tixier M (1996) Cultural adjustments required by expatriate managers working in the Nordic countries. Int J Manpow 17(6/7):19–42

Transparency International (2005) Corruption Perception Index

Transparency International (2017) Corruption Perception Index

Vaiman V, Sigurjonsson TO, Davidsson PA (2011) Weak business culture as an antecedent of economic crisis: the case of Iceland. J Bus Ethics 98(2):259–272

Wade R (2009) Iceland as Icarus. Challenge 52(3):5–33

Chapter 5
Beyond the Daily Catch: Desired Leader Profile in Iceland

It takes time to know people.
Grettir's Saga, c.20

Abstract Scholars and practitioners univocally agree that leadership affects performance and the effectiveness of organizational outcomes (Uhl-Bien et al., Leadersh Q 25(1):83–104, 2014). Interestingly, it was the context of Iceland that emerged in one of the seminal studies confirming the direct relationship between leadership and performance. Through a 3-year analysis of fishing industry and ship performance in particular, Thorlindsson revealed that leadership attributes of different captains could account for 35–49% of the variation in performance (i.e., the catch in this particular case). However, up-to-date discussion on leadership performance has extended beyond the daily catch, and today there is a general consensus that leadership effectiveness depends on the leader's identity and the extent of the schemes and prototypes that he or she holds matches those of his or her followers. The following chapter is an attempt to formulate the desired leader profiles in Iceland.

Keywords Desired leader profile · Leadership · Follower-centric leadership · Iceland

5.1 The Bigger Picture

While previous research has already offered some insights into what constitutes universally to preferred leadership behaviors (House et al. 2004), these preferences can still be nuanced with regard to a particular group or culture, as members of a particular group or culture are more likely to interpret and evaluate situations and events in a similar manner but very differently from how a different cultural group might interpret those same scenarios (Earley 1993). Every context, if it is related to the society, organization, or group, may describe the ideal leader in different ways and transmits the culture and values in its own way (Littrell 2010) and produces leader prototypes that include expected leader features and behavior (Goethals and Sorenson 2007). Yet a noticeable gap exists in the extant literature on the role of cultural contexts, including cultural norms and values in leadership's identity construction processes (DeRue and Ashford 2010). However certain pioneering studies such as results of GLOBE studies (e.g., Javidan et al. 2004) have provided evidence concerning the existence of a reliable relationship between culture and leadership schema content (Shaw 1990). Expectations concerning leadership are in turn associated with cultural values, while "...both cultural values and desired leadership attributes reflect an idealized state of what should be, or an ideal end point" (Dorfman et al. 2012, p. 506). Therefore, embracing cultural values and desired leader attributes becomes an essential step in understanding leadership within a particular cultural context.

Hence, the type of behavior which constitutes a good leader or an "ideal" leader profile has been a central for long, recurring question in the areas of leadership's research and development, including emergence and effectiveness of leader. Descriptions of a desired, preferred, or ideal leader profile reflect the perceptions and expectations of employees who play a fundamental role in leadership by becoming the followers. In this vein, leadership also needs to be regarded as situational, with good leaders being categorized on the basis of the attributes accurately corresponding with the requirements of a particular situation (Hogg 2007). These idealized profiles can have an array of attributes posited by a follower, including physical features, gender, race, and ethnicity (Lord and Emrich 2000). Finally, the followers often play a central role in the evaluation of leadership effectiveness and rating of leaders. Here, leader prototypes often come into play (Lord and Maher 2002) as followers' evaluations are conducted on the basis of leader's actual profile conformity with the leader's prototype that each follower holds (Hogg 2001; House et al. 1997; Yukl 2013).

In this vein, at least two cultural contextual layers need to be taken into account: societal and organizational. The extant literature on leadership in Iceland as a societal, cultural context provides possible valuable insights to understanding two organizational contexts frequently studied in prior research, the business and education sectors. While the prototypes and schemas held by the followers are related to cultural context, each contextual layer may add a level of complexity. First of all, expectations toward particular roles enacted by individuals are often associated with social proxies (Eagly and Karau 2002; Fletcher and Bailyn 2005), including expected behavior for a particular role in a particular environment (Cappelli and Sherer 1991). Examples of such expectations may include specific expectations concerning behavior that are associated with gender and acquired by individuals during the socialization process (Peterson et al. 2001; Gilligan 1982).

In any organizational leadership settings, from business to education sector, multiple functions and conflicting or competing expectations and demands faced by leaders can potentially lead to role ambiguity, associated with the lack of consistent and precise information about the expectations associated with particular role enactment (Kahn et al. 1964) and role conflict (Rizzo et al. 1970), characterized by incongruity or incompatibility in expectations for a particular role. Both role ambiguity and role conflict are related to the environment surrounding of an individual. In the case of leadership, the stakeholders, and primarily the followers, become the referent group of expectations associated with the leader's role in the immediate work environment. The significance of the immediate environment is also related with the encouragement for the formal leaders to engage in distributed leadership covering the whole community and stretching beyond the leader-follower dyads (OECD 2008; Schleicher 2012). While distributed leadership refers to leadership practice, it is the cultural values, in contrast to cultural practices, that actually can enable prediction of leadership attributes (Dorfman et al. 2012).

While it is clear that identification of leader prototypes and schemas is one of the primary steps in understanding the followers' perceptions and, more broadly, leadership as a culturally nuanced phenomenon, to date, these research questions related to these aspects of the leadership remain understudied. As Iceland did not take part in the GLOBE project, the studies on leadership within the nation's cultural context remain nascent. Hence, construction and deconstruction of the desired leader profile can provide a significant and objective contribution. Thus, in this chapter, the fragmented findings on the leader prototypes as a derivative of follower's perspectives are summarized in order to provide an outlook on the desired leader profile in Iceland.

The following sections are built on existing studies that employ a variety of research methods. Particularly, the findings which emphasize the follower-centric perspective are highlighted. The overarching rationale behind this choice is based on a relational approach to leadership (Meindl 1995), which considers that leadership involves a dynamic relationship including reciprocal influence between the leader and the follower (Hogg 2007) and manifests as a process involving both leaders and followers as co-creators and co-producers of leadership (Hunt 1991; Uhl-Bien et al. 2014). Previous research has already established the leader's personality alone to be "a relatively poor correlate of leadership" (Hogg 2001, p. 185). Instead, effective leadership is a process, enacted by both leaders and followers that is grounded in the highly relational interactions between both parties (Antonakis et al. 2004; Yukl 2013). Moreover, recognition of leadership is an outcome of attribute-to-schema comparison (Lord and Maher 1991; DeRue et al. 2009). Likewise, perceived leadership effectiveness is dependent on the situation, circumstances, context, and, of course, the followers themselves. The next sections of this chapter focus on two sectors that require attention with regard to leadership: education and business.

5.2 Desired Leader Profile in Business Settings in Iceland

In order to conceptualize the preferred leader behavior profile in recognition of the culture, Frederick Littrell (2013) applied the Leader Behavior Description Questionnaire Form XII (LBDQ XII) to assess 12 dimensions including Representation, Demand Reconciliation, Tolerance of Uncertainty, Persuasiveness, Initiation of Structure, Tolerance of Freedom, Role Assumption, Consideration, Production

Table 5.1 Preferred leader behavior dimensions defined by the LBDQ XII

Preferred leader behavior dimensions defined by the LBDQ XII	
Factor 1: *Representation* measures to what degree the manager speaks as the representative of the group	Factor 7: *Role Assumption* measures to what degree the manager actively exercises the leadership role rather than surrendering leadership to others
Factor 2: *Demand Reconciliation* reflects how well the manager reconciles conflicting demands and reduces disorder to the system	Factor 8: *Consideration* depicts to what extent the manager regards the comfort, well-being, status, and contributions of followers
Factor 3: *Tolerance of Uncertainty* depicts to what extent the manager can tolerate uncertainty and postponement without anxiety alternatively, getting upset	Factor 9: *Production Emphasis* measures to what degree the manager applies pressure for productive output
Factor 4: *Persuasiveness* measures to what extent the manager uses persuasion and argument effectively and exhibits strong convictions	Factor 10: *Predictive Accuracy* measures to what extent the manager exhibits foresight and ability to predict outcomes accurately
Factor 5: *Initiation of Structure* measures to what degree the manager clearly defines his/her own role and lets followers know what is expected	Factor 11: *Integration* reflects to what degree the manager maintains a closel-knit organization and resolves intermembered conflicts
Factor 6: *Tolerance of Freedom* reflects to what extent the manager allows followers scope for initiative, decision, and action	Factor 12: *Superior Orientation* measures to what extent the manager maintains cordial relations with superiors, holds weight with them, and is striving for higher status

Source: Summarized from Stogdill (1963)

Emphasis, Predictive Accuracy, Integration, and Superior Orientation. These dimensions are presented in Table 5.1.

The study findings have revealed that Integration, Demand reconciliation, Representation, and Initiation of structure are considered by Icelandic followers to be the most important dimensions of the ideal leader profile. In contrast to a large number of other cultural contexts around the globe, the followers in Iceland expressed generally uniform attitudes when describing ideal leader behavior. Certain key follower demographic variables, including gender, education level, and age had no significant effects on the description of an ideal leader. Hence, the ideal leader in the eyes of the follower has to, first and foremost, be able to maintain a close-knit organization and resolve intermembered conflicts (Stogdill 1963). These characteristics suggest that followers expect to experience a healthy team spirit and sense of unity in their work organization and that ensuring such an environment is assumed to be the leader's overarching objective. These findings support the results of the studies in the GLOBE project (House et al. 2004), which highlighted team-oriented leadership as one of the most desired qualities in the Nordic region. The leader's social skills are captured in the integration dimension (Peterson and Seligman 2004), portraying the ideal leader as perceived by the followers to be a highly socially competent individual.

The second most crucial characteristic outlined by the followers, namely, the Demand reconciliation, referring to the degree of leader's ability to successfully reconcile the conflicting demands and reduce disorder (Stogdill 1963). This characteristic is acknowledged by the followers from a relational standpoint even though it primarily considers the individual level. Hence, Icelanders expect to follow a leader who can prevent or at least reduce and resolve various conflicts both within and outside the organization. An additionally highlighted dimension is Representation or the degree to which the leader conveys the voice of the group and serves as its representative (Stogdill 1963) which is also attributed to personality (Peterson and Seligman 2004). In a way, this characteristic refers to charismatic leadership, which is valued in the Nordic countries as it is in a broader international context as a universally desired attribute (House et al. 2004). Representation is complemented with the Initiation of structure, which reflects the leader's ability to define clearly his or her own role within the organization and set expectations for the followers (Stogdill 1963). This finding indicates that followers seek and are in need of clarity, which results in clearer evaluation of performance and more efficient workflow. As such, from the perspective of the followers in Iceland, certain leadership styles, such as distributed leadership, will require specific adjustments in accordance with the general cultural context while still preserving a necessary level of formality that does not breed a sense of hierarchy. Taken altogether, these reflections suggest that the ideal leader is seen as an individual who is able to proactively delegate and assign resources while preserving a considerable sense of the overall direction in organizational progress.

5.3   Desired Leader Profile in the Education Sector in Iceland

School leadership presents a different leadership context where, however, the same tenets exist with leadership being primarily based on relationships and interactions. These interactions take place between principals as formal leaders and subordinates, teachers, as followers with constant interdependence, mutual influence, and varying degrees of reciprocity, as well as the common goals of changing and improving learning and its outcomes (Woolfolk Hoy et al. 2009). Despite the fact that the education sector is usually less often associated with rapid change and turbulence or the challenges of entrepreneurial leadership that call for continuous revisiting of business models, educational leaders, commonly represented by educational leaders, from government officials to school principals, today are facing major challenges internationally (Fullan 2007). A considerable part of these changes is associated with growing and changing expectations of the roles of educational leaders at all levels. For example, the recent Improving School Leadership activity by the Organization for Economic Co-operation and Development (OECD) highlighted improved student learning outcomes as one of the definitive characteristics of school leadership performance. Following this mission, in leadership of contemporary school, leaders and followers, such as principals and teachers, are driven by the same goal of transforming the educational environment for the students toward higher quality (Lárusdóttir 2014). Besides the changing educational needs and demands of the students, these challenges are to a great extent associated with similar conflicting demands, values, and requirements of a myriad of stakeholders, including subordinates (teachers), students, parents, state and federal agencies, officials, unions, and other parties (Bartoletti and Connelly 2013; Hoy and Miskel 2008) that can potentially lead to role ambiguity and role conflict for everyone.

The countries neighboring Iceland, such as the Scandinavian countries, provide a set of favorable insights that are captured in the abovementioned initiative by OECD addressing the improvement of school leadership. Firstly, they reflect the significance of leadership identity formation in Sweden, Demark, and Norway. More specifically, these nations place an extremely heavy emphasis on the promotion of democracy as a fundamental social value (Møller 2009). Secondly, an important distinction in framing a school leader's identity was the differentiation of school leadership from teaching (Møller 2009). Finally, in Norway, the distribution of leadership is highlighted where school leadership is extended to teachers who are expected to take an active role (Møller et al. 2007). However, even though a growing homogenization of approaches to governance is present among these nations, different cultural contexts, even slight ones, can result in distinct practices (Møller 2009). Hence, educational leadership in Iceland is likely to be a distinct practice in its own terms. Unfortunately, the relevant data that is currently available provides room for only a limited overview.

The academic discourse on the urge to transform the leadership in the educational sectors is particularly strengthened by the policymakers (the White Paper by the Parliament of Iceland; Hálfdánardóttir 2014; Óskarsson 2015). To date, however, the study of principal-level leadership in educational sector in Iceland is nascent but encouraged by iterative calls for effective leadership (Hansen 2013) and changing settings such as the nation's growing cultural diversity Statistics Iceland (2018a). Though the work responsibilities of compulsory school principals have been considerably researched over the past two decades, the investigation of instructional leadership of principals is less comprehensive (Hansen and Lárusdóttir 2015). Specifically, there is a considerable lack of research that focuses on managerial leadership in the upper echelon positions beyond the teacher level in schools and individuals who have responsibility for multiple levels of educational institutions (Hansen et al. 2005; Hansen 2013). Most of the extant research is quite narrow, primarily focusing only on such as compulsory school level, while the other three levels (preschool, upper secondary school, and university), specifically investigating the leader-follower dyads that exist within them, remain under-researched (Hansen 2013; Hansen et al. 2005). The findings from a number of available small-scale studies, however, mirror the tendencies observed globally. For example, a study by Lárusdóttir (2014) reflected that educational leaders in Iceland work in an unstable environment, characterized by conflicting demands and competing values of the school stakeholders. This variety of different stakeholders is likely to yield contradicting expectations and demands for the leader (Graen 1976).

At the same time, evaluation of leadership effectiveness in the educational context appears to relate with the leader prototypes and their match with several trends emerging in Iceland. A study by Gudmundsson on the relationship between school authorities and upper secondary school teachers (in this case, followers) in Iceland found that the latter indicated that effective communication with managers (or headmasters), support, encouragement, and teamwork to be of vital importance for headmaster-teacher relationships. At the same time, the teachers who are the followers in this specific context and enact the role of middle leaders report that they are often in a challenging and confusing position, being general members of staff and middle leaders at the same time, additionally denoting the imbalanced communication and trust from their leaders, embodied by the school principals (Lárusdóttir and O'Connor 2017).

The teaching profession in Iceland is overwhelmingly female, with only 22% male in total of individuals employed in the educational sector (Statistics Iceland 2018b), just like in European countries, where 70% of teachers at lower or middle levels are women (European Commission report 2013). Nevertheless, regardless of their gender, educational leaders confirmed care to be the core value in their primary activities and being a pedagogical leader as the primary role (Lárusdóttir 2014). At the same time, a study by Lárusdóttir (2014) has revealed that middle leaders are feeling a lack of power and that their positions are somewhat "positional" and not "influential."

A comprehensive research study by Urboniene et al. (2018) that covered primary, compulsory, and secondary school levels, kindergartens, and after-school programs further outlined followers' expectations of leaders. Consistent with the framework of Stogdill, study of leadership in the business sector, Urboniene et al. (2018) administered the Leader Behavior Description Questionnaire Form XII (LBDQ XII) for educators to assess their standing on the same 12 dimensions of Representation, Demand Reconciliation, Tolerance of Uncertainty, Persuasiveness, Initiation of Structure, Tolerance of Freedom, Role Assumption, Consideration, Production Emphasis, Predictive Accuracy, Integration, and Superior Orientation. The strongest preferences in terms of leadership behavior identified Demand reconciliation, Representation, Integration, Consideration, and Tolerance of freedom as the key dimensions. The least appreciated leader behavior was associated with the Production Emphasis, characterized by overtime work, competition, and urgency to beat the previous work records, what is echoed in the studies of other authors confirming the leaders being overwhelmed with increasing duties and workload (e.g., Hansen 2013; Lárusdóttir 2014), and it is a frequent finding in studies among professional employees in Europe (Schneider and Littrell 2003). These preferences are quite unified regardless of sociodemographic characteristics.

The Demand reconciliation dimension refers to the leader's ability to reduce disorder and reconcile the conflicting demands within an organization. The preference of the followers in the educational sector for the Demand reconciliation dimension reflects their needs in a context with conflicting demands and expectations, potentially leading to role ambiguity and role conflict. Followers expect that their leaders would be able to solve problems efficiently and successfully navigate through the multitude of demands and also to support the staff when in the face of complicated situations. Here, the leader's abilities and skills to nurture the relationships with the followers emerge again as a significant aspect, while leaders are expected to maintain a tightly knit organization, preserve and promote team cohesion, and resolve the arising intermembered conflicts. Furthermore, as educators in Iceland spend a considerable amount of years in a single institution, an emphasis should be put on the sustainability of these abilities and practice in a leader's profile.

Some variation in perceptions and expectations can be seen with regard to the follower's age. The findings of the study indicated a positive even though a weak correlation between age of the follower and his or her leader preferences in terms of Demand Reconciliation and Consideration. Essentially, this translates as older respondents giving higher importance to the leader's ability to solve complex problems efficiently. On a broader level, this refers to the leader nurturing comfort, well-being, status, and contributions of their followers. This is an important outline when the factors such as age of the middle leaders often represented by the teachers come at play: according to the report by OECD (2016), the proportion of the teachers over 50 years of age reached 38.6% of all the teaching staff in 2013.

The followers' appreciation of the Representation of the group dimension indicates their need for a visible representative and a spokesperson on behalf of their group. This is likely to be associated with the vulnerability that the followers likely experience in the face of the significant and often rapid changes posited on the educational sector in general, which in turn can dramatically impact the assigned roles of educators at both national and international levels. In this vein, leaders are expected to attend closely to the comfort, well-being, status, and contributions of their followers—all pinpointing to the charismatic behavior of the leader. These findings are again in line with the observations by House et al. (2004) on charismatic leadership being a universally desired behavior of a leader.

Given the effects of a rapidly changing working environment on the educational sector, the low preference for Production emphasis, which is associated with maximizing output and surpassing previous results, is understandable. Nonetheless, given the many potential factors that can influence one's orientation to Production emphasis, further research in this area is certainly needed.

Finally, the essential preferences are related to empowerment of employees through affording them the Tolerance of Freedom to act of a leader; providing such support and encouragement to their employees is recognized as a core value among educational leaders and central to their identities (Lárusdóttir 2014). Finally, the leader is expected to acknowledge and attend to the double role in the educational sector—for example, the teachers who are simultaneously enacting the roles of both leaders and followers.

The results of this research by Urboniene et al. (2018) have indicated coherence with the structural theoretical approach articulated by Roxas and Stoneback (2004) and unified perspective regardless the gender of the followers. This is consistent with previous findings in the business sector in Iceland (Snaebjornsson 2016) and the high degree of gender equality in Iceland (World Economic Forum 2016). Likewise, the education level of followers did not yield any differences in their preferences for desired leader behavior. Indeed, it is not without a limitation that this particular sample was mainly comprised of professionals holding university education specifically within the education field, inclusive of the field-specific values and norms. Finally, while the research was conducted on primary, compulsory, and secondary school levels, kindergartens, and after-school programs, all of the participating institutions were substantially similar with no apparent differences across the preferred leader profiles.

As the current findings imply, the situation of educational leadership in Iceland echoes the neighboring Scandinavian region that calls for, and already has advanced toward, decentralizing the national educational governance (Ärlestig et al. 2016). Such an approach would allow school principals to engage in more distributive leadership practice that cultivates more active involvement of and collaboration with their teachers. In managerial leadership terms, such practices point to the growing role of the quality of relationships and interactions between the leader and the follower and are marked by their interdependence. Continued research is anticipated to further explore the complexities of effective leadership in school settings. More specifically, by better understanding what followers desire from their leaders, as well as the underlying cultural influences from which these preferences stem, researchers and educational practitioners can better strategize for optimally effective leadership in Iceland's schools.

5.4   Concluding Remarks

Whereas some previous research has found that some countries show low within-country variance in terms of followers' ideal leader behavior, other studies have found significant differences among followers' preferences (Littrell and Snaebjornsson 2016). The cultural context of Iceland is rather unique; there is a broad agreement and almost univocal attitudes in this regard: the followers' preferences toward leader profiles in the business sector in Iceland suggest considerably uniform attitudes in contrast to the observations in international contexts (Snaebjorsson 2016). In a sense, all followers expect to engage with leaders who are highly socially competent and able to maintain effective and empowering communication, assume accountability for the followers, withstand and successfully meet the demanding and often differing performance expectations, support the followers in managing the complexities in their own roles, and resolve conflicts that are likely to arise in any of these areas. The research area that studies leadership in the educational sector further perpetuates no differences in expected leader profiles as a result of sociodemographic characteristics. It further suggests that indeed, to a certain degree borrowing and transferring managerial leadership knowledge and practices from the business sector are viable. These findings yield positive news and potential for the integration of managerial practices and development of leadership on an across-country and across-industry level. The infusion of leadership-fostering programs and policy development in both business and public sectors is not only possible but actually somewhat facilitated within the context of the rather small and homogenous Icelandic society. Certainly, further studies that would monitor the changes in demands and attitudes toward leadership and contribute to the development of nuanced solutions that tackle the possible effects of sectors and industry types are anticipated. As a contribution, such studies would additionally transmit the leadership profile in Icelandic cultural context. To date, however, the extant findings are twofold. First, Iceland represents a unique context where followers and leaders may co-construct and produce a uniform view of a preferred leader profile. Secondly, within the country, they open up broad avenues for consolidation of economic and social capital in order to develop and foster culturally univocal leadership that accurately corresponds with the expectations within the Icelandic society.

References

Antonakis J, Cianciolo AT, Sternberg RJ (2004) Leadership: past, present, and future. In: Antonakis A, Cianciolo T, Sternberg RJ (eds) The nature of leadership. Sage, Thousand Oaks, pp 3–15

Ärlestig H, Johansson O, Nihlfors E (2016) Sweden: Swedish School Leadership Research – an important but neglected area. In: Ärlestig H, Johansson O, Day C (eds) A decade of research on school principals. Springer, Dordrecht, pp 103–122

Bartoletti J, Connelly G (2013) Leadership matters: what the research says about the importance of principal leadership. National Association of Elementary School Principals, Reston, VA, p 16

Cappelli P, Sherer PD (1991) The missing role of context in OB: the need for a mesolevel approach. Organ Behav 13:55–110

DeRue DS, Ashford SJ (2010) Who will lead and who will follow? A social process of leadership identity construction in organizations. Acad Manage Rev 35(4):627–647

DeRue DS, Ashford SJ, Cotton NC (2009) Assuming the mantle: unpacking the process by which individuals internalize a leader identity. Exploring positive identities and organizations: building a theoretical and research foundation. Taylor & Francis, New York

Dorfman P, Javidan M, Hanges P, Dastmalchian A, House R (2012) GLOBE: a twenty year journey into the intriguing world of culture and leadership. J World Bus 47(4):504–518

Eagly AH, Karau SJ (2002) Role congruity theory of prejudice toward female leaders. Psychol Rev 109(3):573

Earley PC (1993) Culture, self-identity, and work. Oxford University Press, Oxford

European Commission (2013) European commission report. Retrieved May 11, 2017, from https://eacea.ec.europa.eu/sites/2007-2013/archiving

Fletcher JK, Bailyn L (2005) The equity imperative: redesigning work for work-family integration. Lawrence Erlbaum Associates, Mahwah

Frederick Littrell R (2013) Explicit leader behaviour: a review of literature, theory development, and research project results. J Manag Dev 32(6):567–605

Fullan M (2007) Change the terms for teacher learning. Learn Prof 28(3):35

Gilligan C (1982) In a different voice. Harvard University Press, Cambridge

Goethals GR, Sorenson GJ (2007) The quest for a general theory of leadership. Edward Elgar, Cheltenham

Graen GB (1976) Role making processes within complex organizations. In: Dunnette MD (ed) Handbook of industrial and organizational psychology. Rand-McNally, Chicago, pp 1201–1245

Hansen B (2013) Transnational influence and educational policy in Iceland. In: Transnational influences on values and practices in Nordic educational leadership, vol 19, pp 49–60. https://doi.org/10.1007/978-94-007-6226-8_4

Hansen B, Lárusdóttir SH (2015) Instructional leadership in compulsory schools in Iceland and the role of school principals. Scand J Educ Res 59(5):583–603

Hansen B, Jóhannsson ÓH, Lárusdóttir SH (2005) Hvaða þættir ráða mestu um hvernig gengur að innleiða aðferðir við sjálfsmat í grunnskólum?: niðurstöður athugana í sex skólum

Hálfdánardóttir A (2014) Aðgengi eða áhugi? Munur á efnistökum og vægi frétta eftir karla og konur (Doctoral dissertation)

Hogg MA (2001) A social identity theory of leadership. Pers Soc Psychol Rev 5(3):184–200

Hogg MA (2007) Uncertainty–identity theory. Adv Exp Soc Psychol 39:69–126

House RJ, Wright NS, Aditya RN (1997) Cross-cultural research on organizational leadership: a critical analysis and a proposed theory. In: Earley PC, Erez M (eds) New perspectives on international industrial and organizational psychology. Lexington Press, San Francisco, pp 535–625

House RJ, Hanges PJ, Javidan M, Dorfman PW, Gupta V (2004) Culture, leadership, and organizations: the GLOBE study of 62 societies. Sage, Thousand Oaks

Hoy WK, Miskel CG (2008) The school as a social system. In: Educational administration: theory, research, and practice. McGraw-Hill, Boston, MA, pp 1–40

Hunt JG (1991) Leadership: a new synthesis. Sage, Newbury Park

Javidan M, House RJ, Dorfman PW (2004) A nontechnical summary of GLOBE findings. In: House RJ, Hanges PJ, Javidan M, Dorfman PW, Gupta V (eds) Culture, leadership, and organizations: the GLOBE study of 62 societies. Sage, Thousand Oaks, pp 29–48

Kahn RL, Wolfe DM, Quinn RP, Snoek JD, Rosenthal RA (1964) Organizational stress: studies in role conflict and ambiguity. Wiley, Oxford

Lárusdóttir SH (2014) Educational leadership and market values: a study of school principals in Iceland. Educ Manage Admin Leadersh 42(4):83–103

Lárusdóttir SH, O'Connor E (2017) Distributed leadership and middle leadership practice in schools: a disconnect? Irish Educational Studies 36(4):423–438

Littrell RF (2010) Comparative value priorities of Chinese and New Zealand business people and their relationships to preferred managerial leader behaviour. Auckland University of Technology

Littrell RF, Snaebjornsson IM (2016) Comparison of managerial leadership behavior preferences across nationalities, industries, and gender. In: Academy of international business 2016 conference, New Orleans, LA

Lord RG, Emrich CG (2000) Thinking outside the box by looking inside the box: extending the cognitive revolution in leadership research. Leadersh Q 11(4):551–579

Lord RG, Maher KJ (1991) Cognitive theory in industrial and organizational psychology. Handb Ind Organ Psychol 2:1–62

Lord RG, Maher KJ (2002) Leadership and information processing: linking perceptions and performance. Routledge, London

Meindl JR (1995) The romance of leadership as a follower-centric theory: a social constructionist approach. Leadersh Q 6(3):329–341

Møller J et al (2007) Successful leadership based on democratic values. In: Day C, Leithwood K (eds) Successful principal leadership in times of change. Studies in educational leadership, vol 5. Springer, Dordrecht

Møller J (2009) School leadership in an age of accountability: tensions between managerial and professional accountability. J Educ Change 10(1):37–46

Organisation for Economic Co-operation and Development (2008) PISA 2008 results. Retrieved from https://www.oecd.org/pisa/pisaproducts/46619703.pdf

Organisation for Economic Co-operation and Development (2016) PISA 2015 key findings for Iceland. Retrieved May 12, 2017, from http://www.oecd.org/iceland/pisa-2015-iceland.htm

Óskarsson E (2015) Nýir stjórnendur á vinnustað í vanda. https://skemman.is/handle/1946/20478

Peterson C, Seligman ME (2004) Character strengths and virtues: a handbook and classification. Oxford University Press, New York

Peterson D, Rhoads A, Vaught BC (2001) Ethical beliefs of business professionals: a study of gender, age and external factors. J Bus Ethics 31(3):225–232

Rizzo JR, House RJ, Lirtzman SI (1970) Role conflict and ambiguity in complex organizations. Adm Sci Q:150–163

Roxas ML, Stoneback JY (2004) The importance of gender across cultures in ethical decision-making. J Bus Ethics 50(2):149–165

Schleicher A (2012) Preparing teachers and developing school leaders for the 21st century: lessons from around the world. OECD, Paris

Schneider J, Littrell RF (2003) Leadership preferences of German and English managers. J Manage Dev 22(2):130–148

Shaw JB (1990) A cognitive categorization model for the study of intercultural management. Acad Manage Rev 15(4):626–645

Snaebjornsson IM (2016) Ideal leader profiles in the Icelandic business sector: evidence of 352 uniformity of followers' attitudes. Tímarit um viðskipti og efnahagsmál 13(2):97–118

Statistics Iceland (2018a) External migration by sex, age and citizenship 1986–2017. https://www.statice.is/statistics/population/migration/external-migration/

Statistics Iceland (2018b) Labour force survey. https://www.statice.is/statistics/society/labour-market/labour-force-survey/

Stogdill RM (1963) Manual for the leader behaviour description questionnaire-Form XII: an experimental revision. Ohio State University, Bureau of Business Research, College of Commerce and Administration, Columbus

Uhl-Bien M, Riggio RE, Lowe KB, Carsten MK (2014) Followership theory: a review and research agenda. Leadersh Q 25(1):83–104

Urboniene L, Kristjánsdóttir ES, Minelgaite I, Littrell RF (2018) The desired managerial leader behavior: leader profile in the education sector in Iceland examined from a follower-centric perspective. SAGE Open 8(2):1–11. https://doi.org/10.1177/2158244018780948

Woolfolk Hoy A, Hoy WK, Davis HA (2009) Teachers' self-efficacy beliefs. In: Wentzel KR, Wigfield A (eds) Handbook of motivation at school. Routledge, New York, pp 627–653

World Economic Forum (2016) Global Gender Gap Report 2016. http://www3.weforum.org/docs/GGGR16/WEF_Global_Gender_Gap_Report_2016.pdf

Yukl GA (2013) Leadership in organizations. Pearson Education, Harlow

Part II
Transforming Leadership: An Entrepreneurial Perspective

Chapter 6
Small, but Mighty: Icelandic Business Environment Before and After the Financial Crisis of 2008

Before financial crisis the leaders of banks were seen almost as heroes, unquestionable, and people would blindly follow their steps. After the crisis, the leaders in banking industry are seen more as humans, managers, professionals.
H. Sigurgeirsson, Personal communication, 6th March, 2018

Abstract In 2008, Iceland resembled the lost land of Atlantis that was steadily going under the water at an increasing pace. What could have become a Plato's legend that turned to reality resulted in a different storyline. Even when events turn to a force majeure, and the magnitude of the turbulence reaches a level of a catastrophe, it is the human factor, which, despite often being a contributing factor in causing the chaos, can also play a vital role in preventing the irreversible consequences. What potentially could be called a miracle is Icelanders' resilience and ability to revert the order. This chapter lays out the story how the crisis shaped the business environment of Iceland in relation to the social aspect that so far has remained less unpacked in the literature covering the crisis.

Keywords Business environment · Financial crises

6.1 The Bigger Picture

As Jónsson and Sigurgeirsson (2017) reflect, in October 2008, "Iceland, for all the wrong reasons, had the world's attention." Marked by the collapse of its three main banks and the national currency within 1 week and accompanying growing political and societal unrest, Iceland, as widely reflected in the literature, seemed to be at the epicenter of an earthquake that spread to the rest of the world. At the same time, this earthquake paradoxically reshaped the Icelandic business environment and its landscape into a dynamic, thriving, and growth-oriented one.

© Springer International Publishing AG, part of Springer Nature 2018
I. Minelgaite et al., *Demystifying Leadership in Iceland*, Contributions to
Management Science, https://doi.org/10.1007/978-3-319-96044-9_6

Some researchers and analysts provided an optimistic perspective, stating that the Icelandic economy had the potential to be restored because of the thriving sectors that still existed at the time, such as fishing industry, energy-intensive industry, agriculture, food production, information technology, and tourism (Karlsson and Steinþórsson 2009). In addition, other assets such as strong national infrastructure, educational institutions, top-level administration, and support teams further buoyed the nation in its effort to withstand the crisis (Karlsson and Steinþórsson 2009).

While much is written and even more is said about the Iceland in the context of the crisis of 2008, many aspects remain to be investigated in order to take away as much as possible from those lessons for building a sustainable future. The preludes and effects of the crisis from an economy standpoint have been widely analyzed and illustrated (e.g., Bergmann 2014; Jónsson 2009; Danielsson and Zoega 2009; Buiter 2009; Jónsson and Sigurgeirsson 2017). However, it is not uncommon for studies on economy to underestimate the role of cultural evolution as a path dependent process, despite it being essential for understanding human behavior (Henrich et al. 2008). In essence, collapse as a term broadly covers a number of different processes with consequences in a multitude of areas, including economics, which, however, mainly stems from sociopolitical sphere (Tainter 1988). While collapse and disintegration of a society always remains a concerning possibility of highest social significance, it calls for studies across different disciplines with sociopolitical complexity as the core (Tainter 1988).

As Sahlins (1985) previously noted, understanding of social phenomena calls for understanding historical events and the cultural meanings which actors do attribute to these events. As Loftsdóttir (2014) explains, for Icelanders themselves, the crisis, as a historical moment, drew a demarcation between "before" and "after" the crisis. When talking about the crisis, Icelanders use the concept *kreppa* that primarily means a contraction and reflects a state or a result of something that happened, rather than a gradual change in the economic situation (Loftsdóttir 2014). This differentiation connotes Schein's (2010) idea that culture can be referred to as a "state" of a particular system before a change takes place. Therefore, there is a significant differentiation in the Iceland's business environment between the states "before" and "after."

There is some evidence illustrating that the economic collapse of 2008 was preceded by sociopolitical and cultural issues that served as the antecedents of the crisis. Before and shortly after the crisis, the Icelandic business environment was permeated by a weak culture (Vaiman et al. 2010; Sigurjonsson et al. 2014) with a general lack of transparency, integrity, and justice (Jónsdóttir and Steinþórsson 2010). Vaiman et al. (2010) contend that a specific form of corruption, fueled by weak business culture and symbiosis of business and politics, rather than traditional corruption, provided room for unethical, self-serving decisions that were made by both business and political elite of Iceland. It is likely, that together with nepotism which is a natural yet unfavorable phenomenon in a relatively small society like Iceland (Ísleifsdóttir and Guðmundsdóttir 2015) where so many individuals are connected through familial ties (Sigurjonsson et al. 2014); gave momentum to the downfall of the economy. This is discussed more in depth in the works of Loftsdóttir

(2014) and Jónsson (2009). Some elements of the organizational culture also remained undefined, with, for example, nearly a half of small- and medium-sized companies reporting not having employee policy (Eðvarðsson and Óskarsson 2012).

In comparison to the great collapses of empires throughout history worldwide, which must be marked by rapidness and substantial loss of sociopolitical structure (Tainter 1988), the crisis of 2008 can perhaps be still considered as more of downfall or decline. This outcome can partly be attributed to the change of a cultural mindset of the society and organizational culture. If among the instigators of the downfall were the Icelandic entrepreneurs who successfully joined the global elite (Loftsdóttir 2014), still, it is a wider community of entrepreneurs as active members of society, who contribute to the recovery. Hence, as Bergmann puts it, "...in the years leading up to the Crash, Iceland had been trumpeted in world business media as an economic miracle" (2014, p. 1), which was also strongly advocated by the Icelandic government, business, and media (Loftsdóttir 2014). Thanks to the favorable economic factors (including tourism inflow and profitable yields in the fishing industry), as well as the changing business environment, the Icelanders managed to achieve a relatively rapid recovery after the crisis (Bergmann 2014), which has changed the potentially bleak environment and transformed the adverse events into the basis for a newly shaped economy. In response to the antecedents and aftermath of the downfall, the previously undermined social responsibility gained its role rapidly across the business practice and education of socially responsible managers. This shift toward social responsibility illustrates a cultural change following the underlying concepts and frameworks developed by Lewin (1951) and Schein (1990–2010). While it is the most difficult to change culture in the organizations (Schein 2010), the disequilibrium caused by the collapse created enough power to induce a cultural shift which was clearly evident in the business environment. In essence, this shift follows Lewin's (1951) classical three-step approach of change known as unfreezing-changing-refreezing, and their characterizations reflect those suggested by Schein (2010). Existing data suggests that this cultural change primarily manifested through restructuring the concept and learning the new concept (Schein 2010) of social responsibility which now manifests through corporate practice and education of socially responsible managers.

6.2 The Cultural Shift in Icelandic Business Culture: Unfreezing and Changing

The direction of the evolution of a particular system is determined by several forces: "(1) technological and physical changes in the strategic environment; (2) changes in the internal dynamics of the social system; (3) historical circumstances that are fortuitous or serendipitous" (Schein 2012, p. 253). While changes in the strategic environment of organizations were undoubtedly present, the evolution of organizations in Iceland to a great extent was evidently shaped by the sudden collapse in

2008. This event became one of the most significant historical circumstances, and the changes in the internal dynamics of the society eventually were transmitted and internalized, including dynamics of the business community and organizations.

6.2.1 Unfreezing

In order for the cognitive structure to undergo major changes, the system must first be subjected to substantial disequilibrium, including a sense of threat, crisis, or dissatisfaction, which induces a coping process (Schein 2010). Edgar Schein identified three different processes that are all required for motivation to change, in line with Lewin's idea of "unfreezing." Firstly, there must be enough disconfirming data present that would lead to strong discomfort and disequilibrium. Secondly, the disconfirming data must be connected to important goals and ideals and eventually cause anxiety and/or guilt. Finally, a sufficient degree of psychological safety is required, associated with the ability to see the possibility of solving the problem and learning something new without loss of identity or integrity. Disconfirming data can be economic, political, social, or personal and refers to pieces of information which indicate some goals being not met or some processes not accomplishing the goals that they are supposed to (Schein 2010). It also evokes anxiety among the members of an organization and signals which change is required in order to avoid negative ramifications (Schein 2010). As Schein (2010) contends, this disconfirming data represents symptoms that in turn require diagnostic work with a focus on the underlying problem or specific issue and its definition and formulation of the new, specific behavioral goals. This analysis involves an assessment of the culture so that one can identify the degree to which the cultural elements have contributed to the problem situation (Schein 2010). At the same time, for the motivation to change and to arise, a belief that new order is achievable and the learning process will not bring too much anxiety is required. In the case of Iceland, the crisis led the society and business community to assess the weak business culture and identify the nepotism and the social irresponsibility as the problematic cultural elements.

Until the crisis of 2008, which resulted in an economic collapse, social responsibility was pursued by Icelandic companies in a limited scope, mainly through philanthropy and cultural, sports, and educational activities (Arnarsdóttir 2009). After the crisis, the situation turned around. Even though the companies were beginning to feel public pressure to begin acting more socially responsible before 2008, the crisis forced this to be a prominent issue, and the companies increasingly felt the public pressure to assume responsibility for their impact on the society and the environment (Jóhannsdóttir et al. 2016). The public debate questioned parliament, government officials, and businesses in general, calling for a redefinition of values and social responsibility-fueled performance and accountability toward their stakeholders (Jónsdóttir et al. 2015).

6.2.2 Changing

Schein (2010) argues that in order for the transformative change to take place, the target of change (e.g., the person or the group) must unlearn something and learn something new. In Iceland, restructuring of the concept of social responsibility and learning it anew was explicitly the case. The external pressure from the society on business environment increased both awareness of the true meaning of corporate social responsibility and the socially responsible corporate practices. In turn, this focus on increasing knowledge and the visibility of the concept has promoted the company motivation and actions (Ólafsson et al. 2016). Despite that there is still a lack of knowledge of corporate social responsibility among Icelandic companies and the governmental support is still limited (Ólafsson et al. 2016), the corporate landscape is more and more gaining the socially responsible shape. For example, many companies have adopted the corporate governance policies, the guidelines for corporate governance issued by the Icelandic Chamber of Commerce (Johannsdottir et al. 2015). In 2011, Festa, the Center for Corporate Social Responsibility, was founded by six companies (Landsbankinn, Landsvirkjun, Íslandsbanki, Rio Tinto Alcan, Síminn, and Össur). By 2013, the number of companies had increased to 29 (Ólafsson et al. 2016). Today, social responsibility in Icelandic business is more highly valued and practiced, and its prominence continues to increase steadily with foci on environmental issues, human resources, impact on society, transparency, business practices, ethical conduct, and charity activities (Ólafsson et al. 2016). This commitment to social responsibility is more pronounced among the larger companies that also experience greater pressure from the environment, prompting in more written policies, connections with the community, and partnerships with stakeholders, in contrast to the smaller companies (Jónsdóttir and Steinþórsson 2010). Finally, the interest of the investment community in sustainable and responsible investment has been growing, leading to the establishment of the Iceland Sustainable Investment Forum (IcelandSIF) in 2017.

In examination of incentives that contribute to, or may contribute to, increased corporate social responsibility and/or environmental responsibility, Kjartansdóttir and Jóhannsdóttir (2015) followed along Hoffman's theory (2000) and identified 11 incentives in Icelandic context. These were public procurement, general procurement, government, legislation, finances, consumers, image, innovation and product development, interest, information and sharing, municipalities, environmental accounting, and community reports. Kjartansdóttir and Jóhannsdóttir (2015) further noticed the little emphasis on competitors, while the companies highlighted the increased demands from consumers and the pressure to develop their products and services, summing up to behavior as a response, rather than initiative, with legislation and authorities being among the major influential factors. On the other hand, when social responsibility in the workplace is considered, the companies do not feel the pressure from the national government as the insights by Ólafsson et al. (2016) further suggest. Instead, many firms mention workers as the driving force of action, as the employees will be more satisfied and perform better in companies with a social focus. The incentives to engage in socially responsible practice also arise in the external environment and manifest through, for example, the role of corporate image.

Government action can also become an agent for social change (Aguilera et al. 2007), with established regulatory mechanisms serving as incentives. In Iceland, an increased legal pressure has been observed to engage in socially responsible practices, affecting companies of particular size and type and promoting integrated reporting which applies to companies of a certain size (view the law) and public interest units (such as pension funds, credit institutions, and insurance companies). It includes information necessary for assessing the development, extent, status, and impact of the company in relation to environmental, social, and employee affairs, company's policy on human rights issues, and how the company is managing corruption and justice (Althingi 2016).

The real transformation ultimately calls for behavior change and thus for a genuine cognitive redefinition and restructuring of concepts and learning new concepts (Schein 2010). The increasingly growing value of corporate social responsibility is Icelandic business context transmitted into the understanding of education. A study involving 1000 managers from the largest Icelandic companies underscored a belief that the weak business culture had penetrated the curricula of universities, accompanied by the lack of courses in corporate social responsibility, corporate governance, and business ethics (Sigurjonsson et al. 2014). Perhaps incidentally, a study in the University of Iceland was conducted in October 2008, assessing how well master's students in business management know the terms related to the eco-friendly or sustainable corporate operations. Two hundred and seventeen students were presented with 15 environmental concepts that addressed environmental literacy on a 5-point scale. The results of the study revealed that the master's students had not attended courses that considered ecological or sustainable management and the environmental impact and that the students' general awareness of these issues was very limited. The students performed best when the concepts of climate change and greenhouse gases were presented, but when they were asked about methods of management that companies used to deal with environment-related problems, the knowledge was very limited (Jóhannsdóttir 2009).

Finally, as Schein (2010) highlights, behavior change can only be lasting if it is preceded or accompanied by cognitive redefinition. The business community in Iceland already identifies the need for such cognitive redefinition of social responsibility. The study by Sigurjonsson et al. (2014) revealed that the business community considers the universities to have a major role in the discourse on business ethics and expects the graduates to have substantial ethical standards before joining the organizations and that this expectation is higher among experienced managers. The responses in this study also signaled a request for a different approach in terms of business ethics education by the universities, that is, business ethics becoming a mandatory and integrated as a part of the curriculum rather than simply a stand-alone course. Even more so, the managers themselves expressed a demand for the reeducation of the current practitioners to navigate them through corporate governance and business ethics, as well as equip them with good role models.

6.3   Concluding Remarks

As it can be seen, the business environment in Iceland was subjected to cultural change as a result of the economic and cultural collapse in 2008; in fact, these changes created a cultural impact that still lasts today. Existing data suggest that many organizations have already gone through the stages of unfreezing and changing. Indeed, the change is still taking place currently. In the change of framework, the final step in the process is refreezing, which involves reinforcement of the new behavior and set of cognitions and gradual stabilization of new beliefs and values (Lewin 1951; Schein 2010). For the refreezing to take place, a genuine internalization of new cognitive constructs and standards of evaluation is required and can be effectively achieved as the learners actively engage in designing the learning process. For the Icelandic business community and society, in general, this implies that close cooperation between organizations and their stakeholders, including communities and the government, is crucial. Currently, the businesses admit the existence of internal barriers that primarily relate to resources, corporate culture, attitudes and factors of technical nature (Ólafsson et al. 2016), company size, and lack of time as a resource (Jónsdóttir et al. 2015). The corporate responsibility standards are therefore required as an intervening condition, and this idea has been supported by the business community and framed by regulatory mechanisms when government action became an agent for social change (Aguilera et al. 2007). As an evident in the study by Sigurjonsson et al. (2014), the managers highlight the lack of indicators for assessing the ethical behavior. Supported by the findings from the corporate environment that stress the role of pressure from society and the government, development of ethical guidelines, as part of the corporate and societal culture, becomes crucial. An important vehicle to increase the business ethics presence in the business environment is education. Content-wise, an underlying idea of the adjusted business education system would be to integrate seamlessly business ethics into existing curricula, as well as require students to examine critically the negative historical experiences during and resulting from the crisis. These interventions, which are in line with suggestions by Warren and Tweedale (2002), would serve as a foundation for educating the future generation of managers as well as reeducating the current one.

References

Aguilera RV, Rupp DE, Williams CA, Ganapathi J (2007) Putting the S back in corporate social responsibility: a multilevel theory of social change in organizations. Acad Manage Rev 32 (3):836–863

Althingi (2016). https://www.althingi.is/

Arnarsdóttir D (2009) Samfélagsleg ábyrgð fyrirtækja: grunnlínurannsókn á CSR umræðu í íslenskum fjölmiðlum. Háskóli Íslands, Reykjavík

Bergmann E (2014) Iceland: a postimperial sovereignty project. Coop Confl 49(1):33–54

Buiter WH (2009) Lessons from the global financial crisis for regulators and supervisors. London School of Economics and Political Science, London

Danielsson J, Zoega G (2009) The collapse of a country. Institute of Economic Studies, Reykjavik

Eðvarðsson IR, Óskarsson GK (2012) Íslenskir stjórnendur: Einkenni, stjórnunaraðferðir og árangur. Bifröst J Soc Sci 3:45–65

Henrich J, Boyd R, Richerson PJ (2008) Five misunderstandings about cultural evolution. Hum Nat 19(2):119–137

Ísleifsdóttir AI, Guðmundsdóttir S (2015) Expatriates in Iceland: culture, the workplace and communication with Icelanders. Int J Bus Res 15(3):61–77

Jóhannsdóttir L (2009) Umhverfislæsi viðskiptafræðinema. In: Hermannsdóttir A, Sigurðardóttir MS, Ólafsson S (eds) Vorráðstefna Viðskiptafræðistofnunar Háskóla Íslands 20. maí 2009, Háskóla Íslands

Johannsdottir L, Olafsson S, Davidsdottir B (2015) Leadership role and employee acceptance of change: implementing environmental sustainability strategies within nordic insurance companies. J Org Change Manage 28(1):72–96

Jóhannsdóttir L, Ólafsson S, Jónsdóttir HD (2016) Rannsókn á samfélagsábyrgð íslenskra viðskiptabanka

Jónsdóttir HD, Steinþórsson RS (2010) Samfélagsleg ábyrgð fyrirtækja og sjálfbærni. In: Hilmarsson E, Ólafsson S, Christiansen T (eds) Vorráðstefna Viðskiptafræðistofnunar Háskóla Íslands, pp 58–68

Jónsdóttir HD, Jóhannsdóttir L, Ólafsson S (2015) Samfélagsábyrgð í íslenskum skaðatryggingafélögum. Tímarit viðskipti efnahagsmál 12(1):64–83

Jónsson Á (2009) Why Iceland?: how one of the world's smallest countries became the meltdown's biggest casualty. McGraw-Hill, New York

Jónsson Á, Sigurgeirsson H (2017) The Icelandic financial crisis: a study into the world's smallest currency area and its recovery from total banking collapse. Palgrave Macmillan, New York

Karlsson G, Steinþórsson RS (2009) Samkeppnishæfni Íslands: Varanleg verðmætasköpun og hagsæld. In: Hermannsdóttir A, Sigurðardóttir MS, Ólafsson S (eds) Vorráðstefna Viðskiptafræðistofnunar Háskóla Íslands. Viðskiptafræðistofnun Háskóla Íslands, Reykjavík

Kjartansdóttir GM, Jóhannsdóttir L (2015) Álit, upplifun og framtíðarsýn ráðgjafa á hvata íslenskra fyrirtækja til aðgerða á sviði samfélagsábyrgðar og umhverfismála

Lewin K (1951) Field theory in social science: selected theoretical papers (edited by Dorwin Cartwright)

Loftsdóttir K (2014) Vikings invade present-day Iceland. 001364112

Ólafsson S, Davíðsdóttir B, Jóhannsdóttir L (2016) Samfélagsábyrgð íslenskra fyrirtækja

Sahlins M (1985) Islands of history. University of Chicago Press, Chicago

Schein EH (2010) Organizational culture and leadership, vol 2. Wiley, New York

Schein E (2012) Handbook for strategic HR: best practices in organization development from the OD network. AMACOM, New York

Sigurjonsson TO, Vaiman V, Arnardottir AA (2014) The role of business schools in ethics education in Iceland: the managers' perspective. J Bus Ethics 122(1):25–38

Tainter J (1988) The collapse of complex societies. Cambridge University Press, Cambridge

Vaiman V, Davíðsson PÁ, Sigurjonsson TO (2010) Revising a concept of corruption as a result of the global economic crisis – the case of iceland. In: Stachowicz SA (ed) Organizational immunity to corruption: building theoretical and research foundations. Polish Academy of Science Commission Regional Departure, Katowice, p 363

Warren R, Tweedale G (2002) Business ethics and business history: neglected dimensions in management education. Br J Manage 13(3):209–219

Chapter 7
Born to Enterprise? Entrepreneurial Intent Among Icelanders

Entrepreneurial attitudes have been found to be important because they express the population's general feelings toward entrepreneurs and entrepreneurship
Ács, Szerb, & Lloyd (2018)

Abstract In recent years, researchers and political figures have increasingly focused on entrepreneurship, emphasizing its role on economic and social growth and development, as well they have discussed how entrepreneurs can improve economies and people's lives by creating jobs, developing new solutions to problems, and creating technology that improves efficiency (Naudé, World Dev 39(1):33–44, 2011, Entrepreneurship and economic development. In: Currie-Alder B, Kanbur R, Malone DM, Medhor R (eds) International development ideas, experiences and prospects. Oxford University Press, 2014; Ács et al. Small Bus Econ 31(3):219–234, 2008, Global entrepreneurship index (GEDI). The Global Entrepreneurship and Development Institute, Washington D.C., 2018; Ács and Szerb, Found Trends® Entrep 5 (5):341–435, 2009; Van Praag and Versloot, Small Bus Econ 29(4):351–382, 2007; Audretsch et al., Entrepreneurship and economic growth. Oxford University Press, New York, 2006; Van Stel et al., Small Bus Econ 24(3):311–321, 2005; Parker, The economics of self-employment and entrepreneurship. Cambridge University Press, Cambridge, 2004; Carree and Thurik, The impact of entrepreneurship on economic growth. In: Handbook of entrepreneurship research. Springer, 2003; Storey, Understanding the small firm sector. Routledge, London, 1994; Leibenstein, Am Econ Rev 58(2):72–83, 1968). In light of this discourse, this chapter covers the case of Iceland that is a matter of great relevance to the cultural characteristics as well as the economic turmoil that took place in the late 2008.

Keywords Entrepreneurial intent · Entrepreneurship · Iceland

7.1   The Bigger Picture

It has been argued that the entrepreneur is sensitive to his environment, being therefore affected by the cultural context of his country. Although individuals with entrepreneurial characteristics may emerge in all societies and cultures, there are some personal features that might be more easily cultivated and frequently displayed as a function of the particular local cultural characteristics of the individual's environment. While the entrepreneur likely possesses certain innate characteristics, he is nevertheless the product of his economic, institutional, and cultural environment (Brancu et al. 2012). Although the importance of sociocultural factors in entrepreneurial decision-making is considered both by multiple studies (Shinnar et al. 2012; Thornton et al. 2011; Drakopoulou Dodd and Anderson 2007; Busenitz and Lau 1996; Shane 1992, 1993, 1995) and by international organizations such as the European Union (EU) (European Commission 2004, 2006), measuring how socio-cultural factors influence entrepreneurial potential is quite difficult. In this sense, culture is defined as a software of the mind, as a collective mental programming (Hofstede et al. 2010), and as a set of values and norms that shape individuals' perceptions about the world and life. This programming is exerted through a lifelong learning process that starts in childhood.

Specific studies have analyzed the question of cultural implications for entrepreneurship. Some have studied to what extent the entrepreneurs' motivations are related to national culture (Ozgen 2012; Shinnar et al. 2012; Gupta et al. 2004; Hayton et al. 2002; Mitchell et al. 2000; Mueller and Thomas 2001; Steensma et al. 2000; McGrath et al. 1992). The conclusions indicate that different cultural contexts do indeed influence the needs that support entrepreneurial behavior. Also, national cultural characteristics can support and/or create higher or lower potential entrepreneurs. Some authors consider it difficult to even conceive of studying or understanding entrepreneurship without considering a more interdisciplinary approach that accounts for individual entrepreneurs' culture (Bayad and Bourguiba 2006; Audet et al. 2005; Gartner 1989).

The national culture is a factor that can influence individuals' motivations, values, and beliefs and through them the entrepreneurial potential. An extensive study by Hofstede et al. (2004) examined the relationship between entrepreneurship and economic factors and cultural and personal variables (level of dissatisfaction), indicating the presence of a relationship between cultural variables and entrepreneurial intent. A more detailed discussion on national culture and entrepreneurship is available in the work by Hayton et al. (2002) who have conducted a synthesis of the empirical studies on this topic. Most of the studies use Hofstede's (1980) model as an analysis framework. The research based on this model (Del Junco and Brás-dos-Santos 2009; Hofstede et al. 2004; Hayton et al. 2002; Mueller and Thomas 2001) indicates that some cultural variables, like high levels of individualism and masculinity, may be associated with a higher propensity toward entrepreneurship. The results of Hofstede et al. (2004) study indicate a link between cultural variables and entrepreneurial intention, especially in relatively poor Western economies, characterized by a large power distance, by low individualism, and often by strong uncertainty avoidance. Mueller and Thomas (2001) conclude that cultural values such as individualism and uncertainty avoidance are significantly related to traits such as internal locus of control, risk-taking, and innovativeness, which are associated with entrepreneurship. Hayton et al. (2002) argue that high individualism, high masculinity, low uncertainty avoidance, and low-power distance are conducive to entrepreneurship. As for Del Junco and Brás-dos-Santos' (2009) study, they underscore that there is an impact of a country's cultural and social values on entrepreneurs' values. At the same time, the authors provide evidence that many EU entrepreneurs show similar values, regardless of their country of origin.

7.2   Icelandic Entrepreneurial Intent as Means for Economic Resilience

It was in October 2008 that Iceland was hit hard by the global financial crisis and the three of the main Icelandic banks were defaulted and the banking collapse was considered the largest experience relative to the size of the economy. The collapse led to significant political unrest and economic depression (Jónsson and Sigurgeirsson 2016). A nation that, according to Moody's has a triple-A rating, now needed a bailout from the International Monetary Fund. At the same time, many organizations declared bankruptcy, and many people lost their jobs and were forced to find new ways to make ends meet and provide for themselves and their families. Many individuals used the opportunity to attend university, while great many others seized the opportunity to start their own businesses.

In a study by Kelley et al. (2011), Iceland was categorized as an innovation-driven country. The study compared 59 national economies, and Iceland scored among the highest in relation to perceived opportunities, perceived capabilities, perceived entrepreneurship as a good career choice, and perceived high status to successful entrepreneurs. Finally, Iceland also scored among the lowest on fear of failure and stood out along with Belgium as having a high number of entrepreneurs who had international customers. Although this report was favorable to the Icelandic entrepreneurial environment, a report published 2 years later by the McKinsey and Company (2012) made the recommendation for Iceland to look for new ways to increase economic growth and support entrepreneurship even further. After the McKinsey report was issued, a few initiatives were taken on behalf of the Icelandic government to encourage and support entrepreneurship. For example, in 2016 special program and initiative was put in place with 22 defined measures such as to decrease the bureaucracy in relation to establish a new company, making the establishment of a new company less expensive along with tax cuts and incentives (Frumkvöðlar 2016).

Starting from the premise that innovative spirit is a prerequisite for entrepreneurship, the EU created the Innovation Union Scoreboard (IUS) that gives a comparative assessment of innovation performance of the EU Member States and the relative

Table 7.1 Position of Iceland in Global Entrepreneurship Index (GEI)

Country	GEI 2018 lower limit	GEI 2018 upper limit	GEI 2018	Rank 2018	GEI rank 2017
United States	77.5	89.7	83.6	1	1
Switzerland	72.5	88.4	80.4	2	2
Canada	73.9	84.6	79.2	3	3
United Kingdom	73.6	81.9	77.8	4	8
Australia	69.0	82.0	75.5	5	7
Denmark	64.8	83.8	74.3	6	5
Iceland	63.6	84.7	74.2	7	6
Ireland	66.8	80.6	73.7	8	9
Sweden	67.1	79.1	73.1	9	4
France	59.9	77.1	68.5	10	13

Source: GEI Report (2017)

strengths and weaknesses of their research and innovation systems. Although Iceland is not a member of the EU, it is a member of the European Free Trade Association (EFTA) along with Lichtenstein, Norway, and Switzerland and, as a result, is included in the report. The Innovation Union Scoreboard measures the quality of national human resources, research systems, innovation-friendly environment, finance and support, firm investors, innovators, linkages, intellectual assets, employment impact, and finally sales impact. Switzerland was ranked the highest on the indicator of strong innovator, followed by Sweden, Denmark, Finland, the Netherlands, and the United Kingdom; Iceland tied for eighth place with Germany on this dimension. However, when looking at the subindex innovation-friendly environment, Iceland scores on top of the chart followed by Denmark, Sweden, Norway, and Finland. Another indicator is the Global Entrepreneurship Index (GEI) by Ács et al. (2018). It gives an overall GEI score for 137 countries. The index summarizes the contextual characteristics of entrepreneurship and measures 14 components that support an entrepreneurial ecosystem. The components are opportunity perception, startup skills, risk acceptance, networking, cultural support, technology absorption, human capital, competition, product innovation, process innovation, high growth, internationalization, and finally risk capital. When looking at the GEI for Iceland, the results show that Iceland is among the top ten countries in the 2018 report, similar to the previous years. As can be seen from Table 7.1, the United States ranks first, while Iceland is an impressive 7 of the 137 nations.

When looking at more specific attributes within the ranking, one measure is entrepreneurial attitudes. This attribute is defined as the general attitude of a country's population toward recognizing opportunities, knowing entrepreneurs personally, attaching high status to entrepreneurs, accepting the risks associated with business startup, and having the skills to successfully lunch businesses. As can be seen from Table 7.2, Iceland is in the top rank followed by the United States, Australia, Finland, Canada, and other countries.

Entrepreneurial attitudes have been found to be important because they express the population's general feelings toward entrepreneurs and entrepreneurship. The

Table 7.2 Entrepreneurial attitudes subindex and pillar values for the first 25 countries, 2018[a]

Country	Attitudes subindex	Opportunity perception	Startup skills	Risk acceptance	Networking	Cultural support
Iceland	82.3	0.947	1.000	0.917	1.000	0.633
United States	80.0	0.864	1.000	0.969	0.569	0.816
Australia	79.2	0.947	1.000	0.717	0.698	0.782
Finland	79.0	0.954	0.986	0.782	0.833	0.885
Canada	77.9 77.4	0.981	0.795	0.708	0.626	0.975
Netherlands	77.4	0.898	0.887	0.877	0.800	1.000
United Kingdom	73.6	0.810	0.573	0.876	0.619	0.928
Denmark	71.9	1.000	0.690	0.748	0.634	0.918
Sweden	71.1	1.000	0.472	0.704	0.740	0.896
Chile	70.3	0.821	0.903	1.000	0.709	0.628
Switzerland	69.5	0.776	0.719	0.879	0.533	0.673
Hong Kong	69.4	1.000	0.581	0.610	1.000	0.680
Austria	67.3	0.780	0.953	0.672	0.552	0.683
Ireland	67.2	0.766	0.966	0.801	0.390	0.780
Norway	66.1	1.000	0.540	0.999	0.473	1.000
Israel	63.3	0.738	0.598	0.481	1.000	0.738
France	61.4	0.502	0.558	0.751	0.673	0.641
Germany	61.1	0.775	0.627	0.657	0.380	0.842
Estonia	57.6	0.896	0.800	0.622	0.493	0.563
Korea	55.6	0.457	0.774	0.905	0.765	0.272
Slovenia	54.4	0.349	1.000	0.843	0.331	0.504
Taiwan	54.0	0.517	0.526	0.587	0.664	0.580
Belgium	53.8	0.679	0.677	0.559	0.349	0.568
Saudi Arabia	53.6	0.611	0.933	0.436	1.000	0.477
Spain	51.3	0.407	0.807	0.692	0.640	0.339

[a]Pillar values are the normalized pillar scores and after the average pillar correction
Source: GEI Report (2017)

benchmarks are to (1) recognize valuable business opportunities, (2) have the necessary skills to exploit these opportunities, (3) attach high status and respect entrepreneurs, (4) handle startup risk, and (5) know entrepreneurs personally (i.e., have a network or role models). Moreover, these people are considered to be able to provide cultural support, financial resources, and networking potential to those who are already entrepreneurs or want to start a business (Ács et al. 2018).

The reason why entrepreneurial intent and entrepreneurial environment are so important to Iceland is that they represent the first step of the entrepreneurial process. In general, the literature studying this aspect of entrepreneurship focuses on analyzing the motivations and personal characteristics of individuals. Seen as an activity that generates innovation, employment, and long-term growth, entrepreneurship is considered as one of the solutions to economic and social problems by governments (Thornton et al. 2011). Creating new companies through private initiative or the development of so-called self-employment means alternative ways of reducing current unemployment rates that were caused by the 2008 global financial and economic crisis. These are some reasons why entrepreneurship has become an increasingly important issue.

7.3   Concluding Remarks

As discussed in the outline of cultural setting presented in previous chapters, Iceland has been argued to score low on power distance, high on individualism, low on masculinity, and medium on uncertainty avoidance and long-term orientation (Guðmundsdóttir et al. 2015). Iceland's language and culture today primarily stem from its early Scandinavian roots, as well as from some traces of Celtic influence. Today, Iceland is a dynamic society with a growing international presence and increased tourist inflow as the country has been discovered for its beautiful nature and amiable people. It is a well-developed democracy with a consumer economy based on fishing as well as tourism, aluminum smelting, and information technology (Statistics Iceland 2016). Icelandic culture has been found to place great emphasis on egalitarianism in general, as equality of socioeconomic status, equality of the sexes, equality of opportunity, and equality of socioeconomic conditions are all considered important values. Respect for authority in business context seems moderate, and the need for autonomy and individual freedom is highly regarded. A solid work ethic has been found among Icelanders; the workweek is among the longest in the world and the vital role of work in obtaining individual achievements (Ólafsson 2003). Icelanders have also been found to react positively and even optimistically to adverse nature comprising the "action poet" psyche of the nation and the "fisherman mentality" (Eyjolfsdotiir and Smith 1996). Icelanders have been found more tolerant of uncertainty than many other nations because of the ever-changing weather, earthquakes, and volcanic eruptions. Thus, Icelanders are considered to be very flexible and positive regarding abrupt changes in the workplace. Entrepreneurship has blossomed ever since Iceland's independence, but many entrepreneurs have either been insufficiently cautious or overestimated their abilities to manage a business of their own (Sigurlaugsson 1993). However, Iceland has gained experience and high ranks on global indexes compared to other countries. It can therefore be concluded that the cultural environment supports entrepreneurial intent as entrepreneurs are seen as a favorable role to take on where people can demonstrate their independence and are not afraid to take risks. Such a tendency and advancement, along with successful regional and global leadership cases, presented in the next chapters of this book, open up new possibilities for growing entrepreneurship and internationalization.

References

Ács ZJ, Szerb L, Lloyd A (2018) Global entrepreneurship index (GEDI). The Global Entrepreneurship and Development Institute, Washington D.C.

Audet J, Riverin N, Tremblay M (2005) L'influence de la culture d'un pays sur la propension entrepreneuriale de ses citoyens (le cas du Canada). Paper presented at the Congrès annuel du Conseil Canadien de la PME et de l'Entrepreneuriat, Waterloo

Bayad M, Bourguiba M (2006) De l'universalisme à la contingence culturelle: Réflexion sur l'intention entrepreneuriale. 8ème congrès international francophone en entrepreneuriat et PME CIFEPME 25: 26–27

Brancu L, Munteanu V, Gligor D (2012) Study on student's motivations for entrepreneurship in Romania. Procedia Soc Behav Sci 62:223–231

Busenitz LW, Lau C-M (1996) A cross-cultural cognitive model of new venture creation. Entrep Theory Pract 20(4):25–40

Del Junco JG, Brás-dos-Santos JM (2009) How different are the entrepreneurs in the European Union internal market?—an exploratory cross-cultural analysis of German, Italian and Spanish entrepreneurs. J Int Entrep 7(2):135–162

Drakopoulou Dodd S, Anderson AR (2007) Mumpsimus and the mything of the individualistic entrepreneur. Int Small Bus J 25(4):341–360

European Commission (2004) Action plan: the European agenda for entrepreneurship. Commission of the European Communities, Brussels

European Commission (2006) Entrepreneurship education in Europe: fostering entrepreneurial mindsets through education and learning. Commission of the European Communities, Oslo

Eyjolfsdotiir HM, Smith PB (1996) Icelandic business and management culture. Int Stud Manag Organ 26(3):61–72

Frumkvöðlar (2016) Viðskiptablaðið: a special issue on entrepreneurship.

Gartner W (1989) Who is an entrepreneur? Is the wrong question. Entrep Theory Pract 13(4):47–68

Guðmundsdóttir S, Guðlaugsson Þ, Aðalsteinsson GD (2015) Icelandic national culture compared to national cultures of 25 OECD member states using VSM94. Stjórnmál og Stjórnsýsla 11 (1):19

Gupta V, MacMillan IC, Surie G (2004) Entrepreneurial leadership: developing and measuring a cross-cultural construct. J Bus Ventur 19(2):241–260

Hayton JC, George G, Zahra SA (2002) National culture and entrepreneurship: a review of behavioral research. Entrep Theory Pract 26(4):33–52

Hofstede G (1980) Culture's consequences: national differences in thinking and organizing. Sage, Beverly Hills, CA

Hofstede G, Noorderhaven NG, Thurik AR, Uhlaner LM, Wennekers AR, Wildeman RE (2004) Culture's role in entrepreneurship: self-employment out of dissatisfaction. In: Brown TE, Ulijn JM (eds) Innovation, entrepreneurship and culture: the interaction between technology, progress and economic growth, pp 162–203

Hofstede G, Hofstede GJ, Minkov M (2010) Culture and organizations, software of the mind, intercultural cooperation and its importance for survival. McGraw Hill, New York

Jónsson Á, Sigurgeirsson H (2016) The Icelandic financial crisis: a study into the world's smallest currency area and its recovery from total banking collapse. Palgrave Macmillan, New York

Kelley DJ, Bosma N, Amorós JE (2011) Global entrepreneurship monitor: 2010 global report. Global Entrepreneurship Research Association (GERA)

McGrath RG, MacMillan IC, Scheinberg S (1992) Elitists, risk-takers, and rugged individualists? An exploratory analysis of cultural differences between entrepreneurs and non-entrepreneurs. J Bus Ventur 7(2):115–135

McKinsey & Company (2012) Charting a growth path for Iceland

Mitchell RK, Smith B, Seawright KW, Morse EA (2000) Cross-cultural cognitions and the venture creation decision. Acad Manag J 43(5):974–993

Mueller SL, Thomas AS (2001) Culture and entrepreneurial potential: a nine country study of locus
    of control and innovativeness. J Bus Ventur 16(1):51–75
Ólafsson S (2003) Contemporary Icelanders: Scandinavian or American. Scand Rev 91(1):6–14
Ozgen E (2012) The effect of the national culture on female entrepreneurial activities in emerging
    countries: an application of the GLOBE project cultural dimensions. Int J Entrep 16:69
Shane S (1993) Cultural influences on national rates of innovation. J Bus Ventur 8(1):59–73
Shane S (1995) Uncertainty avoidance and the preference for innovation championing roles. J Int
    Bus Stud 26(1):47–68
Shane SA (1992) Why do some societies invent more than others? J Bus Ventur 7(1):29–46
Shinnar RS, Giacomin O, Janssen F (2012) Entrepreneurial perceptions and intentions: the role of
    gender and culture. Entrep Theory Pract 36(3):465–493
Sigurlaugsson B (1993) Frá handafli til hugvits (From Manual skills to mental skills). Framtikarsn,
    Reykjavik
Statistics Iceland (2016) Iceland in figures 2017
Steensma HK, Marino L, Weaver KM (2000) Attitudes toward cooperative strategies: a cross-
    cultural analysis of entrepreneurs. J Int Bus Stud 31(4):591–609
Thornton PH, Ribeiro-Soriano D, Urbano D (2011) Socio-cultural factors and entrepreneurial
    activity: an overview. Int Small Bus J 29(2):105–118

Chapter 8
What's Next? From Tourism Bubble to the Future of Business Leadership in Iceland

It often happens that things go by turns.
The Saga of Thrond of Gate (Færeyinga Saga), c. 31

Abstract Just about the time when Iceland's future could not have been more obscure and tenuous, a series of unplanned and unprecedented events brought a constellation of economic revival opportunities. As it is quite common for Iceland, given the proper context, the threats have turned into chances. The low-cost flight options from Europe and the United States, the immediate downfall of Icelandic krona in 2008, and the Eyjafjallajökull volcano eruption in 2010 all made Iceland a destination spot on the maps of many world travelers. These events gave rise to the tourism in Iceland that for decades was mainly considered to be only a secondary socioeconomic activity. In the aftermath of the crisis of 2008, tourism became an industry that gave new roots to economic revival and growth of the country. Nowadays, the ultimate arising question is, "What will be the next economic boom for Iceland?" This chapter synthesizes the insights of 13 experts on the tourism industry in Iceland, its role in the economy and in society in general, and the future possibilities it sets for leadership.

Keywords Tourism industry · Leadership · Iceland

8.1 The Bigger Picture

The inbound tourism in Iceland had actually started to grow before the financial crisis of 2008. For example, the increase in tourist inflow over the prior years was 12.9% in 2006 and 14.8% in 2007 (Icelandic Tourist Board 2015, 2017). Following the crisis, an initial substantial decline was observed; yet, the trend soon recovered, with an increase ranging from 15.8% to 29.1% over the period of 2011–2015 and 38.3% in 2016 alone. The direct tourism industry's contribution to GDP rose from 3.8% in 2011 to 8.4% in 2016 (OECD 2018). For a country that had historically

© Springer International Publishing AG, part of Springer Nature 2018
I. Minelgaite et al., *Demystifying Leadership in Iceland*, Contributions to
Management Science, https://doi.org/10.1007/978-3-319-96044-9_8

predominantly relied on fishing and aluminum industries, the new economic history began in 2008 with the tourism sector at the forefront. This shift in reality is well expressed by Olöf Yrr Atladóttir, the Director General of the Iceland Tourist Board (2017), who has made statements such as "Tourism is the factor that got us out of the recession and placed us where we are now," "We couldn't foresee this tremendous growth in interest for Iceland," and that "We are just realizing what tourism is. It's a totally different industry from all others." In this vein, the public attitudes, perception of tourism as a phenomenon and a viable industry, and its enactment on a public, governmental, and entrepreneurial level today all play a pivotal role in the future of the Icelandic economy and society in general.

This chapter aims at tracing the shifts in attitudes, Icelanders' current perceptions of tourism, the effects and future potential for tourism as an industry, its boundaries and limitations, and the leadership interventions required to stabilize and sustain the industry's growth. At present, the future landscape for tourism is still quite ambiguous and relatively unknown. As relatively little formal data exists to fully explain the developments that led to tourism's growth or guide decision-making for its future, we employed expert opinion as a research method (Rowe and Wright 2001) as a means to address these gaps. The expert opinion method is based on samples of individuals possessing superior knowledge about specific knowledge (Roper et al. 2011) and relies on plurality of expertise for a range of insights (Krueger et al. 2012). We therefore invited 13 experts from the fields of economics, environmental studies, marketing, and tourism industry who are directly engaged in the topic of Icelandic tourism. Specifically, we relied on the insights of these subject matter experts to address the following points:

1. The attitudes of Icelanders toward the tourism in Iceland prior to 2008 as well as 10 years after
2. The effects of the tourism industry on Iceland's economy, society, nature, culture, education, and other domains familiar to these experts
3. Their perception as to whether or not a "tourism bubble" currently exists in Iceland
4. Their forecasts about the future of the tourism industry in Iceland

The next sections synthesize the findings from these expert interviews.

8.2   The Attitudes of Icelanders Toward the Tourism in Iceland

All experts note a substantial shift in the attitudes of Icelanders toward the tourism that rapidly grew in their country. At first, they considered tourism somewhat as merely an act of hospitality toward the rare guests that visited the nation. However, since that time, Icelanders have realized that tourism can become a whole industry in and of itself that can help to pull the economy out of the crisis it had recently experienced. Today, the tourism, as a phenomenon, has been surrounded by diverging attitudes.

As one expert recalls, in the 2000s, there were intense debates concerning the land use, accompanied with "tensions between energy development as a means of job creation/development, in rural areas versus nature conservation." At that time, tourism was already considered by many to be a possible alternative that could simultaneously foster employment, rural development, and environmental conservation. However, tourism was still viewed somewhat as more of a supplementary business to complement the main industries like fisheries, heavy metals, and financial services. As experts recall, prior to 2008, Icelanders held positive attitudes toward tourism and, as one interviewee noted, were "…even mildly curious as people thought it was fun to see foreign visitors." These foreign visitors at the time would mainly be "budget-minded backpackers whom Icelanders made fun of for their 'eccentric' customs and behaviors. To some, these odd visitors were even considered to be a bit of a 'nuisance'. But over time, the general attitude of society was marked by a surprising shift from asking "Why would they want to come to Iceland?" to asking those very people "How do you like Iceland?"

As one interviewee noted, Icelanders did not seem to think that their country would one day "become a mainstream tourist attraction." For some locals, who, as one expert suggests, "were quite proud of the country and its unique qualities in regard to tourism" and were pleased "to hear something nice about the country" from the guests, it was a social, cultural interaction, and the tourists would sometimes be perceived as the "friends of Iceland ('íslandsvinir')." Even though tourism "was viewed as an integral part of the economy," it would often be not considered to be an industry or even a major leverage for the economy. Instead, it tended to be perceived more as a "third sector in the economy, behind fisheries and banking." Accordingly, very limited national discourse on potential "opportunities, challenges, and impact on nature and society" followed. As experts contend, even the key socioeconomic role of tourism would be considered in vein of employment possibilities for Icelanders residing in more remote and sparsely populated areas outside Reykjavik.

One expert alludes to the unexplored opportunities due to lack of demand: the tourism "was growing slowly but with no real impetus, and the Icelandic economy was seemingly so strong that there was no real need to investigate new growth sectors." After 2008, the tourism unfolded as an industry, "before the society had a chance to acclimate itself," with mixed feelings, mainly associated with the reviving economy as a positive outcome on the one hand and the risk of spoiling nature as a negative outcome on the other side. Likewise, Icelanders experienced similar mixed attitudes toward the tourists themselves. Alongside the generally positive attitude, some locals were pleased to "see more life and different cultures in the streets," whereas others showed "benign indifference," as one expert frames it, while others yet expressed clearly negative attitudes. An important remark to be made in this regard is that in order for an Icelander to be able to form an attitude about a stranger and define how to address him or her, one needs to understand what type of a person he or she is. Hence, the undefined behavior of tourists and their associated effects often leave Icelanders puzzled. This attitude was previously echoed by Atladóttir (Enelow 2016):

> You can go out and fish and you go and get your fish and then come back. There's somebody in the factory that prepares it, and then it's sold. That, of course, is a tremendous economic impact, but then everybody goes home. The fish aren't bothering you out in the streets, asking where the restaurants are, and aren't using your buses or utilizing a lot of the public goods. They aren't sitting in your swimming pools.

Overall, the positive attitudes toward the tourism industry prevail, as a "significant part of the current and future economy of Iceland." As one expert notes, tourism industry is "now respected as one of three main pillars of the Icelandic export sector (along with fishing and aluminum), the main source for new jobs, and carries a growing political clout." Yet, as one expert contends, "there are many Icelanders who resent the growth in tourism, or do not feel that its economic merits justify the many societal costs." Other experts add a certain degree of "skepticism and some hostility" is present, with regard to sustainability of the industry and infrastructure, including "obnoxious and rude behavior and the danger they create on the roads" from some tourists who seem to "come to 'pollute' Iceland and 'take advantage'" of the locals, especially in the downtown of Reykjavik and southern Iceland. Such views are especially prevalent in the regions, where some locals feel that the tourists are crowding them out. What Icelanders have seen so far, as the experts note, are the overcrowded infrastructure of the country, increased real estate (housing) prices, and limited possibilities for native Icelanders to experience and enjoy their country on their own (Statistics Iceland, 2015–2017). Artifacts of growth, as seen through the eyes of some Icelanders, include observations that "shops have shifted towards those catering for tourists"; "city skyline is replete with cranes and building sites, as more and more hotels are being built"; and "key sites are often very overpopulated with visitors." While some locals try to "to get most of the tourism boom in the past years without focusing on needs of people already living here," others seem to experience resentment. They begin to avoid the overcrowded nature spots or "object to the number of cruise ships visiting their towns" that "sometimes double the local population in the smaller towns," such as popular ports like Ísafjörður, Grundafjörður, and Akureyri. At the same time, some industry players are striving to prevail over these negative attitudes. In fact, these negative attitudes have a strong grounding, discussed further.

8.3   The Effects of the Tourism Industry in Iceland: Is There a Bubble and Will It Burst?

As noted in the previous section, the tourism industry has become a driver of Icelandic economy, especially since 2011, strengthened by the increased purchasing power from 2013. Experts distinguish among three main channels:

1. Economies of scale, as in such a small country, the increase in tourism leads to higher volumes of sales by Icelandic companies and growth in productivity
2. Appreciation of currency appreciation, for as the Icelandic krona appreciates, Icelanders gain higher purchasing power through lower-priced imports
3. Demand effects in some key areas, such as housing and labor

Tourism has been bringing major foreign currency influx, where the total is more than fishing and aluminum industries taken in together, earning a highly important role in the economy of Iceland. The increase in tourism has both opened up an array of opportunities and a set of accompanying challenges. Therefore, the effect of tourism is based on the two sides of the same coin, as the experts highlighted further. On the one hand, the rapid tourism growth ultimately strengthened the Icelandic krona and the purchasing power of individuals. The locals have also been provided with options for engagement in the industry directly, in the related industries, or through activities complementing their primary sources of income, such as renting their property. At the same time, the tourism industry has grown to a degree of nearly crowding out other export industries.

Secondly, tourism has left an imprint on urban and natural development. Certainly, Reykjavik was among the first destinations influenced by tourism, including high flows of tourists and gentrified infrastructure. As one expert notes, Reykjavik "is definitely a lot better place to live in now and we owe it to tourism." Rural areas have also been affected, where nature is the main driver for touristic inflow. The Icelandic nature and landscapes fascinate many yet increasingly suffer from high intrusion, including overcrowding and vehicle traffic in the preserved areas (see also, OECD 2017). As experts note, the close monitoring of environmental questions is required, including adequate conservation plans and tourism taxes to support the nature preservation.

The effects on cultural life and activities are also notable. The tourism effect on Icelandic culture has given rise to a diverse selection of food industry (hotels, restaurants, cafes, commonly referred to as HORECA) options. However, as some experts note, the growth of tourism inflates the demand for lower-skilled jobs in the HORECA industry, especially in contrast to university-level education. Similarly, this industry is typically characterized by low-level compensation and unfavorable working conditions for employees, many of whom are immigrants. In turn, some locals express their discontent regarding restaurants and other service companies that do not serve clients in their native language.

The pace of upsurge in tourism raises a concern that the rapid growth could eventually lead to a bursting of the bubble. Some experts consider the tourism bubble to be present and note that the exponential year-on-year growth is already flattening out. That said, the majority of experts believe that tourism growth is not itself associated with a bubble. However, in combination with other factors, it might lead to an overheating of the economy in some markets most affected by growth of the sector, such as the housing market. Hence, the economic upturn may be not stable, although it can be controlled while given proper actions. As one expert notes:

The main thing for Iceland is that tourism is a new pillar of the economy, it represents a welcome diversification in a country where we basically lived off fishing. But you could argue that tourism has become too big and it represents a systemic risk for the Icelandic economy just like the banks were. But there is little vision for creating and developing new sectors of the economy.

The experts differentiate between midterm and long-term expected effects of the tourism growth. The short-term and sudden positive impact that unfolded after 2008 has been a coincidentally successful event that requires additional input in order to scale these effects over the mid and long term:

> So, the growth of the tourism industry has been almost like a free lunch for the state—since the foreign visitors are just using the infrastructure that is already in place and pay a lot of taxes. In the short term, the surge in tourism after 2011 came at a very favorable time. Icelandic economy had shrunk considerably after the banking collapse of 2008 and the export industry was stagnant despite a much lower currency. The increased export revenue came at little cost. All the infrastructure was already there. In the medium term. It's the end of free lunch.

Some experts suggest that the pace of the growth may gradually slow down over the next years but will overall still remain stable. Over time, the industry is expected to reach maturity: "In the long run, tourism will be stable and integral part of the overall economy, still with considerable growth potential at sustainable rates." The experts contend that tourism is a growing phenomenon worldwide and believe that Iceland always had a long-standing potential as a destination for years to come, thanks to unique nature and high degree of safety, and the relatively small proportion of worldwide tourists that Iceland needs to attract as a means to its tourism capacity. As one expert puts it, empowered by low fare flights and unlimited possibilities to explore the world, "people will venture into countries that before were considered off the beaten track." Nevertheless, despite the positive forecast of its potential, many experts do not consider the tourism sector to be a right candidate for leading the growth in Iceland.

Currency fluctuations may pose a risk and interfere with any planning, leaving many experts skeptical: "I don't see Iceland creating a sustainable tourism industry in the long term with the gyrations of the Icelandic krona. The only realistic solution is to join the EU and adopt the Euro." The experts also note that the short-term success is fragile and prone to effects of a number of external factors, as well as the local action. For example, the revival of Icelandic krona or an awakening of any natural disaster will also hamper the tourism sector:

> It is expensive to stay in Iceland and most visitors view a trip to Iceland as a once-in-a-lifetime experience. The pool of potential new visitors is becoming smaller and the Icelandic króna has become ever stronger in recent years. The question is what happens next? And, particularly, what happens if a natural disaster dramatically reduces visitor numbers. This is overdue, with [volcanoes] Barðarbunga, Katla, Öræfajökull, and Hekla all threatening major eruptions. These could disrupt international airspace for many months, or at the very least make the country appear too risky to visit. What then for the industry and the Icelandic economy? The problems would likely be very similar to the Icelandic banking crisis of 2008, as much of the new accommodation in the city is financed by debt and needs the current level of visitors in order for vast sums of borrowing to be repaid. Could these hotels ultimately

collapse and then be converted back into studio accommodation for locals? There is a real sense that Icelanders are making the most of the boom whilst it lasts, knowing it cannot last forever.

The size of the country that gives the tourism its potential on the one hand can be another limiting factor at the same time. While the tourism industry in Iceland needs to compete only for a fraction of the tourists worldwide, its capacity is also limited, setting the boundaries for growth over the long term:

> The population of Iceland is almost too small to support the infrastructure and specialization needed for a developed economy. Foreign visits have similar effect as a population increase, without the welfare costs. The main thrust of the taxation in Iceland is indirect, both through a very high value-added tax and levies on alcohol and gasoline which one has to pay to use the road system. Iceland would e.g. be unable to maintain an international airport with the current flight frequency or number of destinations without the foreign visits ... Iceland cannot welcome an unlimited number of tourists—as it will create burden for the population as well as the precarious nature. In not so distant future, Iceland will probably place limits to the growth of the tourism sector.

However, the key factors limiting the industry and growth, according to most experts, are primarily related to management and development of infrastructure and thus are within the local control. As one expert frames it, "long-term, there will always be a role for tourism in Iceland, but it could be that the here and now represents a once-in-a-generation golden harvest." Another expert adds: "If tourism declines in Iceland, it will be our own fault." Hence, the future is to be defined by Icelanders themselves:

> The future is what you make it. If there isn't a major international war or economic crises of some sort tourism will continue to grow worldwide. Icelanders have a choice of creating a sustainable industry in the long term which will create a lot of prosperity. That requires vision, planning and implementation in the long term.

Another expert extends this question to the strategy level: "in the long term there should be a holistic national tourism strategy developed, with relevant measures to see if we are on the right track regarding strategy implementation." These challenges will need to be addressed strategically by the National Tourist Board and governmental agencies:

> The future is good, but it is important that Icelandic authorities form some sort of tourism strategy, as regards what kind of tourists we want, taxation, entrance fees etc., infrastructure investment. In the SR tourism may continue to increase, but MR and LR looks bleaker.

Shall there be no strategy, the very same inflow of tourists that troubles some locals is likely to cause mirrored in the anxiety among the tourists, too. As one expert frames:

> Every tourist wants to be special and expects to find the untouched Iceland, however, finds 30 busses at Gullfoss or Þingvellir, Seljalandsfoss or Blue Lagoon. People will eventually lose interest in Iceland as it is now. Also, it is very expensive for the tourists as well as locals for what it has to offer. In the past years Iceland is focusing mostly in Luxury tourism and for the average travelers it will be more and more difficult to travel here.

Experts identify that substantial progress and development are still required with regard to limited infrastructure, nature preservation, cultural heritage, lack of employees with required competences, compensation schemes, effects on the real estate market, and other aspects, including companies considering the challenges associated with the rapid growth. Hence, in order to capitalize on the short-term positive effects, and translate them into long-term competitiveness, a consolidated approach from the governmental agencies and the businesses is required. Experts call for greater consolidation within the sector, "as service providers have to deal with higher currency, higher domestic costs and increased competition." The opportunistic entrepreneurial intentions and actions will reach their limit, and the entrepreneurs will need to engage in sustainable practice, including "more professionalism within the industry and companies stop thinking in short-term profit maximization and start thinking about how to grow the tourism industry as a sustainable industry in Iceland."

Obviously, the strategy is to be implemented in close cooperation between the governmental agencies and the companies:

> In terms of the effects of tourism a lot will depend on policy-making and effective implementation and how companies manage some of these issues on their part. I think it should give pause for thought that despite nature being Iceland's main tourism product not enough is done to ensure its protection.

8.4   Concluding Remarks

As it becomes evident in the expert opinions, the stabilization required to turn short-term gains into long-term competitiveness calls for a sustainable approach to further development. Sustainable development should be embraced through holistic approach, well-framed by Jóhannesson et al. (2011, p. 375): "...where economic, environmental and social factors are not treated as separate entities." With accountability expected at all levels and degrees of engagement in tourism industry, specifically including governmental agencies, businesses, and the individuals who stand at the forefront, the urge for sustainable leadership arises.

As noted in the previous chapters of this book, the crisis of 2008 has already yielded a number of lessons in social responsibility, encouraging the society and business communities to reconceptualize their activities. Ten years later, the strengthened economy and tourism sector calls for sustainable development not only building on the footprints of the past ramifications but also with a perspective on the future. Firstly, increased awareness by the social actors of the actual role they have on the construction and interpretation of the context, including the forces and values behind it (Fergus and Rowney 2005), is necessary. Furthermore, responsible and sustainable development requires the businesses to step from entrepreneurial leadership on a mission to create value in the market, even if it is driven by pragmatism (Surie and Ashley 2008), and engage in sustainable leadership. Here, sustainable leadership is inquisitive beyond the shared needs, goals, and values of moral leadership (Burns 1978) and normative behavior addressed by ethical leadership (Trevino et al. 2000;

Brown et al. 2005). It calls for a sustainable approach toward the future that reflects the best outcomes for the environment and society (Jutras 2009), "improving the lives of all concerned" (McCann and Holt 2010, p. 209).

This type of leadership has a strong emphasis on the future generations, through "meeting the needs of the present generation without compromising the ability of future generations to meet their needs" (WCED 1987, p. 43). Following this strand, it also poses a demand for participatory type of leadership that engages all stake-holders of the outcomes in decision-making. Such an approach to leadership may also consolidate the stakeholders and contribute to creation of value networks (Lord and Brown 2001) for the future sustainable development of Icelandic economy and society. Finally, referring back to the relatively small size of the country, Iceland can become a new case study for the model of sustainable leadership in action, where it is pursued by all stakeholder groups in concert.

References

Brown ME, Treviño LK, Harrison DA (2005) Ethical leadership: a social learning perspective for construct development and testing. Organ Behav Hum Decis Process 97(2):117–134

Burns JM (1978) Leadership. Harper and Row, New York

Enelow S (2016) 5 lessons from Iceland and the perils of overtourism. https://skift.com/2016/10/25/5-lessons-from-iceland-and-the-perils-of-overtourism/. Accessed 29 Apr 2018

Fergus AH, Rowney JI (2005) Sustainable development: epistemological frameworks & an ethic of choice. J Bus Ethics 57(2):197

Icelandic Tourist Board (2015) Report

Icelandic Tourist Board (2017) Report

Jóhannesson IÁ, Norðdahl K, Óskarsdóttir G, Pálsdóttir A, Pétursdóttir B (2011) Curriculum analysis and education for sustainable development in Iceland. Environ Educ Res 17 (3):375–391

Jutras C (2009) The ROI of sustainability: making the business case.

Krueger T, Page T, Hubacek K, Smith L, Hiscock K (2012) The role of expert opinion in environmental modelling. Environ Model Softw 36:4–18

Lord RG, Brown DJ (2001) Leadership, values, and subordinate self-concepts. Leadersh Q 12 (2):133–152

McCann JT, Holt RA (2010) Servant and sustainable leadership: an analysis in the manufacturing environment. Int J Manag Pract 4(2):134–148

OECD (2017) OECD economic survey: Iceland 2017. OECD Publishing, Paris

OECD (2018) National accounts of OECD countries: main aggregates, vol 1. OECD Publishing, Paris. https://doi.org/10.1787/na_ma_dt-v2018-1-en

Roper AT, Cunningham SW, Porter AL, Mason TW, Rossini FA, Banks J (2011) Technology forecasting. In: Forecasting and management of technology, 2nd edn. Wiley, Hoboken, NJ, pp 15–39

Rowe G, Wright G (2001) Expert opinions in forecasting: the role of the Delphi technique. In: Armstrong JS (ed) Principles of forecasting. Springer, New York, pp 125–144

Surie G, Ashley A (2008) Integrating pragmatism and ethics in entrepreneurial leadership for sustainable value creation. J Bus Ethics 81(1):235–246

Trevino LK, Hartman LP, Brown M (2000) Moral person and moral manager: how executives develop a reputation for ethical leadership. Calif Manag Rev 42(4):128–142

WCED (1987) Our common future. The brundtland report, world commission for environment and development. Oxford University Press, Oxford

Part III
Transforming Leadership: Gender Issues

Chapter 9
Gender and Leadership in Iceland: The Journey to the Top of the Global Gender Gap Index

...I think there is something that is very distinct about Iceland which makes the society flat in general ... there is no Mr. and Mrs.
Anonymous interviewee

Abstract The fact that Iceland has been acknowledged at the top of the Global Gender Gap Index for 7 consecutive years has raised interest not only among scholars and practitioners but also the media. A range of documentaries has been produced, and international periodicals such as the Guardian, Al Jazeera, Reuters, BBC, Washington Post, and others have covered the story on why this is the case. In this chapter, Icelandic society's impressive journey to the top of the Global Gender Gap Index is described.

Keywords Global Gender Gap Index · Gender equality · Iceland

9.1 The Bigger Picture

The Global Gender Gap Index was first introduced by the World Economic Forum in 2006 as a framework for capturing the magnitude of gender-based disparities and tracking progress toward rectifying them over time. The Index benchmarks national gender gaps on economic, education, health, and political criteria and assigns country rankings that allow for effective comparisons across regions and income groups. These rankings are designed to create global awareness of the challenges posed by gender gaps and the opportunities created by reducing them. The methodology and quantitative analysis behind the rankings are intended to serve as a basis for designing effective measures for reducing gender gaps (World Economic Forum 2017). The Global Gender Gap Index examines the gap between men and women in four categories: *economic participation and opportunity*, *educational attainment*, *health and survival*, and *political empowerment*.

© Springer International Publishing AG, part of Springer Nature 2018   81
I. Minelgaite et al., *Demystifying Leadership in Iceland*, Contributions to Management Science, https://doi.org/10.1007/978-3-319-96044-9_9

Economic Participation and Opportunity
This category is based on three concepts: the participation gap, the remuneration gap, and the advancement gap. The participation gap is captured using the difference between women and men in labor force participation rates. The remuneration gap is captured through a ratio of estimated female-to-male earned income and a qualitative indicator gathered through the World Economic Forum's Executive Opinion Survey based on wage equality for similar work. Finally, the gap between the advancement of women and men is captured through the ratio of women to men among legislators, senior officials, and managers, as well as the ratio of women to men among technical and professional workers (World Economic Forum 2017).

Educational Attainment
This category focuses on the gap between women's and men's current access to education through ratios of women to men in primary-, secondary-, and tertiary-level education (World Economic Forum 2017).

Health and Survival
This category provides an overview of the differences between women's and men's health through the use of two indicators. The first is the sex ratio at birth, which aims specifically to capture the phenomenon of "missing women" prevalent in many countries where there is a strong preference to have sons over daughters. The indicator examines the differences between women's and men's life expectancy.

Political Empowerment
This index measures the gap between men and women at the highest level of political decision-making through the ratio of women to men in minister-level and parliamentary positions. Also, it includes the ratio of women to men regarding years in executive office (prime minister or president) for the last 50 years (World Economic Forum 2017).

It is evident that being placed at the top of the Global Gender Index for such as a small society with relatively young traditions in human resource relationship management and leadership is a great accomplishment. It demonstrates how a general society's values of egalitarianism have translated into the work environment.

9.2   The Icelandic Case

Iceland has been on the top of the Gender Gap Index since 2009. Iceland has the highest labor force participation within the OECD countries. In 2016, participation rates were 83.4% for women and 89% for men (OECD 2018). In 2017, 199,600 or 81.2% of the population in the age range of 16–74 were active in the labor market, and the unemployment rate was only 2.6% (Statistics Iceland 2018).

The average working hours for the age group 25–74 in the period 2003–2018 was 33.1 for women and 41.2 for men (Statistics Iceland 2018). Thus, Icelanders' full-time work and dual-earning households are the norms which the state and municipalities support that by providing public access to day-care for children (Snorradóttir et al. 2014).

The incremental progress of gender equality can be attributed to the solidarity of women and human rights defenders challenging and protesting the historic monopoly of power resting in the hands of men. Furthermore, the progress toward gender equality can be attributed to women taking the initiative and creating alternatives to the patriarchal culture that was predominant. Also, making the invisible realities of women visible, most importantly discriminatory practices including sexual harassment and abuse were a critical driving force. Lastly, Iceland's progress can be attributed to women and men sharing decision-making power with each other and gradually having more men supporting gender equality (Marinósdóttir and Erlingsdóttir 2017). When the history of gender equality in Iceland is analyzed, it not only reflects a long journey through which many women struggled for an equal voice and treatment but one that has made considerable progress through female as well as male advocates.

9.2.1   The History of Gender Equality in Iceland

The nineteenth and twentieth centuries in Iceland were marked by a multitude of social, political, and economic changes. The historical perspective of women's movement and developments is presented below, and based on information from Jafnréttisstofa or the Centre for Gender Equality, which is a national bureau (2012). As can be seen from the history of gender equality on the political front, the solidarity of women through political movement has been crucial in promoting gender equality in Iceland.

Before the middle of the eighteenth century, women in Iceland as elsewhere had very limited formal power. In 1850, the first step was taken as women acquired the same inheritance rights as men. In 1869 the first women's association was founded, and advancements took place in the legal system giving the limited right to widows and unmarried women to vote in 1882. In 1886 girls earned the right to education at the single college in Iceland. This period was marked by developments in Icelandic society that led to an increased profile and mobility of women: a women's college was founded (1874), and the first women's rights organization was founded (1894), as well as the Icelandic Women's Association, i.e., an organization with principle goal of fighting for women's rights, including women's suffrage. These were initial steps that allowed for future developments and laid the ground for the future success of Iceland in gender equality issues.

The first few decades of the twentieth century were marked with many critical social and political changes. Icelandic married women gained their financial competency at the beginning of the new century. In 1902 women with voting right gained local suffrage and in 1908 gained the right to hold local office, which resulted in four women being elected to the city council in Reykjavik the same year. This was a great victory for the founders of the women's suffrage movement in Iceland. 1909 was crowned with all Icelandic women gaining the right to vote and run for office in local elections. In 1907 the Women's Rights Association of Iceland was founded, and Bríet Bjarnhéðinsdóttir is one of the leaders of the women's rights movement in Iceland, but she had worked with the International Woman Suffrage Alliance (IWSA). In 1911, women acquired full equal access to education, public grants, and public office. These times paved the way for women's increased access to political office. During this period, women's group's contribution and influence on social issues continued to grow. In 1922, the first woman, Ingibjörg H. Bjarnason, was elected to parliament. In 1948, a male Parliamentarian, Hannibal Valdimarsson, drafted a law on the gender equality of women and men; ironically, this proposal was thrown out based on the assumption that actual discrimination had not been thoroughly researched or demonstrated to exist. Despite that women comprised only 1% of all council members in Iceland in 1958, first women mayors were elected in 1957 and 1959 in Kópavogur municipality closed to Reykjavík and Reykjavík, respectively. In order to address the gender pay gap, in 1961, parliament approved the first law on wage equality with the ultimate aim to bridge the gap by 1968. This, however, has taken longer than anticipated.

The first Icelandic female cabinet minister was appointed in 1970. While full gender equality was still not achieved, these were monumental achievements. "Red Stockings" movement was established the same year, as a reaction to women's right and feminists' movements taking place all over the world. "Red Stockings" movement was a women's liberation movement, which is a critical, radical force raised further awareness on various gender equality issues. Progress toward equality in organized religion was made during this time, as the first woman was ordained as a priest of the National Lutheran Church in 1974. Despite these advances, it was 1975, dubbed UN International Women's Year, when a number of hallmark events occurred. On 24 October 1975, more than 25,000 Icelandic women took a day off, from both paid and unpaid work positions, and went on a strike. They undertook such an action to emphasize the importance of women's contributions to the economy. Also, that same year, a law guaranteeing 3 months' maternal leave was approved, a new law more favorable to women, eliminating a restriction on abortion, securing reproductive and maternal health was passed, and the Women's History Archives was founded. The year 1976 was marked by passing the first equality and foundation of the Gender Equality Council. However, after the parliamentary election in 1979, women were still only 5% of the parliamentarians. This fact made women in Iceland ponder what could be done to change the situation.

The 1980s were characterized by continuous velocity and substantial changes in gender equality issues. Vigdís Finnbogadóttir was elected the fourth President of the Republic of Iceland in 1980. This marked a new era as Vigdís Finnbogadóttir was not only the first woman to be democratically elected as head of state for Iceland but of the entire world. Vigdís Finnbogadóttir had served as the Artistic Director of the Reykjavík Theatre Company from 1972 to 1980, later the City Theatre. She was also a member of the Advisory Committee on Cultural Affairs in the Nordic countries where she served as chair from 1978 to 1980. She had previously taught French at the University of Iceland and hosted French courses at the national television; she first became nationally recognized as such. In this period Vigdís Finnbogadóttir had been steadily increasing her scope of leadership and visibility by taking on these roles. Vigdís Finnbogadóttir as a female candidate obtained considerable support from women in 1980, particularly women's rights activists. Vigdís Finnbogadóttir was narrowly elected over three male opponents and served as the fourth President of Iceland from 1980 to 1996 (Snaebjornsson 2016). She became very popular as was reflected in the fact that Vigdís Finnbogadóttir remains the longest-serving elected female head of state of any country to date. Vigdís Finnbogadóttir was at the time, she was elected, divorced and was the first single woman in Iceland who was allowed to adopt a child. While she served as president, she was an advocate for girl's education, language diversity, and women's rights as well. She is still regarded as a cherished leader and a role model both in Iceland and internationally.

The year 1980 was a watershed year as not only was Vigdís Finnbogadóttir elected but a political party called Kvennalistinn or the Women's Alliance participated in the municipal elections in Reykjavík and Akureyri, a town in the north. Women's participation increased from 6 to 13% among all council members in the country in 1982. The Women's Alliance (*Kvennalistinn*) was founded in 1983 with the main purpose to increase women's liberation and representation of women in the political arena. During the inception of Kvennalistinn women accounted for only 5% of members of parliament, but after the taking part in the first election, the number advanced to 15%. Female enrollment in universities also steadily rose during this decade, and by 1984, women had become the majority of new students at the University of Iceland. Other notable achievements of women's advancement occurred in 1986 when the first woman became a member of the Superior Court, Iceland's highest court, for the first time, and in 1988 when a woman became the first Speaker of parliament. In 1999 after relentless work from inside parliament and influence made on the political debate agenda of the traditional political parties, the Women's Alliance ceased to exist (Marinósdóttir and Erlingsdóttir 2017).

During the 1990s progress continued on various fronts and political activities continued. From 1994 to 2002 council seats held by women increased from a quarter to a third. Furthermore, in 1995 women occupied one-fourth of all parliamentary seats, and in 1999 they accounted for 35% of all members of parliament.

Despite the substantial and historical advancements that had been made during the previous decades, public support for gender equality issues began to stagnate. As a response in 2003, the Feminist Association of Iceland was founded and organized numerous initiatives raising public awareness on various gender issues and keeping it at the forefront. In 2003, Icelandic fathers gained the right to nontransferable 3 months' paternal leave; this excluded mothers that had the right for 6 months' maternity leave to take the father's months as leave. During this decade many more women became pioneers and leaders in their respective sectors. On 24 October 2005, to celebrate the 30th anniversary of the women's strike or the women's day off, close to 50,000 women rallied in Reykjavík and in various towns around Iceland. In 2009, Jóhanna Sigurðardóttir was the first woman in Icelandic history to become prime minister, and at the time there was an equal number of women and men cabinet ministers.

The largest network of women in Iceland, the Association of Women Business Leaders, Félag Kvenna í Atvinnulífinu (FKA) was established in 1999. Initially, it was only for female business owners with the intent to promote and prepare them for promotions and entry into leadership positions in companies. Today this network has broadened its membership to include other professional women's network (Association of Women Business Leaders in Iceland (FKA) 2018). Other professional networks with similar goals have been established both for business leaders and professional networks of women that work in the same industry. Among other gender-related issues, these networks of women were particularly active in pushing for more women representatives on corporate boards.

As a result of FKA's and other agencies' efforts, Iceland passed a law on gender-based quotas for corporate boards in 2010. Women and managers felt the need to increase the number of women in economic decision-making. Norway had introduced gender quotas, and many were keen on taking up similar legislation in the country. Building upon but extending beyond the Norwegian "role model" regarding board composition, this law stated that 40% of each gender must be represented on corporate boards of directors in all state-owned enterprises, publicly traded firms, and private limited companies with 50 or more employees. No other country has legalized such extensive requirements for firms (Arnardottir and Sigurjonsson 2017). In the year, women made up 20% of all managers on the labor market and 24% of all corporate board members (Snorradóttir et al. 2014). There was some skepticism toward gender quotas, especially among male managers (Rafnsdóttir and Þorvaldsdóttir 2012). The main argument for implementing the law on quota was that, although progress had been made in terms of women representation, women's numbers were still relatively lacking and thus the economy, overall, was not adequately represented by the women. There has been a positive relation between corporate board size and the representation of women on them (Snorrason 2012) since the adoption of the legislation, which seems to point to beneficial changes on several fronts. The Icelandic experience of implementing the gender quota has revealed that mandatory regulation is a likely an important key to the successful increase of female representation around the board table (Arnardottir and Sigurjonsson 2017). In 2016, women accounted for 48% of elected representatives in parliament (since recent elections it has dropped to 38%). After more than 100 years and the hard work and dedication of women pioneers and their supporters, there is almost political equality in Iceland today (Fig. 9.1).

Just before the allegations against Harvey Weinstein in the United States came to light, the Government of Iceland had been shaken to its core after convicted sex offenders had their "civil standing" restored under legislation from the nineteenth century through the terminology "restoration of honor." Information regarding the cases, withheld initially and later released, constituted a breach of trust in the minds of one of the smaller coalition partners in the government, resulting in the dissolution of the government. In September, the respective clause in the law was repealed (Marinósdóttir and Erlingsdóttir 2017). For the moment, it is evident that the social media is creating a wave of protest where women are speaking out, repeating "#metoo," which created much attention in Iceland as elsewhere.

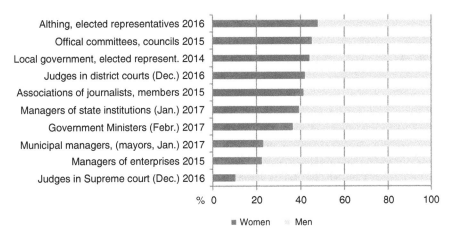

Fig. 9.1 The gender representation in leadership positions. Statistics Iceland (2017)

As gender disparities had existed for decades, Iceland has moved to address this specific issue by introducing laws on equal pay certification. This legislation is based on a tool called the Equal Pay Standard, which aims to eliminate the adjusted gender pay gap. The intention of the government to implement the Equal Pay Standard through legislation was widely debated in Iceland, but it has brought the gender equality debate into mainstream politics and policy-making, away from the margins where it often resides (Marinósdóttir and Erlingsdóttir 2017). Specifically, the standard will apply to all companies and institutions with at least 25 full-time staff positions. Implementing the standard will empower and enable employers to indeed implement a management system of equal pay according to the principle of equal pay for equal work and work of equal value. They will thereby comply with the act on the equal status of men and women and fulfill the demands of international treaties, such as the International Labor Organization Conventions, the Beijing Platform of Action, and the Convention to Eliminate All Forms of Discrimination Against Women (CEDAW).

9.3   Concluding Remarks

As was stated at the beginning of the chapter, the Global Gender Gap Index examines the gap between men and women in four categories: economic participation and opportunity, educational attainment, health and survival, and political empowerment. As can be seen in the case of Iceland, it has been a long road filled with challenges and tremendous effort to be able to earn and keep its seat at the top of the Index. The stepping stones have been both big and small. The hallmark event of October 1975 showed women in Iceland what solidarity could bring about when over 25,000 of them went on strike and almost caused the wheels of society to come to a halt. This led to the Women's Alliance and eventually to the election of Vigdís Finnbogadóttir as the first female President to be elected. The last decades of the twentieth century women's focus turned to the pay gap and access to power in general. Since the turn of the new millennium, further discussion and push for legislative changes have led to major changes regarding women representation on executive boards and equal pay. These initiatives, as well as the current #metoo movement, are signs of progress that can be attributed to earlier efforts in the previous decades. Gender equality is still an important point of discussion and certainly merits and requires continued attention. However, Iceland's top position at the Global Gender Gap Index demonstrates that even in the context of young organizational traditions, with great effort, gender equality can be attained.

References

Arnardottir AA, Sigurjonsson TO (2017) Gender diversity on boards in Iceland: pathway to gender quota law following a financial crisis. In: Seierstad C, Gabaldon P, Mensi-Klarbach H (eds) Gender diversity in the boardroom. Palgrave Macmillan, Cham, pp 75–101

Association of Women Business Leaders in Iceland (FKA) (2018) Félag kvenna atvinnurekstri. http://fka.is/. Accessed 29 Apr 2018

Jafnréttisstofa (2012) Information on gender equality issues in Iceland

Labour force participation rate indicator (2018) OECD Publishing. Accessed 29 Apr 2018

Marinósdóttir M, Erlingsdóttir R (2017) This is why Iceland ranks first for gender equality. World Econ Forum. https://www.weforum.org/agenda/2017/11/why-iceland-ranks-first-gender-equal ity/. Accessed 29 Apr 2018

Rafnsdóttir GL, Þorvaldsdóttir M (2012) Kynjakvótar og mögulegar hindranir á leið kvenna til æðstu stjórnunar. Íslenska þjóðfélagið 3(1):57–76

Snaebjornsson IM (2016) "President Vigdís": the end and the beginning of women's agenda in Iceland. In: Erçetin ŞŞ (ed) Women leaders in chaotic environments. Springer, Cham, pp 35–47

Snorradóttir Á, Rafnsdottir GL, Tómasson K, Vilhjálmsson R (2014) Lay off: the experience of women and men in Iceland's financial sector. Work 47(2):183–191

Snorrason JS (2012) Yfirlit um stöðu og áhrif jafnari kynjahlutfalla við stjórnun og í stjórnum fyrirtækja. Stjórnmál Stjórnsýsla 1(8):93–107

The Gender Representation in Leadership Positions (2017) https://www.statice.is/publications/ iceland-in-figures/. Accessed 29 Apr 2018

Unempoyment rate (2018) https://www.statice.is/publications/news-archive/labour-market/labour-market-statistics-4th-quarter-2017/. Accessed 29 Apr 2018

World Economic Forum (2017) The global gender gap report 2017. Switzerland, Geneva

Chapter 10
Before and After: Effect of Gender Quota on Icelandic Landscape of the Boards of Directors

If Anything can save the world, women can.
Vigdís Finnbogadóttir

Abstract Women and men do not participate in the national or global economy to the same extent. One of the critical factors in gender equality is access to the boards of directors in both private and public companies, as this is where the highest levels of power are concentrated. Sometimes the result of this historical tendency to exclude women is accompanied by an allusion to "smoke-filled rooms," where important decisions are made by powerful people. However, with a release of a law to establish gender quotas in Icelandic boards of directors, both the smoke and the men-only corporate boards vanished away in the largest corporations.

Keywords Gender quota · Gender equality · Boards of directors · Iceland

10.1 The Bigger Picture

The contribution of women directors to corporate value creation has been widely studied (Vinnicombe et al. 2008; Torchia et al. 2011; Noland et al. 2016). Researchers have supported the importance of increasing diversity and bringing more women on boards, with some studies indicating that doing so might lead to increases in companies' profitability (McKinsey and Company 2012). Scholars have particularly pointed out that for women to be seen as legitimate board members, they need to move from being the tokens to a critical mass (Kanter 1977; Torchia et al. 2011; Nekhili and Gatfaoui 2013). Many would agree that corporate governance and company performance are of tremendous importance for any company. The board of directors is critical to governance, as it forms crucial strategic, operational, and financial decisions. The key role of the board of directors is advancing the business strategy with the management team and setting the policy objects, and they are involved in planning and managing resources. In sum, the board of directors

© Springer International Publishing AG, part of Springer Nature 2018   89
I. Minelgaite et al., *Demystifying Leadership in Iceland*, Contributions to
Management Science, https://doi.org/10.1007/978-3-319-96044-9_10

undertakes responsibility for the main decision-making within the organization (Adams et al. 2010). Boards are also physical representations of organizations; they are the face of the company to the public and investors. Thus, women's presence on boards reflects "who the company is." The emphasis on the importance of women representation on boards of directors has been recurrent in academic research as well as among feminist activists (e.g., Vinnicombe et al. 2008; Terjesen et al. 2015; Wang and Kelan 2013; Noland et al. 2016). In practice, women worldwide have not succeeded in attaining equal representation compared to men on corporate boards of directors. In 2015, across 67 countries, women comprised only 10.3% of board directors (Terjesen et al. 2015). Thus, the pressure on policymakers and business leaders increased in response to changing attitudes about women inclusion and public pressure to address the often severe imbalances. As the diversity on corporate boards has been recognized with regard to economic performance, gender equality has gained attention among business leaders and scholars.

In Iceland, attention to corporate quotas has been growing over the past years. A major factor that stimulated this was when Norway passed legislation in 2003 that required at least 40% of public limited state-owned and inter-municipality companies' board memberships be women. The rationale for this quota-driven regulation was directly aimed to increase female leadership in the corporate field. Iceland followed this approach in 2010, establishing a similar target of 40% female representation to be reached by 2013 (Pande and Ford 2011).

This chapter discusses the quota system adoption in Iceland and the effects it has had on boards from the standpoint of female leaders. For this study, a focus group was conducted, involving eight women who have been serving on a number corporate boards both before and after the legal regulation was implemented. Three out of eight focus group participants have also served as the CEO's of large Icelandic companies.

10.2   The Impact of Gender Quotas in General

The use of corporate quotas has led to an increase in female representation among nations that have established such legislative mandates. Overall, there has been an increase in women serving on multiple boards in Norway. However, it has not necessarily been reflected in a proportional increase in the number of female leaders. In Norway, there has been some evidence of resistance or even dismissal of these quotas by companies that do not support the law. As a means to avoid compliance with the quota, some companies have chosen to become private instead of public limited firms, and some have even moved their registration to the United Kingdom (Pande and Ford 2011). According to Pande and Ford (2011), women who are experienced in board membership may be more often selected to serve on boards of multiple companies. However, it has not been proven that the more substantial number of women on boards correlates with the more substantial number of females as top executives in these companies.

It is believed that membership heterogeneity increases the number of possible viewpoints and thus leads to better governance decisions (Vinnicombe et al. 2008; Nekhili and Gatfaoui 2013). Theories on diversity in company boards are based on the argument that women and men differ in their managerial approaches and skills. In the leadership literature, women are often characterized as exercising more democratic and transformational or inspirational style of leadership compared to men (Eagly and Carli 2003; Guðmundsdóttir 2017). Perhaps relatedly, women who are appointed to boards are more likely to be allocated to public affairs or corporate social responsibilities (Nekhili and Gatfaoui 2013). Primary findings illustrate that companies which have more women on boards might be driven by a different strategy before the quotas were applied (Pande and Ford 2011). For example, evidence on the impact of corporate board quotas has shown that in Scandinavian countries, corporate gender quotas led to a short-term loss of profits, primarily driven by increased investment in employees. Women seem to be willing to invest more in the wellness of employees, what can be reflected in greater spending on employee beneficial programs. Extant research also suggests that female directors enhance the decision-making process within the board, enhance the quality of monitoring, and hence strengthen the corporate governance control (Vinnicombe et al. 2008). However, more research is needed regarding the long-term effects of corporate gender quotas on the economic performance of companies (Vinnicombe et al. 2008).

When analyzing the criteria for the selection of women to corporate boards, educational credentials and work experience are prominent attributes. An international survey conducted in 2015 revealed that more than 80% of professional female leaders held a university degree and 38% held an advanced degree (Noland et al. 2016). Experience is also significant, and the literature finds that women's years of leadership experience directly correlates with improved organizational results (Pande and Ford 2011). The appointment process is often driven by candidates' personal acquaintances with the existing board members, and the personal support for a new candidate is often an important prerequisite to being appointed or recruited to serve on the board level. Hence, the social capital of the candidates is of crucial value. Serving on multiple boards is a frequent characteristic of directors (Nekhili and Gatfaoui 2013). Women board directors in Norway also seem to perceive themselves as having more influence, receiving more information, and being more engaged in social interaction since the quota law was implemented (Elstad and Ladegard 2012). It can be argued that those women that were selected on boards after the quota law benefited from their multi-board directorships and extensive network ties.

As one of the chapters in this book discusses, the World Economic Forum's Global Gender Gap Index, which aims to capture a society's willingness to allow women to participate in education, the labor force, and public life, directly addresses the local status of women. However, this index does not examine percentages of women on boards or in the executive ranks. When looking into factors that potentially impede appointment of women to leadership positions, particularly when they are on par with men in other criteria such as education level and participation in the labor are similar, motherhood emerges as a prime factor in a majority of studies. In most societies women, to varying degrees, are more likely than men to take on dual roles and assume both career and family responsibilities; in many cases, this is an expectation for career-oriented women. In Iceland, even though childcare is provided by the municipalities for children of 1–2 years of age, research has shown that it is still primarily women who bridge the time between maternity leave and the child's eligibility for a kindergarten (Velferðarráðuneytið 2018). Even in societies that exhibit less of a cultural bias against women's participation in the technical and professional workforce, women by and large undertake a more significant share of childcare and household responsibilities. Women may need to reduce turn down their career ambitions or put their careers on hold in order to devote more time to family care; again, they are usually expected to do so. This is evident in both business and academic contexts (Rafnsdóttir et al. 2015; Rafnsdóttir and Heijstra 2013). Research has indicated that mandated maternity leave is not correlated with female corporate leadership, but on the other hand, paternity leaves are actively correlated with the female share on board seats (Noland et al. 2016). Thus, policies that place a disproportionate burden of childcare on women are the barrier to women's corporate advancement.

10.3   The Impact of Gender Quotas in Iceland

On 15 May 2009, in response to the underrepresentation of women in higher-level business positions, and especially on corporate boards, the Icelandic Association of Women Entrepreneurs (FKA), Iceland Chamber of Commerce (VÍ), and the Confederation of Icelandic Employers (SA) signed a collaboration agreement expressing the necessity of increasing the share of women in corporate governance of Icelandic companies. In March 2010, the Icelandic government followed the Norwegian example and approved amendments to the legislation on public limited firms and private limited firms. These amendments require companies in Iceland with over 50 employees on a yearly basis to have at least 40% of each gender represented on their corporate boards of directors from September 2013 onward. Following the path of Norway, Iceland was the second country in the world to put a law of this kind into effect (Lög nr. 13/2010).

The collapse of the Icelandic banking system in 2008 has led to an increased demand for more transparent and improved corporate governance. The increased awareness of good corporate governance seems to become a widespread tendency as more companies have been using instructions and manuals for corporate governance (Arnórsdóttir 2012). According to a new report created for the Ministry of Welfare in Iceland, there has not been a significant difference since the gender quota law was reinforced the representation of female board numbers only increased from 24% in 2014 to 26% in 2016 (Velferðarráðuneytið 2018). Size of the company is an important variable in this equation, as companies with fewer than 50 employees have the lowest percentage of women on their board or 25.6%. In companies that have 50–99 employees, the figure is 27.2%, while in companies with 100–249 employees, it rises to 35.1%. Only in the largest companies, with 250 employees or more, has the proportion of women on boards reached the targeted 40% (Velferðarráðuneytið 2018). In 2016, 23.9% of board directors of the biggest companies were female in Iceland (Velferðarráðuneytið 2018). In the last 16 years, female CEOs had only increased by 6%, but in 2016, they represented 22.4% in the smallest companies yet only 13.1% of the largest ones. In the financial sector at the beginning of 2018, only 9 CEOs were female compared to 81 who were male (Velferðarráðuneytið 2018).

According to the study on "gender equality in business management" (Rafnsdóttir et al. 2015), a typical Icelandic male manager is 49.6 years old. He typically has an advanced university degree, often in business or economics. He is married, has three or more children on average, and works 51–60 h a week. A typical Icelandic female manager is 44.9 years old, also has a graduate degree in similar fields, is married, has two children on average, and works 41–50 h a week (Rafnsdóttir et al. 2015). This reflects the noted difference between women and men in light of family duties, as men leaders work more extended hours at their jobs, whereas women leaders devote hours to their homes. Just under 32% of women and 40% of men agree that women have less freedom to pursue their career because of the responsibilities they typically assume for their families and children. In a question concerning the work-life balance as an avenue to better gender balance in top management positions, notable gender differences are observed. The results indicate that 75% of women but only 57% of men believe that the distribution of parental leave is necessary, while 82% of women and only 59% of men believe an equal division of family duties between parents is important (Rafnsdóttir et al. 2015). This highlights that gender imbalance is not as simple as organizations not appointing women to top positions; it is also a simple function of expectations of homelife and spousal expectations/support. Before women can engage in career advancement, they might have to fight this battle in their own homes and with their own families.

Just over a half of women, or 53%, compared to 33% of men, think that recruitment of women into a management position is not a priority within the business sector. The equality principle assumes that men and women with equal competence should be equally represented in top positions across the business sectors. However, the largest gender imbalance is found among executive management ranks in Iceland. The gender discrepancy in middle management was slightly smaller, in 2014 (Rafnsdóttir et al. 2015). Such an imbalance evokes considerations about differences in employment procedures. When the question is raised whether recruitment for management positions relies too heavily on informal networks, 73% women and only 39% men agree with the statement. When asked whether the business sector is dominated by men with insufficient trust in women, just under a half, or 49% of women agree with the statement as compared to 25% of men.

In 2014, board members participating in the study on gender equality in business in Iceland were asked if they had noticed any changes in board operations after the

Table 10.1 Overview of the focus group participants

Name	Age	Number of boards	Education
Kristin	67	Over 10	Pharmacist
Emma	49	8	PhD in business
Viktoria	64	Over 10	Business degree
Hekla	50	5	Business degree
Eva	53	4	Business degree
Maria	46	6	Law
Freyja	49	Over 10	Economist
Julia	49	Over 10	Business degree

law on the quota. Many respondents were not in a position to answer that as they had not been serving before the enforcement of the law. Additionally, 16% of female and 17% of male respondents answered that the board they served on was not affected by the law. The majority of men, or 60%, but only 28% of women stated that no noteworthy change had occurred in the board's operations following the law. More women than men claimed to have noticed improvements or 34% of female and 14% of male respondents. Hence, the study results suggest that women were the ones to perceive and experience the differences most.

10.4   Women on Corporate Boards: Different Issues on the Agenda

The focus group initiated for this study involved eight female participants, whose basic demographic and board participation data are presented in Table 10.1 (the names were changed to preserve confidentiality). The criteria for selection was that they had served for an extended time on corporate boards and had served on multiple boards as well as having the experience both before and after the gender quota law was issued.

Half of the women who participated have been serving as CEOs, and five of them dedicate most of their working time for the operations of the boards in which they are now involved. All participants have extensive top management experience, and some have been appointed on more boards after the law enforcement. The findings of the focus group have been organized into five categories: shifted board agenda, increased dynamic diversity, enhanced networking on boards, role models enacted by female board members, and a backlash pronounced last year. The findings are further discussed according to each category.

Shifted Board Agenda   All participants agreed that after more women were selected for corporate boards, the agenda and issues changed. "I am not sure if it is the women who changed it or the ethos of the time after the financial crisis of 2008. However, the pressure on transparency and social responsibility has increased enormously," noted Freyja. Participants unanimously agreed that the quota law had dramatically weakened the "old boys' network" and that the board's decision-making process improved overall. "Gender equality is almost not an issue anymore because everybody agrees on the importance of it," suggested Viktoria. More stakeholders are involved, and the importance of sustainability is one of the issues that all participants agree on and thus discuss more frequently. Another issue that all participants highlighted is the increased role of proper governance. "I do not know if this has to do with more women on boards, but at least I feel that we have made a difference and that on the whole, the boards are more professional than before," said Emma. According to participants, most corporate boards in Iceland have a specific performance evaluation system that they turn to regularly, a practice which emerged in the last decade. All participants agreed that they greatly emphasize both gender equality and staff issues and certainly more than they used to.

Increased Dynamic Diversity "I think that most would agree that it is more fun working in a diverse environment," said Julia. All participants contended that having diversity on boards ensures a dynamic environment that can also enhance creativity. "The leadership becomes more varied and more points of view get included," said Kristin. "Even though it takes time to change the culture . . . It can even be said that we have a new generation of men that are as equal-minded as women," added Maria. Thus, female board members themselves experience positive feedback from their environment. This shows how more diverse ideas can help people think in new ways they never thought possible. There seems to be a synergistic effect as people who are exposed to new ideas are more likely as a group to build upon each other's perspectives and thus create solutions that a single person would not have developed independently.

Enhanced Networking on Boards All participants agreed that appointment to corporate boards had had a positive influence on their careers. Half of the focus group participants are professional board members; they see both pros and cons associated with engaging this profession. "You get a little lonely as you are deciding to do something and that is exciting, and then there are others that do what needs to be done," said Freyja. All of them agreed that they had much more opportunities after the gender quota, and some of them are sure that if the economic crisis of 2008 had not occurred, the law would never have been passed. Women in Iceland are a part of an international community called Women Corporate Directors (WCD) Foundation, which is the world's largest membership organization and community of women corporate board directors. Most of the women in the group belong to both the Icelandic and the international networks. Participants noted their association with the community made a big difference that helped them to make new connections on both personal and professional levels with women who shared a similar mindset and, perhaps most importantly, made it easier to recommend and provide names when new board membership opportunities opened.

Enactment of Role Models All participants shared their awareness of the importance of having their own role models as well as the responsibility they felt for being role models for other women. According to participants, the law has strongly shaped their position and enhanced the possibilities to strengthen the corporate female portrait. Icelandic boards of directors typically consist of five members and the focus group participants confirm that they feel a difference after the legal regulation. "*I could feel a great difference when there were three women in one of the seven boards that I was a member of. There was a change in the culture and the attitude*," said Maria. The participants confirmed trying to include more women on boards and ensure that companies realize the process of women development up to the career ladder.

Backlash The women who participated in the focus group were concerned that they were experiencing some form of backlash and in particular that the "*#metoo*" revolution had made many men uncomfortable. Even though all participants supported the issue wholeheartedly and were sure of its purpose, they could feel a backlash in the boardroom. They acknowledged that the issue of "*#metoo*" was crucial and that it was necessary to take part in highlighting the mistreatment of women when they are not given equal rights, let alone positions of power. On the other hand, the participants confirmed they could feel that men were unsure of how they should react and this led them to reflect on the "good old days" when gender politics may have been less contentious or so much at the forefront of society. The participants also related these questions to the issue of judgment. They all agreed that women in business are treated differently by the media and the society. "When a woman CEO makes a mistake, it is blown out of portion both in politics and business," said Eva. They all claimed to be familiar with cases where women were blamed for making a wrong decision while men were more likely to "get away with it." Nevertheless, the participants believe that women are more honest in the media and elsewhere and are often made to pay for their actions.

10.5   Concluding Remarks

This chapter has illustrated that most of the issues women are facing on corporate boards worldwide are similar in Iceland as they are elsewhere. Even though after the law on the 40% quota, Iceland is demonstrably more progressive in these areas compared to other nations, there is still a set of questions that need to be addressed. Some of the women who made their way to corporate boards have had the opportunity to serve on multiple boards, what has created the so-called "golden skirts" effect with a new generation of women who work solely as professional board members. The agenda and dynamics of boards tend to change when women are included on them; moreover, the pressure to offer greater transparency of board functioning and activities is evident. Women bring different perspectives and interests to the discussion. For example, social responsibility and sustainability are not solely a female concern, but active engagement of women on boards is associated with a more intense consideration of the questions. Just as in Norway, female board directors in Iceland perceive themselves as having more influence, receiving more information, and being more engaged in social interaction after the quota regulation was implemented. Time will reveal if a backlash is only temporary and if women in business need to be aware of not losing what has been won. It is important to consider general public acceptance and promotion of women in upper management, males supporting their spouses and co-workers more. Iceland has put great value on egalitarianism, and as thus people need to support advances in gender equality at boards and in general on all levels. The attention Iceland has given to gender balance has focused on and had positive results for women; perhaps the scope will expand to include other issues such as gender identity and transgender or gender fluidity, again not necessary but a legitimate question to consider in the name of gender equality in the future.

References

Adams RB, Hermalin BE, Weisbach MS (2010) The role of boards of directors in corporate governance: a conceptual framework and survey. J Econ Lit 48(1):58–107

Arnórsdóttir RE (2012) Gender quota on corporate boards in Iceland. Attitudes within the Icelandic business community, Copenhagen

Eagly AH, Carli LL (2003) The female leadership advantage: an evaluation of the evidence. Leadersh Q 14(6):807–834

Elstad B, Ladegard G (2012) Women on corporate boards: key influencers or tokens? J Manag Gov 16(4):595–615

Guðmundsdóttir ÁE (2017) Sterkari í seinni hálfleik. Spennandi umbreytingar og heillandi tækifæri í framtíðinni. Bjartur, Reykjavík

Kanter RM (1977) Men and women of the corporation. Basic Books, New York

McKinsey & Company (2012) Unlocking the full potential of women at work, New York

Nekhili M, Gatfaoui H (2013) Are demographic attributes and firm characteristics drivers of gender diversity? Investigating women's positions on French boards of directors. J Bus Ethics 118 (2):227–249

Noland M, Moran T, Kotschwar B (2016) Is gender diversity profitable? Evidence from a global survey. Working Paper series. Peterson Institute for international Economics

Pande R, Ford D (2011) Gender quotas and female leadership. Harvard University

Rafnsdóttir GL, Heijstra TM (2013) Balancing work–family life in academia: the power of time. Gend Work Organ 20(3):283–296

Rafnsdóttir GL, Axelsdóttir L, Diðriksdóttir S, Einarsdóttir Þ (2015) Women and men as business leaders in Iceland. Jafnréttisstofa, Raykjavik

Terjesen S, Aguilera RV, Lorenz R (2015) Legislating a woman's seat on the board: institutional factors driving gender quotas for boards of directors. J Bus Ethics 128(2):233–251

Torchia M, Calabrò A, Huse M (2011) Women directors on corporate boards: from tokenism to critical mass. J Bus Ethics 102(2):299–317

Velferðarráðuneytið (2018) Skýrsla félags- og jafnréttisráðherra um stöðu og þróun jafnréttismála 2015–2017. Reykjavík

Vinnicombe S, Singh V, Burke RJ, Bilimoria D, Huse M (2008) Women on corporate boards of directors. Edward Elgar, Cheltenham

Wang M, Kelan E (2013) The gender quota and female leadership: effects of the Norwegian gender quota on board chairs and CEOs. J Bus Ethics 117(3):449–466

Chapter 11
The Untold Story of Gender Quota Effects in Iceland

From a business perspective, it's just finding the right person who can deal with the problem. That's where you start.
Anonymous interviewee

Abstract Following the pioneering movement in Norway, a law requiring the gender quotas to be established on corporate boards was amended in 2010 in Iceland. This event could legitimately be called an uprising in the fight against the shadow of the so-called *Octopus*—the fourteen patriarchs who in the middle of the twentieth century "were said to control the politics, bureaucracy, judiciary, and economy of Iceland and shared the spoils among themselves" (Kelsey 2016, p. 13; Boyes 2009; Johnson et al. 2013). Whether the *Octopus* has been slowly reincarnated in corporate boardrooms or instead, it has become a mystical creature wrapped in legends and still remains a valid question. This chapter unveils an untold story on the gender quota effects that was shared by six male board members with long-standing corporate experience. This story could have equally been revealed to either a male or a female interviewer. Yet, it could only be shared once the female board members stepped out of the room. This revelation unfolded in an atmosphere of complete privacy, when male board members, often pre-accused with gender bias, once asked to describe the law on gender quota in one word, put forward all the candor, and stated: "It is biased against males."

Keywords Gender quota · Gender equality · Gender diversity · Iceland

11.1 The Bigger Picture

A backlash regarding women's involvement in a variety of social institutions has long been a concern among scholars, practitioners, and society (e.g., Johnson et al. 2013; Kelsey 2016). Despite being highlighted as a pioneer against this backlash, together with Norway, egalitarian Iceland is still underperforming in terms of gender

© Springer International Publishing AG, part of Springer Nature 2018
I. Minelgaite et al., *Demystifying Leadership in Iceland*, Contributions to
Management Science, https://doi.org/10.1007/978-3-319-96044-9_11

diversity in the upper echelons (Rafnsdóttir et al. 2015; Halrynjo et al. 2015). Even with the adoption and implementation of the law establishing gender quotas, board-rooms have still often been dominated by men (Centre for Gender Equality 2012), and the males in dominant leadership positions often have been accused of attempts to "transgress proclaimed values of accountability, transparency, and equality" (Johnson et al. 2013, p. 196). The law, in essence, states that public and private limited companies with over 50 employees are required to include both genders on the corporate boards and preserve the proportion of each gender of at least 40% if the number of board members exceeds three (Centre for Gender Equality 2012).

Indeed, when the change in gender representation on the corporate boards in Iceland is considered, the numbers suggest a certain degree of ambiguity. By the end of 2015, women comprised 25.9% of corporate board members in Iceland (Statistics Iceland 2016), constituting a slight difference from 22 to 24% present over the 10 years from the 2000s (Snorrason 2012). The socially significant yet statistically limited increase toward balanced gender participation suggests a discussion whether the roots of imbalance are solely related to gender bias. Traditional male-only "chummy networks" (Johnson et al. 2013, p. 185) put aside, an additional array of possible causes may have been at play. For example, corporate board membership has always been associated with top-level skills and competences. It was not until the first wave of migration in 1990s, when women began to be actively considered as high education- and career-seekers. Marking the first period of substantial migration in the country, during this time, Icelandic women notably departed from their jobs in the fishing industry, often in rural areas, in search for higher education and career opportunities (Júlíusdóttir et al. 2013). Years after, however, an imprint on incon-gruence between gender roles (Eagly and Karau 2002) may still be present. Further-more, the difference between gender equality as a societal-level value and an individual-level value, and the potential gap between the gender equality and gender diversity, may be both affecting the attitudes and behaviors as Sund and Snaebjornsson (2017) suggest.

Gender equality, as a value, inevitably entails ethical considerations, especially in the light of law amendment. According to Lawrence Kohlberg, a pioneering devel-opmental psychologist who is perhaps most well-known for his theories of moral reasoning and moral development, enactment of values through behavior cannot be discerned from moral reasoning, accompanied by rationale and logic. Moral reason-ing is based on cognitive moral development, which encompasses three different levels: preconventional, conventional, and principled (Kohlberg and Kramer 1969). It is at the conventional and principled levels of cognitive moral development when an individual shifts from his or her own interests and positive or negative conse-quences (often taking a form of rewards or punishments) to a more developed sense of morality. At these two levels, the concept of what is ethical, moral, and "right" comes into play, accounting for the beliefs and interests of society and ultimately universally applicable values. However, in this light, a potential cultural clash around gender balance takes place. In the middle of this clash, women are often viewed as an underrepresented force overshadowed by men. Yet, there is a chance that the situation is related to the different upbringings and development of current males who are on corporate board members and the women who are not. This development has been very likely grounded in a different cultural setting, where women were mainly active as caretakers of the family, rather than corporate activists, entering the boardrooms and setting their equal competences and experience on the table to open up new perspectives and shape the corporate governance standards.

This chapter was undertaken as a deeper investigation on the gender equality in the boardroom that may be missing in a larger public discourse. For the purpose of this chapter, a focus group with six male participants who have long-standing backgrounds and experiences on corporate boards of the leading Icelandic companies was conducted. The three sides of the untold story on gender quota effects soon emerged, highlighting the different perspectives by men and women toward the corporate landscape in the past, the proper corporate board design methodology, and the enactment of the law on gender quotas. The findings of the focus group are accordingly nested under three categories and discussed further.

11.2   The Untold Story of Gender Quota Effects

One of the underlying reasons behind the law was a national urge for a balanced gender representation on the corporate board of companies. The male participants stated that before the law on gender quota was introduced, the gender proportions on corporate boards were not considered specifically, although they were not complexly ignored, either. "I don't think there was really a measurement of it before the law. I mean, I think there was also [a sentiment that] 'yes, we need to have, you know, women on those boards.' But of course, since we got the law, now you need to have 40–60% balance on the board," Brynjar argued. Today, the law is enacted, as Brynjar commented, "It has really become a norm or something that everybody complies to." All of the focus group participants confirmed that they have been observing a change once the law on gender quota was passed in 2013 in Iceland, both in their own and other companies. As Baldur recounted, "...I saw many companies pushing out senior board members to be able to take out women board members to comply with the laws, so, it definitely has an impact."

As it has been discussed in the previous chapters, the effects of the gender quota law in action confirm the growing numbers of women on boards of directors and the shift toward greater gender balance. The male focus group members reiterated this effect, as summarized by Haraldur:

> ... When I look at people being elected to board at the moment, I see more and more names of women that I didn't recognize before. So, yeah ... we have already, these few years after the law was implemented, more female names popping up. And I think it's a good thing because it gives them the experience needed to move forward.

In the extensive discourse concerning the specific law and its effect, there an untold part of the story remains on the male side. In many ways, this is due to the reality of an inconvenient truth. The male board members do acknowledge the effect of the law in general, however, outline some precautions. This feedback is not to be mixed with complaints, however, even if there were some during the first years after the law was passed. Male board members base their position on the needs of the business, as Baldur explained:

> I think the change itself is not really negative. But I think the promise that follows the legislation—that this will so beneficial to companies and profitability, that it was really a good business decision—has not been proven. I have seen no indication of businesses in Iceland where women quota has been implemented to have increased profitability or financial results.

While any negative feedback toward enforcement can often be perceived and presented as resistance of males against limitations of their power, indeed, perceptions of men are driven by a different set of arguments. As Dagur commented: "I mean, a female can be just as clever as any male. And then I want to vote for her on my board because of her cleverness not because she is wearing a skirt." These insights unravel the underlying principle that male board members often support— selection of talent and capability regardless of gender. Once deeper discussions with female and male board members are initiated, it becomes evident that men and women have a different relationship with the past, present, and the future of the corporate board practice.

11.2.1   Diverging Perspectives Toward the Past

Some participants consider that the scarce representation of women on corporate boards back in 1990s was essentially associated with a lack of competences and skills. Haraldur characterized the boards mostly as "middle-aged to older males." Brynjar commented: "One issue that was used is that there was a shortage on supply of women who were available or willing, or some would say, capable to sit on board. This was the excuse of many men CEO's or men ownership—well, there were no women available with either this education or this knowledge or these skills. . ."

However, by the 2000s, the landscape and perceptions of women's capabilities and motivations had become very different, due in part to what Haraldur characterized as the "young culture coming in":

> It used to be like that. But in this century, I don't think it is that way anymore. But last century, it was like that. Women were looked at like, 'What are you doing here'? I mean, this is the male club and things are like that. Women were also looked at, 'What's wrong with you? Do you want to be a male?' I have to go all the way back to 1990s to remember that attitude. In this century, I guess from 2000 on, it has been changing rapidly.

While female board members still recall board activities in the 2000s as being dominated by men and offering little access for women, male board members generally do not recollect any significant differences that would be exclusively related to gender. One of the focus group participants remembers male environment mostly. Another focus group participant, Armann, shared, however: "Of the boards,

I can recall that there always had been a mixture of both sexes as far as I can remember … I presume it's been a majority of men, but it's probably been sort of around a third of women at least, or up to a half. So, it's been mixed over the years." At some point, participants may have different or inaccurate memories toward the gender balance. Other participants noticed, for example, that women may had been in an inferior position when making their way toward the board membership. However, they tend to highlight the roots of the problem different than bias toward gender, as a remark by Baldur illustrates:

> I don't think that males have more or better skills than women. But I think it goes down, like I just said before, that men are more, let's say, networked to other men. So, they'd say, 'Well, I know this guy, this guy, this guy, and this guy. So, let's compare the skills they have and if no one suggested a woman, then no woman was suggested. That was probably a mistake, but it was, let's say. I think of the past of the people I have been working before and in those terms, I think, in some cases, women didn't have a fair chance.'

Hence, the male board members tend to associate the possible underrepresentation of women with the downside of networking-based board member selection techniques, usually taking place in immediate social circles, rather than the gender bias. According to the male focus group participants, this technique, in turn, is driven by a different approach toward sustainable board design, based on the search for proper competences, rather than convenience of a network.

11.2.2   Diverging Perspectives Toward the Board Design

The focus group findings reveal that male board members have assumed a different approach toward board composition. This approach, in fact, embraces diversity but primarily concerns the right combination of competences and experience, rather than strategically designing the board to ensure appropriate representation of gender, age, race or ethnic background, or other demographic variables. Secondly, the participants' approach to board composition follows a loyalty-to-the-shareholder tradition, that is, respecting the shareholders' right to select to whom they should entrust the governance of their company. "From a business perspective, gender is not an issue. Not at all. From a business perspective, it's just finding the right person who can deal with the problem. That's where you start,"—Elvar argued. He further elaborated:

> I think that what I've seen is that if you are a skilled person, it doesn't matter whether you are a man or a woman. If you have an eye on the ball and you have the qualification and you know what you are doing—you're going to get elected. So, it doesn't matter who you are, where you come from, if you have the skills—you succeed.

In line with Elvar's perspective, Dagur summarized, "That is what I would like to see in a board if I was a CEO today—board members who are really business-minded. Not—men or women—that is not a question." Armann reflected:

> …when you try to form a board, whether you have a number of shareholders or a single shareholder, you try to get a diversified board … if you are thinking of a long-term success

of the business. You want to have a diversified board. You don't want people of the same education, the same age or the same background, because diversity brings some value.

The compliance with the needs of the company and the rights of the shareholders is an overarching concern in the board composition, according to the logics of the traditional approach to board membership. Baldur recalled the time before the law on gender quota was enforced:

...my perspective at that time and many of those male colleagues ... we thought about that ... This was a little bit of a strange situation where there is no longer a question of the shareholders controlling who the board members are. So, as it's taking away the ownership rights of the public companies we thought that it is still important to have the right combination of skills rather than the right combination of gender. So, I think at that time I was not supportive, but I understood where they were coming from. But in my mind, it is always a question of whether the women have the same opportunities of buying equities and buying their own board seats as everybody else does.

Baldur further reiterated an approach that is based on a proper combination of competences, skills, and experience, regardless their source:

I also acknowledge that finding the right person is not always easy—[A right person] with the right skills needed for the company. So, sometimes people support a woman, it could be a young woman with limited experience in the workforce, but she may have the right connections or the right backers, and I am not saying that this does not happen with men, too. But I think in general, if we are talking about larger companies, it should be about the skills set and the experience because the management is the daily drive of the business, the board needs to be a sounding board, the police, the follow-up on the corporate governance, and the quality of the work of the management, and then you need a space. I have been on boards, where you have board members who have not said a single sentence during any board meetings for a long period of time. So, what are they for? They are useless. And this applies to both men and women.

He also illustrated how the competence-driven logic approach translates into board design:

On the board, we were trying to fulfill a structure of ownership...where the largest shareholders put people in-charge to carry out the mandates they set. Or if there is more academic people on board, then it is a question of skills. So, we want somebody with legal knowledge, maybe a couple of people with business skills and then individuals with skills related to the business in which the company operates. So, people were looking more for necessary skills, rather than age or gender. And as far as I remember, I don't think there have been any problems... Definitely, there was no bias or prejudice when it came to skills, whether it was women or men. So, I think there was none, and I think there is an easy combination, but I think also, in general, putting a board together is a little bit like putting a workplace together—you pick people you know. And more men, no men, and more women, no women.

When commenting on the situation after the law was actually passed, Armann echoes a similar viewpoint:

I admit women do sometimes have different perspectives which may be attributed to gender rather than anything else. One of the things, if you have a board of three or four or five or six or seven, you really need to make sure that you have diversity in terms of experience, diversity in terms of educational and professional background, diversity in terms of age which I think is much more important than gender. If you have nothing but men in their sixties, you probably run the business into the ground at some point because they tend to have a perspective that is lacking what's happening in the ... generation that is following them. Equally, if you have nothing but people in their thirties, they are no longer on the ground because they haven't seen enough in their working life to go good decision. But if you have a board which consists of people from late twenties and into their late seventies—the whole range—then you will have a successful board. Now, personally, I have always been on a board and worked with women and found it to be very good. But to force people to choose somebody on the basis of their gender, I think it is not a sensible thing when you ignore all the other things that you need to think about. The second reason is shareholder rights. If you have a company, for example, owned by three women, why in the world if they have to find two men to join their board if they grow in size? They would probably want to run their own company. I think shareholders should have the right to nominate [members] according to the shareholders' agreement—and they should have to. They should have the right to nominate their own directors who they believe are the most capable to carry the business forward.

Focus group participants also underscored that the complexity of the law enactment does raise concerns with regard to the standard shareholder rights, as Elvar summarized:

It creates a level of complexity, which is ... it creates a cost ... The company structure is very simple. You own a share and you have a vote. And you can appoint people, and you have a vote. And then there is a general meeting. And in the general meeting the shareholders can vote who is going to be on the board of the company. Based on your number of shares, it's where you get your power to vote. So the corporate structure itself doesn't have a view on gender at all. It shouldn't have a gender at all. Because it is just a place, it is a structure to have those who hold risk and interest of the company to execute their rights which is the govern itself of the company. They have the rights to appoint their representatives who are responsible for running the operations of the company. So the law before was just a structure as it should be, which is, the investors are the ones who appoint and then you have the annual meetings—everybody can nominate somebody for the board. And then there's the election, and the election takes care of determining who is on the board. So that's just the sort of a neutral process which is mainly based on how much ownership you have in the company and how much you can rightfully have a say in running the company. And so, when the gender law is put into law, you get a dimension which goes against the democracy inside the companies and making gender a specific issue; and that just creates a complexity and preference which has nothing to do with the main purpose of shareholding that is you are just in terms of power in running the companies.

In sum, the law on gender quota collides with the traditional perception of the board composition, design, and procedures that were held by male board members. As a result, a set of diverging perspectives, contrasting the ones held by women, developed toward the gender quota enforcement.

11.2.3 Diverging Perspectives Toward the Law on Gender Quotas

Rather often, the law on gender quotas is perceived as a harness of male power and aimed at balancing inequities in attaining leadership positions. While existing studies confirm its positive outcomes, discussed in the previous chapters, such a harness is juxtaposed with some perceptions, often only shared privately. The criticism against the gender law is yet again driven by the logics of the board composition design, held by men. "I didn't believe in it. I don't think it is important. I think it is important that people have skills and I think this quota will go away,"— commented Baldur. This key clash of interpretations and support for the law is further captured in Armann's point of view:

> It is a mistake in the sense that I know the intentions are good but as it often happens, good intentions have unforeseen consequences. And it may lead to the difficulty in getting the right board in terms of the right skills that you want to bring to that particular board. And let's say, you have a particular board of five and one is retiring, the most important thing is to find somebody who may bring the same skills that have been really valuable and the rest of those the remaining board has. And to limit that to one sex or the other is making the search much more difficult in some cases.

From the male point of view, the regulation that is exercised by the gender quota policy, at times, hampers the underlying principle of selecting the board members who most accurately match the needs of the company. "One will have to recruit an independent board member just because it's not the right gender. The enforcement of the law it gets very, very complicated in many ways, it's difficult to comply," Elvar reflected. Brynjar elaborated further:

> ...I think in many cases, people have said, 'Well, in case I need to have two, a minimum of two or three independent directors on my board, let's just pick some women ... Not really randomly. Let's go out and find some independent women and have them bring on board.'

Such a practice further extends to a set of new bias in selection procedure, the focus group findings suggest. As discussed in the previous chapters, women feel disadvantaged by the board member selection procedures that heavily rely on networking and word of mouth. In turn, male focus group participants reflect that under the gender quota regulation, networking-based selection procedure yields a limited pool of options, again undermining the portfolio of competences for a given board. Brynjar reflected:

> However, if you see what happened shortly after the quota law, you that found a pool of women who were joining the boards was not very big. So, you saw the same women showing up on many boards. <...> So, it's like, 'okay, do you know some woman?' ... 'Yeah, Yeah, she's sitting on this board, maybe she would be willing to come on our board.'

As a result, it was not the diversity that increased, but the gender proportions that were inflated, with the same women serving on multiple boards. In this regard, men tend to consider that such a practice further translates into an even more complex case of intersectionality, with potential barriers for young, aspiring women to make their way to the boardroom and forced to compete with experienced, professional female board members. Finally, the male board members with extensive experience tend to consider that if one is to address the gender equality issues, an even more multilevel approach is required. Brynjar argued:

> The problem is that we see, of course, the numerical effects on the board that are complying with the law. But there's no really a measurement with the management team. Because my

view is that, you can change the board. But yeah you can change the board, but to really change the companies, you really need to change the management team. Or you need to make sure that is a triggering effect into the management team.

In sum, all points brought up by male board members point at a skepticism toward what Kelsey (2016, p. 18) labeled "a strategy that reflects the Nordic focus on the masculine culture of business," and the possibility to solve the challenges of effective board performance by solely following the regulation. While these challenges are shared by societies around the world, they include particular historical and cultural roots need to be rectified. Such an attempt has been undertaken by introducing a specific regulation in the Icelandic system. The speculations by the male board members seem to be in line with the warnings outlined by Kelsey (2016), who highlights that:

> Appointing women to boards or as traders in the hope they will feminize the goals, values and operations of the finance industry, without addressing the systemic drivers of financialized capitalism, seems remarkably naive. The finance industry cannot become emasculated without financialized capitalism ceasing to operate. When women become insiders, the culture requires them to conform. (p. 18)

11.3 Concluding Remarks

As the study based on limited sample presented in this chapter illustrates, male board members do understand the logic behind the quota; however, there are also responses that represent skepticism toward the gender quota policy. However, the roots of it stem from the clash of the conventional business rationale and the law that mandates specific action. As one of the focus group participants, Baldur summed up: "I don't believe in it. I have belief in the freedom of [both] the government and the business. So, all women boards, all men boards—I don't think it as a problem." Hence, the story of the gender quota regulation in Iceland illustrates how the lack of ascribed procedures that enforce the law and also accurately reflect the challenges faced by the boards in practice can leave those affected with a sense of enforcement. Coupled with a sensitive issue of gender, this perception through the eyes of men seems to connote an arranged marriage in the boardroom, where partnerships may compromise the most accurate match, based on required background, competences, and experience. Finally, once the male and female board member perspectives are considered, it becomes evident that a suppressed tension exists between the sides. The source of this tension seems to stem from the diverging perspectives toward the principles of board design and composition. In this vein, the extant situation calls for a new discourse concerning the guiding principles of implementation, and a new set of recommendations that would be developed by all the corporate gender balance stakeholders, including policymakers, practitioners, and society. While particular concerns are raised by the participants of the study, the pioneering initiatives undertaken by Norway and Iceland set an important milestone in embracing gender diversity and equality.

References

Boyes R (2009) Meltdown iceland. How the global financial crisis bankrupted an entire country. Bloomsbury, London

Centre for Gender Equality (2012) Gender equality iceland: information on gender equality issues in Iceland. The Centre for Gender Equality Iceland, Akureyri

Eagly AH, Karau SJ (2002) Role congruity theory of prejudice toward female leaders. Psychol Rev 109(3):573

Halrynjo S, Teigen M, Nadim M (2015) Kvinner og menn i toppledelsen: Ringvirkninger av lovkrav om kjønnsbalanse i bedriftsstyrer? Virkninger av kjønnskvotering i norsk næringsliv. Gyldendal Akademisk, Oslo

Hlutfall kvenna í stjórnum stórra fyrirtækja stendur í stað milli ára (2016) https://hagstofa.is/utgafur/frettasafn/fyrirtaeki/stjornir-og-framkvaemdastjorar-fyrirtaekja/. Accessed 29 Apr 2018

Johnson JE, Einarsdóttir Þ, Pétursdóttir GM (2013) A feminist theory of corruption: lessons from Iceland. Politics Gend 9(2):174–206

Júlíusdóttir M, Skaptadóttir UD, Karlsdóttir A (2013) Gendered migration in turbulent times in Iceland. Norsk Geografisk Tidsskrift-Norwegian J Geogr 67(5):266–275

Kelsey J (2016) A gendered response to financial crisis: what can others learn from Iceland? Oñati Socio-legal Ser 6(1):8–25

Kohlberg L, Kramer R (1969) Continuities and discontinuities in childhood and adult moral development. Hum Dev 12(2):93–120

Rafnsdóttir GL, Axelsdóttir L, Diðriksdóttir S, Einarsdóttir Þ (2015) Women and men as business leaders in Iceland. Jafnréttisstofa, Reykjavik

Snorrason JS (2012) Yfirlit um stöðu og áhrif jafnari kynjahlutfalla við stjórnun og í stjórnum fyrirtækja. Stjórnmál Stjórnsýsla 1(8):93–107

Statistics Iceland (2016) Iceland in figures 2016, vol 21. Statistics Iceland, Reykjavík https://www.statice.is/media/49863/icelandinfigures2016.pdf

Sund B, Snaebjornsson IM (2017) When "we" and "I" don't value the same: understanding the Nordic gender diversity paradox. Paper presented at the EURAM 2017, Glasgow, UK, 21–24 June, 2017

Part IV
Leadership in Action: Specific Cases

Chapter 12
Moving Icelandic Companies Global Through Visionary Leadership: The Case of Alvogen

Being an entrepreneur is romantic, but the idea of being an entrepreneur is not nearly the same as actually being one.
Anonymous interviewee

Abstract In his article published in the MIT Sloan Magazine, Harvard Business School professor William R. Kerr (2016, p. 62) notes: "Innovators such as Airbnb, Upwork, Alvogen, Rocket Internet, and Bloomberg New Energy Finance have more in common with one another than they have with traditional players in their own industries." The linking factor among these organizations is their global approach. On this list, the Iceland-based company Alvogen, a rapidly growing generic pharmaceutical company operating in 35 countries, is now producing over 350 pharmaceutical products for global markets and has an annual turnover that exceeds $1.2 billion. Indeed, the company was born global, led by CEO Robert Wessman who has been characterized as a low key, yet, charismatic and inspiring leader who exudes complete confidence in himself and passion for his goals. These traits are so pronounced that the entrepreneur, venture capitalist, and professor Daniel Isenberg (2008) notes in his articles in Harvard Business Review: "Over my career I've met many first-class directors. In my opinion, Robert is among the top four or five. Even Bill Gates and Elon Musk at Tesla could learn a lot from him." This chapter unveils the entrepreneurial mindset of Robert Wessman, the CEO and visionary leader of Alvogen, and its transcendence to the core team.

Keywords Robert Wessman · Alvogen · Leadership · CEO · Iceland

12.1 The Bigger Picture

In 1934, Joseph Alois Schumpeter, a former Harvard University professor often referred to as the most influential economist of the twentieth century, was one of the first to recognize the importance of entrepreneurs and entrepreneurship for a nation's

© Springer International Publishing AG, part of Springer Nature 2018   111
I. Minelgaite et al., *Demystifying Leadership in Iceland*, Contributions to
Management Science, https://doi.org/10.1007/978-3-319-96044-9_12

economic growth. He openly discussed the importance of "wild spirits," and doing things in a new way, he also argued that the innovation and technological change of a nation fundamentally is originated with entrepreneurial activities. Since then, many scholars have emphasized the importance of the entrepreneur's role in development of new venture creation and have often characterized them as the ones who take risk, start new companies, exploit new opportunities, and ultimately create value (Collins and Moore 1970; Shapero 1975; Webster 1977). Schumpeter described entrepreneurs as individuals who attempt to "reform or revolutionize the pattern of production by exploiting an invention," and this, he argued, was only found in a very small fraction of the population (Schumpeter 1934, p. 132).

Since Schumpeter's writings on the "wild spirits," interest in entrepreneurial individuals has continued to grow (Baron and Ward 2004; Gaglio 2004; Hayton et al. 2002; Hayton and Kelley 2006; Kuratko et al. 1997). Among these, many related topics of interest are included what entrepreneurs actually do (Mueller et al. 2012), entrepreneurs operating specifically within the public sector (Luke and Verreynne 2006), entrepreneurs within small- and medium-sized enterprises (Carland et al. 2007; Freel and Harrison 2006; Zahra et al. 2004), and entrepreneurs' activity in global corporations (Birkinshaw 1997, 1999). In line with who they are and how they behave, scholars have explored whether a set of individual entrepreneurial traits exists. While some scholars have been in support of this trait approach, others have not (Brockhaus and Horwitz 1986; Gartner 1985; Gürol and Atsan 2006; Koh 1996; Littunen 2000).

Yet others argue that identifying a cluster of relevant traits may be more useful to assess the entrepreneurial personality than focusing on a single characteristic (Cromie 2000; Gürol and Atsan 2006). Traits refer to the mix between biological factors and environmental factors, that is to say, traits have been argued to predispose us to act in certain ways, yet experiences and environmental factors can play an influencing role as well. It has been argued that there are multiple factors which determine one's overall personality. Over the decades, there have been many different views on what makes up a personality, specifically the constructs that underlie it and lead to individual differences. Gordon Allport, considered by many to be the father of trait theory, initially identified over 18,000 distinct traits. Obviously, meaningful applications of such a vast number of traits are not practical. Fortunately, other theorists continued to study trait theory, among them Raymond Cattell and Hans Eysenck, whose collective works ultimately led to the reduction of meaningful Ramalu et al. (2010) traits to five.

In the areas of personality and trait research, a set of five factors, commonly known as "The Big Five," are widely accepted "the" complete constellation of personality traits. While this number is a drastic reduction from Allport's number, factor analyses have found that all personality attributes can be traced to one of the Big 5. These five factors are extraversion, agreeableness, conscientiousness, emotional stability, and openness. Researchers such as Caligiuri (2000) and Hogan et al. (1996) have suggested that individuals possessing high levels of some of the five personality traits will be better suited for the work in the international environment because they can better adapt work and nonwork lives to international arena.

Extraversion has been linked with traits such as being talkative, energetic, and assertive. It has been argued that extroversion is linked to the ability to learn new customs and ways in the new surroundings, communication with people from different backgrounds, and individuals are more likely to adjust to the global surroundings (Caligiuri et al. 2009; Black 1990). Agreeableness has been linked with traits such as being sympathetic, kind, flexible, and affectionate. Ramalu et al. (2010) argued that individuals who possess this element can be found more attentive to customs and norms and more sensitive in their efforts to interact with people in new environments. They have further been linked to the ability to solve disputes and work toward mutual understanding (Caligiuri et al. 2009; Black 1990; Tung 1981; Bhaskar-Shrinivas et al. 2005) because they tend to be more easygoing and adaptable to new people and surroundings. Conscientiousness has been linked with traits such as achievement orientation, organization, and reliability. Shaffer et al. (2006) suggested that individuals who are motivated to be organized and are task-oriented have an easier time adjusting to new environments of work. Hogan et al. (1996) argued that this trait might help those in international business arena to achieve their goals and to get along with host nationals. Emotional stability has been linked with traits such as being tense, moody, and anxious. Researchers such as Black (1988) and Gudykunst (1998) have, for example, argued that emotional stability plays a big role in overall adjustment in the host country. Further, emotional stability might help the international manager or, in this case, the global entrepreneur to face and tolerate the cultural differences, meet job expectations, and get along with host county nationals. Interacting with people from different backgrounds can be stressful, and it can be beneficial to understand as well as to behave in a culturally relevant manner (Hogan and Holland 2003). Openness, the fifth factor, has been linked with other traits such as having a wide range of interests and being imaginative and insightful. Apart from the quite broad Big Five model, other researchers such as Ciavarella et al. (2004) propose different models that include traits, for instance, the strong need for autonomy, high tolerance for risk, proactivity, innovativeness, market aggressiveness, and someone who is driven by self-realization rather than by money itself. Yet, other researchers argue that in order to understand the nature of the entrepreneurial personality, one must understand the role of the environment as well as the personality characteristics (Alstete 2002; Greve and Salaff 2003) and the characteristics of the entrepreneurial personality (Ciavarella et al. 2004; Llewellyn and Wilson 2003; Zhao and Seibert 2006).

Gartner (1989) has argued that it is not enough just to have specific traits to be labeled an entrepreneur. Using his definition "an entrepreneur is a creator of organizations," he further has argued that we should look at what the entrepreneur does rather than who the entrepreneur is: that is, we should rather be examining the behavior than looking at the traits. A topic of entrepreneurial orientation (EO) has emerged along these lines. EO essentially covers the entrepreneurial process, how entrepreneurship is undertaken, and the methods, practices, and decision-making styles used to act entrepreneurially (Lee and Peterson 2000). Anderson et al. (2015) suggested that EO is a firm-level strategic orientation which captures an organization's strategy-making practices, managerial philosophies, and firm behaviors that are entrepreneurial in nature. According to Lumpkin and Dess (1996), EO consists of five main dimensions. The first dimension is innovativeness, which explains how firms engage in and support new ideas as well as experiment with new processes that may lead to new ideas or products. The second dimension is risk taking. It is one of the characteristics that is widely associated with entrepreneurial behavior and associated with an individual who is willing to accept uncertainty. The third dimension is proactiveness, which is associated with seeking for new ways or opportunities, whether in line with the current business or not, as well as the urge to be ahead of the competition. The fourth dimension is autonomy, which refers to independent actions of an individual or a team in bringing the vision to life. Finally, the fifth dimension is competitive aggressiveness; it refers to the company's effort to outperform the industry competitors and rivals (Lumpkin and Dess 2001). Studies show that organizations with a higher level of EO tend to have better organizational performance (Rauch et al. 2009; Moreno and Casillas 2008), and Cho and Jung (2014) found, for example, that metacognition had a significant positive impact on EO and that EO played a strong mediating role in the relationship between entrepreneurs' metacognition and their firm performance.

A growing number of entrepreneurs aim to have a presence on a global scale, grounding their business models in globalization from day one. They and their executive teams therefore have to interact, socialize, and build trust across borders from the very beginning. Scholars such as Dencker et al. (2009) and Ellis (2011) have argued that the ability to manage external interactions with key stakeholders in foreign countries can be a major determinant in a firm's international success. In relation to this debate, increased attention has been given to Earley and Ang's (2003) construct of cultural intelligence (CQ). The concept is based on Sternberg's (1986) triarchic theory of human intelligence and defined as an individual's capability to effectively manage in the international arena (Earley and Ang 2003). Cultural intelligence is suggested to be a multidimensional construct targeted at assessing an individual's competence in dealing with situations of cross-cultural interactions arising from differences in race, ethnicity, and nationality (Earley and Ang 2003; Earley et al. 2006). At the individual level, a person's norms and values are an important aspect of the self, as they guide what features of the social environment the person attends to and what in it he or she values. A person coming from a collectivist society is more likely to have strong group-based values, as suggested by Hofstede (2001), and is more likely to avoid situations requiring personal actions (Gudykunst et al. 1996). Such a person is likely to evaluate individual idiosyncratic behavior negatively. As such, cultural adjustment may be impaired by one's cultural values and norms. Cultural intelligence seeks to understand inter-individual differences in the ability to adapt effectively to new cultural settings (Ang et al. 2006; Earley and Ang 2003; Templer et al. 2006; Thomas and Inkson 2004) by using four facets suggested by (Earley and Ang 2003).

These four facets are metacognition, cognition, motivation, and behavior. The metacognitive facet of CQ reflects the mental processes that individuals use to acquire and understand host cultural knowledge, including knowledge of and control over individuals through processes relating to culture (Earley and Ang 2003). This factor of CQ has been related to capabilities such as monitoring, planning, and revising mental models in relation to cultural norms (Ang et al. 2007). For example, a US national scoring high on this factor might be in a better position to understand and digest the non-facial expressions, limited personal space, and directness that has been associated with Icelandic behavior. While metacognitive CQ focuses on higher-order cognitive processes, cognitive CQ reflects knowledge of the norms and practices in the host culture developed from training, education, and personal experiences. This includes knowledge of different legal, social, and economic factors in the host country (Triandis 2004), as well as the knowledge of cultural norms and values (e.g., Hofstede 2001). According to Earley and Ang (2003), it is not sufficient to have knowledge of another group's ways of dealing with the world. According to Earley et al. (2006), expatriates must be able and motivated to use this knowledge and produce a culturally appropriate response; and there are three primary motivators included in this facet. They are enhancement, growth, and continuality. Enhancement is the will to have a good feeling about oneself, growth is wanting to challenge and improve oneself, and continuality is the desire for continuity and predictability in one's life. The motivation facet therefore reflects the individual's capability to learn about and function in culturally diverse settings. Chen et al. (2012) focused on the motivation aspect of CQ as the sole factor that promotes cross-cultural sales performance. Motivational CQ refers and reflects the level of self-efficacy that prevents people from giving up when they face difficulties in intercultural learning or interactions (Chen et al. 2012). The behavioral facet of CQ refers to the behaviors that a person engages in and reflects a person's capability to acquire or adapt behaviors appropriate for a new culture. For example, behavioral CQ reflects the individual's ability to exhibit appropriate verbal and nonverbal actions when interacting with host nationals. Being an entrepreneur in the global arena will require the ability to adapt to variety of cultural situations while doing business with individuals who look, believe, and think in different ways. Expanding to new and foreign markets requires, therefore, a culturally intelligent global entrepreneur who can quickly gain trust and provide the right product in the right packaging with the right message to consumers.

12.2 The Case of Alvogen

Alvogen, a rapidly growing generic pharmaceutical company, has its headquarters in Reykjavík, Iceland. It is located in a new building on the grounds of the University of Iceland, in a new Science Park just opposite the School of Business. The dynamic CEO and Chairman of the Board Robert Wessman was born and raised in Iceland; he has managed to build two major generics companies before turning 50 years of age. When visiting the company's headquarters, one immediately finds a focused and dedicated work environment, composed of work spaces that are open, bright, and meticulously organized. Alvogen has experienced exceptionally high growth since it was Wessman took the helm in 2009 and has been reported to be among the fastest growing companies in the industry. With 2800 employees worldwide, fast-to-market approach, and a sister company, Alvotech is aiming to be a global leader in the biosimilar industry (World Finance 2018). Alvogen has been awarded in various industry awards for customer orientation and reliability in customer service including the prestigious DIANA awards 5 years in a row, the Cardinal Health Leadership awards, and the Healthcare Distribution Alliance Business and Leadership awards. Those awards honor pharmaceutical and consumer product manufacturers for excellence in their product introductions, trading partner relationships, supply chain operations, and commitment to innovation. The company has also been recognized for its branding and marketing practices and is a recipient of the International Brand Impact Awards as well as being named Company of the Year and the Best Business Development Company of the Year and recognized for its Corporate Social Responsibility Initiatives at the annual Global Generics and Biosimilars Awards.

Robert Wessman was born in 1969 in Reykjavik Iceland. He has his office on the top floor with large windows that gives him a clear view overlooking the city of Reykjavík and its neighboring towns. The office is spacious, nicely decorated, and includes Wessman's inversion table he periodically uses to stretch and a Harley Davidson motorcycle. A large painting by the Icelandic artist Erro, an Icelandic postmodern artist known for his powerful and sometimes provoking works, decorates the wall behind Wessman's desk. This work like Erro's other paintings, which happens to portray women, is colorful and simultaneous and also shows both power and strength. Although the motorcycle gives a masculine impression, the coffee station just outside Wessman's office has lit candles. Complementing the coffee and water services, there are healthy snacks such as fruit and nuts. At the time of the visit for the interview, there were boxes full of chocolate Easter eggs located in the reception areas, ready to be given to employees and keeping with the Icelandic tradition of giving local-made Easter eggs for Easter. In Icelandic culture, it is not always the egg that is important, but the accompanying little note inside it. Drawing from the old Icelandic sagas, it sometimes offers advice or a saying with a wise proverb of sorts. For example, a person might draw an egg with a note that says, "Hver er sinnar gæfu smiður," meaning "Every man is the maker of his own fortune," which alludes that shaping one's own fortune, one should not rely on the help of others. Another example is "Á misjöfnu þrífast börnin best"—"Children will thrive best on varied diet/life." These little notes are often the discussion over Easter dinner with friends and relatives; the tradition and sayings are passed on from one generation to the next.

Before the establishment of Alvogen, Robert Wessman took over as the CEO of a struggling pharmaceutical company in Reykjavík at the age of 29. At the time, the company was called Delta but later renamed Actavis. In just a few years, Wessman managed to lead Actavis to become a major player in the global generics market. This phenomenal growth was achieved through integrating over 30 acquisitions with a formula of moving quickly, fast decision-making, and focused strategy execution and putting an effort into understanding the value of the owners and local cultures. In 2008, Wessman decided to leave Actavis after a fallout with the chairman and major stakeholder just before the economic crisis that hit Iceland in November of that same year. Determined to develop a next-generation generic pharmaceutical company, he flew to New York to meet with generic drug developers. At a New York restaurant with potential investors, Wessman shared his future vision on a paper napkin. Now for the second time, Wessman took on the role to develop the most successful generic pharmaceutical company in the industry. Today, Alvogen is a 9-year-old, generic pharmaceutical company focusing on difficultly made generic pharmaceuticals. But Wessman was not done; in 2013 he established Alvotech, a sister company to Alvogen. Alvotech is a biologics manufacturing facility now located at the headquarters in Reykjavík in a new building that was opened in 2016. The first monoclonal antibodies are expected to be launched in 2020, with confidence in the biosimilar and a number of biological products losing their exclusivity. Wessman is confident that Alvogen along with Alvotech can now become the market leaders.

To gather information for this case study on Alvogen and Alvotech, interviews with Wessman and few of his executive team were conducted. Along with the interviews, a questionnaire was sent to all 100 leadership team-level members, 67 of whom responded. The purpose of the questionnaire was to get a further insight into preferred leadership style, level of entrepreneurship, Big Five, and CQ. Demographically, more than a half of the respondents had a master's or doctoral degree, 40% of the respondents were women, and in total represented a mix of Asian-Pacific (22%), North American (26%), and European (52%) nationalities.

When they were asked to describe their leadership style in the questionnaire, the majority of executive team overwhelming preferred a leadership style labeled as "inspirational leadership." In other words, they preferred leaders who have a visionary approach to leadership and are able to communicate to their employees the vision and direction, but do not dictate how they're going to get there. They encourage their team members to use their own initiative to solve a problem or to meet the target. This does not come as a surprise as according to Wessman, the leader's greatest asset, regardless of whatever business the leader is in, are the people. As Wessman shared during the interview, "A leader needs to engage the right people and unite them around a clear and specific vision, empower them to act, and inspire them to achieve something that others have not achieved before." One of his executive team members shared that Wessman came from a middle-class family, his father ran the local hotel, and his mother was working as a beautician. During his early years, Wessman took various jobs while growing up, from peeling potatoes to delivering suitcases or morning papers to hotel guests. Later he became a teacher assistant in statistics while completing his Bachelor studies in business at the University of Iceland. One executive team member reflects: "I think that what has shaped who he is today, is the approach, that no job is too small or irrelevant." He goes on to say, "I always remember when Robert held his first staff meeting with employees at Actavis when he was only 29 years old and had just taken over as CEO. He was holding his first staff meeting and the first question he got was, "How old are you?" the interviewee recalls. He further emphasized Wessman's ability at that point to communicate his vision to employees: "That is his strength... to communicate the vision, both in good times and bad." He further explained how Wessman would not hesitate to discuss matters across hierarchical lines and that he could frequently be found having discussions with employees at all levels. Another executive noted, "He is really a hard worker with great analytical skills, he is fast and takes decisions quickly," reinforced by another executive: "We are not in this business for status quo and the sky is not the limit." As Wessman later commented, "We're setting new standards in our industry and not only driving the change, but being the change, for that you need a strong vision."

When asked about the organizational culture, Wessman recounted how he, along with two of his current executives who had joined him at the beginning, sat together in his office on the first day: "This was a crazy idea... no one was waiting for this company... we wanted to create a next generation pharmaceutical company and it was our understanding that the culture had to be very specific and had to have the entrepreneurial uniqueness with the ability to scale and execute." Wessman then explained how they shaped the character of Alvogen and how they consciously aimed at starting as a global company from day one. As one of the executives recollects: "We behaved and acted like a global company so when we were hiring, we were very bold. Wessman new how he wanted to change the industry and the people they targeted had years of experience, were categorized as best in their industry but on the other hand had to take a risk to join Wessman in developing something new." When discussing the effort in looking for individuals with entre-preneurial intent, one executive said: "Being an entrepreneur is romantic, but the idea of being an entrepreneur is not nearly the same as actually being one." The executive then added: "We filled the company of entrepreneurial minded people."

Results of the survey on entrepreneurship conducted at Alvogen illustrate that the company's aim to fill itself with entrepreneurs has paid off and that the company's entrepreneurial climate is still cultivated by the top leadership 9 years later. As can be seen from Fig. 12.1, the leadership team scores high on all the items. Most notably

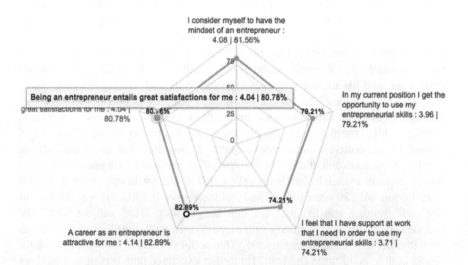

Fig. 12.1 Entrepreneurial attitudes of executive directors at Alvogen

on the statements "I consider myself to have the mindset of an entrepreneur," "A career as an entrepreneur is attractive for me," and "Being an entrepreneur entails grate satisfaction for me" all have a score of 4.0 or more on a scale from 1 to 5.

The study results confirm the vision of Wessman: "I encourage my executives to be entrepreneurial, that is the people we look for they need to be independent but still be able to work in a group." An executive further explained their aim in the recruitment process to sort out those who like the idea of being an entrepreneur from those who actually are. In relation to the Big Five traits, employees at the executive level score highest on conscientiousness and agreeableness and then openness followed by extraversion and emotional stability. Hence, the results suggest that the executive level place high emphasis on effort and persistence, are likely to be highly driven, and constrain high discipline along with being organized; they are also likely to be more compliant and conforming but at the same time affect their longing for high performance and being adaptable to change. These trades have contributed greatly to the success of Alvogen, according to Wessman, where the ability to execute and get things done is critical for success of a fast-growing global company in an exceptionally competitive marketplace.

When asked further about the organizational culture, it became clear that the national culture plays some role. The low-power distance in Iceland along with Wessman upbringing in believing that no job is irrelevant and the organization structure is flat. As Wessman explains: "Our hierarchy is low and if you look at the organizational chart it is flat so we can take information fast and effectively." He continues: "If you look at the competitive organizations their organizations charts are much more complex than ours"—he explained what he set out in the beginning, representing fast and transparent culture. The interviews reveal that the organizational culture was strategically designed to be global from its very first day. Diversity plays a big part within this culture, and Wessman explains that "We are in the forefront of gender equality here in Iceland and in fact in our industry globally and weather deliberate or not around half of our executives are females and that is not the standard in this male dominant industry." He further contends that 90% of the profits are coming from countries were women are country managers. One of the executives explains that when creating the cultural artifacts, the team chose the yellow color to represent the sun:

> We decided on the sun as we are global and all have the sun in common . . . The sun does not get lost in translation reflecting on the passion, care and drive, power, strength, happiness and other values that come represent the color yellow. The culture is then tight to the STARMAP that is the fundamental strategy while the vision is to be a leading global company and preferred partner in all their operating markets. The STARMAP consists of five elements or, best people, best portfolio, best quality, best service and low cost.

As Wessman explained, the STARMAP is connected to everything they do, the weekly meetings, the metrics, progress tracking, and evaluations. As Wessman said in relation to the corporate culture, "If you don't live it then you might as well skip it. We believe in these five pillars that it will make us the best in the industry and all our operation culture evolves around it." When asked how the core team communicates the culture to global locations, Wessman describes that they have cultural champions in each location. One of the executives describes that employees who take on this voluntary role meet four times a year to coordinate their activities. At the same time, they have a considerable amount of freedom to improvise in accordance to their local culture: "They are able to decide on events that they lead in each country the way they consider is the best, and of course, we reinforce this from top down but in reality the development and execution is from bottom up and we always make sure that the cultural events are integrated. Everything we do is aligned with the STARMAP."

Wessman further explains that the core team is completely aware of the differences persistent in every country: "When people start at Alvogen it is like sports… we have a certain culture in the field that we want our players for follow. Alvogen hosts about 60 nationalities and 3000 employees … we need to have the same vision … Alvogen is one company in 35 counties but not 35 companies in 35 countries." Given that Wessman's vision was for Alvogen to be a global player from the start, high CQ has always been an imperative for its leaders. As one of the executive recalls:

> We had a rather large team coming over to Iceland from Asia, we were had not really thought about the protocol, and had just made sure we had the right number of chairs etc. But when they saw the meeting room and setup they went back to the cars while we rearranged and figured out who was going to sit where, and alike.

CQ is a critical competency that allows entrepreneurs to develop good relationships with foreign networks ties. In particular, in terms of cognitive CQ and metacognitive CQ, entrepreneurs' ability to appreciate the criticality of understanding and anticipating the behaviors and customs of other cultures greatly enables them to meet the social expectations of their foreign business partners, customers, and various other stakeholders. In demonstrating this sensitivity, entrepreneurs are much better equipped to establish trusting relationships with their global partners, which is often the first essential step in developing subsequent business arrangements. Despite some challenges in the company's early global initiatives in Asia, the current study's results indicate that Alvogen's executive team scores high on cognitive CQ and motivational CQ (Fig. 12.2). This indicates that the leaders tend to rely less on what might be stereotypical assumptions to assess what is appropriate in a culture and instead use inductive reasoning to learn and make more informed judgments about the given behaviors. As one of the executives explains: "We only hire the best and most often those individuals have 15–20 years of experience in the global arena." Even still, simply understanding the importance of intercultural sensitivity does not guarantee success. The high score on motivational CQ represents the level of self-efficacy that individuals exhibit when dealing with the natural and expected difficulties in intercultural learning and interactions. Rather than become frustrated and revert to "their" way of doing this, people high on motivational CQ persevere and remain committed to working through the learning process. Along with the leaders' high scores on conscientiousness and agreeableness, these results are not surprising as individuals who score high on agreeableness are often less offensive when placed in new or unfamiliar cultures and find it easier to acclimate to them. Wessman further explains that during acquisitions, Alvogen tends to appoint local

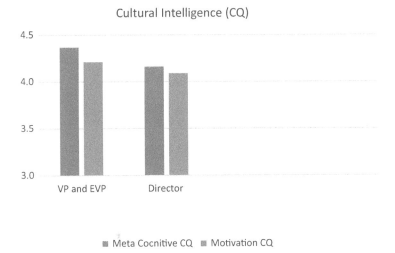

Fig. 12.2   Cultural competence at Alvogen

individuals as the new country manager and local business unit leaders: "They are the best intervals to build trust in a newly acquired companies and communicate the vision." He further explains that by hiring or keeping a local CEO, trust becomes so much more than if Alvogen were to send one of its own to the new location. In addition, there are practical business advantages to this strategy. For example, this approach eliminates the time a "new outsider" would need to get adjusted to the country or region. In addition, it enhances the likelihood of gaining the new employees' trust and commitment to Alvogen's strategy and vision since they are hearing it from someone who is familiar with them and their location. He further contends that they are given full support from the Alvogen Academy and support from the integration teams. Those teams are interdisciplinary teams including members from both Alvogen and the newly acquired company. The aim of the teams is to identify ways to execute on integration priorities and synergy realization bottoms up for a fast, sensible, and hands-on execution versus a high-level corporate directive. This way, individuals are responsible for key areas of the business on both sides and work together toward a common goal, speeding up the actual integration of people and processes.

As Hall (1959) has argued, mental capabilities for cultural understanding and motivation must be associated with the ability to exhibit appropriate verbal and nonverbal actions, based on cultural values and norms of specific settings. This further emphasizes the importance of having a wide and flexible repertoire of behaviors when communicating with host nationals, both in delivering and receiving messages. Rockstuhl and Ng (2008) suggest individuals' flexibility in adjusting their behavior to suit people from different cultures which allows them to gain trust more easily because it enhances the sense of familiarity and similarity in the relations, highlight the awareness of subtle cultural differences, and increase predictability of behaviors. Finally, when entrepreneurs understand the unique social and business norms and protocols in each country and demonstrate appropriate behaviors that signify to their foreign partners that they are appreciative and respectful of cultural differences, they send a clear signal that they are worthy to be trusted to engage in business ventures. This can greatly and positively affect the extent to which the entrepreneurs are perceived by foreign partners in terms of credibility.

12.3   Concluding Remarks

If leadership in Iceland, as discussed in other chapters of this book, often serves as an example of a "small can be big" approach, then the case of Alvogen accentuates the importance of long-standing vision in leadership development. Robert Wessman, together with his core team, has adopted such an approach from the first day when they have established Alvogen. Put another way, they have adopted and promoted visionary leadership from the start. In addition, this case illustrates how visionary leadership, with a strong emphasis on entrepreneurship, can transcend to the members of the core team. In this vein, Robert Wessman who has not only once but three times led his companies, Actavis, Alvogen, and Alvotech become a major global player. It is a saga on visionary and contagious leadership that unfolded in a context of a country with 337,780 inhabitants to become a legitimate worldwide presence.

References

Alstete JW (2002) On becoming an entrepreneur: an evolving typology. Int J Entrep Behav Res 8 (4):222–234

Anderson BS, Kreiser PM, Kuratko DF, Hornsby JS, Eshima Y (2015) Reconceptualizing entrepreneurial orientation. Strateg Manag J 36(10):1579–1596

Ang S, Van Dyne L, Koh C (2006) Personality correlates of the four-factor model of cultural intelligence. Group Org Manag 31(1):100–123

Ang S, Van Dyne L, Koh C, Ng KY, Templer KJ, Tay C, Chandrasekar NA (2007) Cultural intelligence: its measurement and effects on cultural judgment and decision making, cultural adaptation and task performance. Manag Organ Rev 3(3):335–371

Baron RA, Ward TB (2004) Expanding entrepreneurial cognition's toolbox: potential contributions from the field of cognitive science. Entrep Theory Pract 28(6):553–573

Bhaskar-Shrinivas P, Harrison DA, Shaffer MA, Luk DM (2005) Input-based and time-based models of international adjustment: meta-analytic evidence and theoretical extensions. Acad Manag J 48(2):257–281

Birkinshaw J (1997) Entrepreneurship in multinational corporations: the characteristics of subsidiary initiatives. Strateg Manag J:207–229

Birkinshaw J (1999) The determinants and consequences of subsidiary initiative in multinational corporations. Entrep Theory Pract 24(1):9–36

Black JS (1988) Work role transitions: a study of American expatriate managers in Japan. J Int Bus Stud 19(2):277–294

Black JS (1990) The relationship of personal characteristics with the adjustment of Japanese expatriate managers. Manag Int Rev 30:119–134

Brockhaus RS, Horwitz P (1986) The psychology of the entrepreneur. In: Sexton DL, Smilor RW (eds) The art and science of entrepreneurship. Ballinger, Cambridge, MA, pp 25–48

Caligiuri PM (2000) Selecting expatriates for personality characteristics: a moderating effect of personality on the relationship between host national contact and cross-cultural adjustment. Manag Int Rev 40:61–80

Caligiuri PM, Tarique I, Jacobs R (2009) Selection for international assignments. Hum Resour Manag Rev 19(3):251–262

Carland JW, Hoy F, Boulton WR, Carland JAC (2007) Differentiating entrepreneurs from small business owners: a conceptualization. In: Entrepreneurship. Springer, Berlin, pp 73–81

Chen XP, Liu D, Portnoy R (2012) Marketing strategy-performance relationship: an investigation of the empirical ling in export market ventures. J Mark 58(1):1–21

Cho YS, Jung JY (2014) The relationship between metacognition, entrepreneurial orientation, and firm performance: an empirical investigation. Acad Entrep J 20(2):71

Ciavarella MA, Buchholtz AK, Riordan CM, Gatewood RD, Stokes GS (2004) The Big Five and venture survival: is there a linkage? J Bus Ventur 19(4):465–483

Collins OF, Moore DG (1970) The organization makers: a behavioral study of independent entrepreneurs. Appleton-Century-Crofts, New York

Cromie S (2000) Assessing entrepreneurial inclinations: some approaches and empirical evidence. Eur J Work Organ Psy 9(1):7–30

Dencker JC, Gruber M, Shah SK (2009) Pre-entry knowledge, learning, and the survival of new firms. Organ Sci 20(3):516–537

Earley PC, Ang S (2003) Cultural intelligence: individual interactions across cultures. Stanford University Press, Stanford, CA

Earley PC, Ang S, Tan J-S (2006) CQ: Developing cultural intelligence at work. Stanford University Press, Stanford, CA

Ellis PD (2011) Social ties and international entrepreneurship: opportunities and constraints affecting firm internationalization. J Int Bus Stud 42(1):99–127

Freel MS, Harrison RT (2006) Innovation and cooperation in the small firm sector: evidence from 'Northern Britain'. Reg Stud 40(4):289–305

Gaglio CM (2004) The role of mental simulations and counterfactual thinking in the opportunity identification process. Entrep Theory Pract 28(6):533–552

Gartner WB (1985) A conceptual framework for describing the phenomenon of new venture creation. Acad Manag Rev 10(4):696–706

Gartner W (1989) Who is an entrepreneur? Is the wrong question. Entrep Theory Pract 13(4):47–68

Greve A, Salaff JW (2003) Social networks and entrepreneurship. Entrep Theory Pract 28(1):1–22

Gudykunst WB (1998) Applying anxiety\uncertainty management (AUM) Theory to intercultural adjustment training. Int J Intercult Relat 22(2):227–250

Gudykunst WB, Matsumoto Y, Ting-Toomey S, Nishida T, Kim K, Heyman S (1996) The influence of cultural individualism-collectivism, self construals, and individual values on communication styles across cultures. Hum Commun Res 22(4):510–543

Gürol Y, Atsan N (2006) Entrepreneurial characteristics amongst university students: some insights for entrepreneurship education and training in Turkey. Educ Train 48(1):25–38

Hall J (1959) A description of deep space net facilities, operations, and capabilities. Technical Report, California Institute of Technology, United States

Hayton JC, Kelley DJ (2006) A competency-based framework for promoting corporate entrepreneurship. Hum Resour Manag 45(3):407–427

Hayton JC, George G, Zahra SA (2002) National culture and entrepreneurship: a review of behavioral research. Entrep Theory Pract 26(4):33–52

Hofstede G (2001) Culture's recent consequences: using dimension scores in theory and research. Int J Cross Cult Manag 1(1):11–17

Hogan J, Holland B (2003) Using theory to evaluate personality and job-performance relations: a socioanalytic perspective. J Appl Psychol 88(1):100

Hogan R, Hogan J, Roberts BW (1996) Personality measurement and employment decisions: questions and answers. Am Psychol 51(5):469

Isenberg DJ (2008) The global entrepreneur. Harv Bus Rev 86:107–111

Kerr WR (2016) Harnessing the best of globalization. MIT Sloan Manag Rev 58(1):59

Koh HC (1996) Testing hypotheses of entrepreneurial characteristics: a study of Hong Kong MBA students. J Manag Psychol 11(3):12–25

Kuratko DF, Hornsby JS, Naffziger DW (1997) An examination of owner's goals in sustaining entrepreneurship. J Small Bus Manag 35(1):24

Lee SM, Peterson SJ (2000) Culture, entrepreneurial orientation, and global competitiveness. J World Bus 35(4):401–416

Littunen H (2000) Entrepreneurship and the characteristics of the entrepreneurial personality. Int J Entrep Behav Res 6(6):295–310

Llewellyn DJ, Wilson KM (2003) The controversial role of personality traits in entrepreneurial psychology. Educ Train 45(6):341–345

Luke B, Verreynne M-L (2006) Exploring strategic entrepreneurship in the public sector. Qual Res Account Manag 3(1):4–26

Lumpkin GT, Dess GG (1996) Clarifying the entrepreneurial orientation construct and linking it to performance. Acad Manag Rev 21(1):135–172

Lumpkin GT, Dess GG (2001) Linking two dimensions of entrepreneurial orientation to firm performance: the moderating role of environment and industry life cycle. J Bus Ventur 16 (5):429–451

Moreno AM, Casillas JC (2008) Entrepreneurial orientation and growth of SMEs: a causal model. Entrep Theory Pract 32(3):507–528

Mueller S, Volery T, von Siemens B (2012) What do entrepreneurs actually do? An observational study of entrepreneurs' everyday behavior in the start-up and growth stages. Entrep Theory Pract 36(5):995–1017

Ramalu SS, Rose RC, Kumar N, Uli J (2010) Doing business in global arena: an examination of the relationship between cultural intelligence and cross-cultural adjustment. Asian Acad Manag J 15 (1):79–97

Rauch A, Wiklund J, Lumpkin GT, Frese M (2009) Entrepreneurial orientation and business performance: an assessment of past research and suggestions for the future. Entrep Theory Pract 33(3):761–787

Rockstuhl T, Ng K-Y (2008) The effects of cultural intelligence on interpersonal trust in multicultural teams. In: Ang S, Van Dyne L (eds) Handbook of cultural intelligence: theory, measurement, and applications. M.E. Sharpe, New York, pp 206–220

Schumpeter J (1934) Theory of economic development. Harvard University Press, Cambridge, MA

Shaffer MA, Harrison DA, Gregersen H, Black JS, Ferzandi LA (2006) You can take it with you: individual differences and expatriate effectiveness. J Appl Psychol 91(1):109

Shapero A (1975) The displaced, uncomfortable entrepreneur. Psychol Today 9(6):83–88

Sternberg RJ (1986) A triarchic theory of human intelligence. In: Human assessment: cognition and motivation. Springer, Dordrecht, pp 43–44

Templer KJ, Tay C, Chandrasekar NA (2006) Motivational cultural intelligence, realistic job preview, realistic living conditions preview, and cross-cultural adjustment. Group Org Manag 31(1):154–173

Thomas D, Inkson K (2004) Cultivating your cultural intelligence. Secur Manag 48(8):30–33

Triandis HC (2004) The many dimensions of culture. Acad Manag Exec 18(1):88–93

Tung R (1981) Selection and training of personnel for overseas assignments. Columbia J World Bus 16(1):68–78

Webster FA (1977) Entrepreneurs and ventures: an attempt at classification and clarification. Acad Manag Rev 2(1):54–61

World Finance (2018) Retrieved May 2, 2018, from https://www.worldfinance.com/2018/page/16

Zahra SA, Hayton JC, Salvato C (2004) Entrepreneurship in family vs. non-family firms: a resource-based analysis of the effect of organizational culture. Entrep Theory Pract 28 (4):363–381

Zhao H, Seibert SE (2006) The Big Five personality dimensions and entrepreneurial status: a meta-analytical review. J Appl Psychol 91(2):259

Chapter 13
A Comedian Who Changed the Leadership Script in Reykjavik: The Case of Jón Gnarr

The atmosphere in the workplace was just turned around.
Anonymous employee of Reykjavík City Council

Abstract This chapter is a case study of the leadership exercised by Jón Gnarr, a famous comedian who later served as the mayor of Reykjavik through 2010–2014. This profile is based on the reflections and insights shared during seven open-ended interviews with official city leaders who had closely worked with Jón Gnarr in the political arena. Evidence suggests that Jón Gnarr emerged as a leader due to extreme social and economic factors, which led to the election of the Best Party and thus shaped an unorthodox leader. At the same time, the descriptions provided by his followers portray an image of a leader that closely matches the theories of authentic leadership and has made a lasting impact. When Jón Gnarr stepped into the role of the mayor of Reykjavík, he used new tactics that had not been seen before with trust, respect, and care as the underlying values, out-of-the-box behavior patterns, original communication style, and intuition. Thus, he inspired his followers to change their own communication style. Finally, the case laid out in this chapter contributes to our understanding of authentic and unconventional leadership as an efficient vehicle in unusual circumstances.

Keywords Authentic leadership · Mayor of Reykjavik · Jón Gnarr

13.1 The Bigger Picture

From a research standpoint, for a long time, a great portion of leadership literature covered analysis from the position of the leader and hence focused on the leader or the effects that an individual in the role has on followers (Bass 1985, 1998; Blom 2016; Korzynski 2014). This tendency, combined with a strong preference for quantitative research methods (Mahsud et al. 2010; Bryman 2004; Blom 2016), eventually resulted in a rather unbalanced understanding of the concept of leadership

© Springer International Publishing AG, part of Springer Nature 2018
I. Minelgaite et al., *Demystifying Leadership in Iceland*, Contributions to Management Science, https://doi.org/10.1007/978-3-319-96044-9_13

(Blom and Alvesson 2014). As the field was developing and growing, more actors and factors were added to the leadership picture, including greater attention to followers, leader-follower relationships, broader groups of leadership stakeholders, and the related factors. Thus, environmental factors such as culture, meaning, norms, and for recent decades, feelings, thinking, and values that are laid down through communication, became more evident (Blom and Alvesson 2014; Kotter 1985).

The penetration of leader-centric perspective sometimes referred to as "romantic" view on leaders, often portraying them as heroes (Diddams and Chang 2012; Meindl 1995; Sinclair 2007; Guðmundsdóttir 2011), was arguably dominant until the first global financial crisis of the twenty-first century. A shift in the leadership discourse arose together with the uncertainty and corporate scandals that shook the leadership domain at the time of financial crisis of 2008, prompting both scholars and practitioners to investigate what kind of leadership builds and promotes sustainability, including transparency and trust. In this landscape, Iceland was found in an unfavorably particular position: once its three major banks collapsed in just 1 week in October 2008, it experienced the most profound and most rapid ramifications (Danielsson and Zoega 2009). Different leaders were required for a new era.

13.2   Theoretical Underpinnings

Leadership is a process between the leader and followers, which, depending on its nature, can be viewed through a number of theoretical lenses. The case presented in this chapter documents an example of authentic leadership in action, which foundations are discussed in this section. The elements of authentic leadership consist of self-awareness, unbiased processing, authentic behavior, and authentic relational orientation (Ilies et al. 2005).

When the environment is chaotic, there is a tendency for followers to call for a change in leadership or other types of leadership behaviors (Williams et al. 2012). In the 1990s, the theory of transformation or transformational leadership was one of the first theories to provide a framework of leadership when uncertainty was high. There are four components of transformational leadership: firstly, *idealized influence*—the leader serves as an ideal role model for followers; the leader gains respect by doing what needs to be done. Secondly, *inspirational motivation*—the leader has the ability to inspire and motivate followers. These first two combined are what constitute the transformation of what Bass names the leader's charisma. Thirdly, *individualized consideration*—transformational leaders, according to the theory, demonstrate genuine concern for the needs and feelings of followers. Thus, they bring out subordinate's best efforts. Fourthly, *intellectual stimulation*—transformational leader challenges subordinates to come up with creative solution (Burns 1978).

According to the theory, transformational leaders empower their followers by inspiring them through intellectual motivation and encouraging them to develop themselves further, thus increasing their follower's productivity (Bass 1999). Burns

(1978) and Bass (1985) pointed out a gap in the literature as it was more geared toward the transactional model of leadership. The transactional model, according to them, stated that the roles of the leader were setting goal, supporting employees, and ensuring that the job gets done through specific performance appraisal systems or giving out "carrots" in exchange for the right behaviors. According to Bass (1998), leaders should strive to reach employees at an emotional level as a means to help them achieve beyond what they ever thought was possible. Instead, within the transformational model, the contributing factors are charismatic leadership, inspirational leadership, and visionary leadership. Leaders who are charismatic and can inspire their followers to look toward the future are, according to Bass (1998), transformational. The theory of transformational leadership was of great importance, and the following theories have underpinnings that are highly related to it (Avolio et al. 2009; Mahsud et al. 2010). It continues to be important, and it is necessary for the dynamic nature of modern organizations as well as employee's expectation that leaders will help them achieve their personal and professional goals.

Among them is the theory of authentic leadership, with its differential emphasis on what it means to be "authentic" or, as Avolio and Gardner (2005) refer to on examples of Greek philosophers, what it is "to thy self be true" (p. 5) and how authenticity influences leadership and leaders (Avolio and Gardner 2005; Ladkin and Taylor 2010). Authentic leadership model is based on both philosophy and psychology with the works by Erikson and Maslow among the central pillars. Erik Erikson, the German psychoanalyst, was one of the first to attempt to analyze human's life, from birth to old age, as a series of distinct and consecutive stages. Abraham Maslow was an American humanist psychologist, but based on his (1954) theory, self-actualization is the highest form of how individuals can succeed in reaching their furthermost potential, great self-knowledge of one's talents and skills as well as an understanding of the effect one has on others, and be able to have power over one's behavior by being conscious of the impact that people have on themselves and others. Maslow suggested that those who reached the self-actualization had stronger ethical values and needs; values are important components of authentic leadership. Carl Rogers, who was an influential figure in the development of education and psychology, in his work referred to authenticity as he stresses that people need to live in the moment and stretch and grow constantly (1957). Avolio and Gardner (2005) applied Maslow's theory stating that in order to be an authentic leader, the individual has to know oneself well and behave in accordance with the authentic self, related to inner thinking and emotions. Scholars have pointed out that it could be more appropriate to use the term "working selves" or "possible selves" (Ladkin and Taylor 2010). Thus, the life story of the leader enters the picture as a valuable research tool (Shamir and Eilam 2005). This is connected to Erikson's life stages and Rogers's work where they state that through experience, people grow and this growth is what leads to a leader's style, outlook, and relationship with followers.

Authentic leadership stresses that a leader who is authentic usually uses a process where both positive and highly developed organizations motivate self-knowledge and development with discipline in a positive way for both themselves and followers (Avolio et al. 2009). Thus, it is clear that the underlying theme of authentic leadership is that a leader's personal life experiences, thoughts, emotions, and values shape the leader. Another critical point in the theory is how leaders are actually developed. Shamir and Eilam (2005) pointed out that it is important to analyze the life story in order to understand this process and its outcomes. By analyzing the leaders' life stories, researchers can better understand how leaders' values and identities were formed. Biological factors are sometimes also taken into account, and genetic issues and upbringing are analyzed, but it is generally considered that environmental factors play a more significant role in leaders with their life experience being a strong factor in shaping them (Avolio et al. 2009).

Thus, exactly how leaders behave and compose themselves is an essential factor in leadership, including, how they explore, understand, and process feelings and emotions about their true inner selves. The use of the body language is noticeable in the literature as it is a significant factor in communication and it can be argued that trust between leaders and followers is transmitted through body language (Sinclair 2005; Ladkin and Taylor 2010) and given that authentic leaders may require a talent in acting as they need to be able to draw out emotional responses and bring them forward. Additionally, leaders should be aware of how others see them and how they relate to others or communicate and how to be leader-like or how to take on the role that followers need (Quinn et al. 2000). In this vein, values are also important such as kindness, honesty, commitment, appreciation, and respect which are the foundations of the theory of authentic leadership (Michie and Gooty 2005).

In recent times, scholars within positive leadership strand have developed a broader sense of leadership picture by focusing on the factors that contribute to the empowerment of followers in organizations. Fredrickson (2001) has shown that those who are on the whole positive have more psychological resources to learn and grow and therefore expand themselves. This is the underlying theme that scholars within positive leadership build on when discussing how leaders develop (Avolio et al. 2009). Authentic leadership builds up more self-consciousness and self-control and positive behavior on behalf of leaders and followers. They show a tendency to be hopeful, optimistic, and resilient (Avolio and Gardner 2005). Research within authentic leadership has indicated that those who score high in authentic leadership among subordinates show more commitment toward their organizations and have stronger ethical values. They also seem to be able to build up respect, trust, and employees' participation and integrate them into their communication style and self-understanding (Diddams and Chang 2012; Avolio et al. 2009). A noticeable gap in the literature is authentic leaders' awareness of their weaknesses. It is possible that leaders are more successful by focusing on other factors (Walumbwa et al. 2008). Leaders are often more focused on achieving results, because authentic leaders have more insight and are truer to themselves and they are more inclined to understand and accept their weaknesses and then work to improve them. The recent theory of servant leadership that has already gained acknowledgement among scholars and others (Gunnarsdóttir 2011) has many similarities with and, to a certain degree, complements authentic leadership. The originator of the theory, Robert Greenleaf, puts forward the idea that a leader should be a servant in his or her role as a leader (Guðjónsson and Gunnarsdóttir 2014).

Servant leadership is thus about helping others achieve their goals by offering development, support, and cooperation with the well-being of their followers always at the forefront of the leader's mind (Jónsdóttir et al. 2011). Servant leaders need to be able to have high self-awareness. This is similar to authentic leadership as both theories stress bringing out the best in people as transformational leadership does as well.

Leader-membership exchange theory (LMX) is based on the social exchange theory, which adds up to the equation of authentic leadership by analyzing the relationship between followers and leaders that develops over time and yields mutual benefits (Mahsud et al. 2010). The high quality of the relationship between leaders and followers is grounded in mutual trust, respect, and kindness. If the relationship is strong, followers are willing to work harder, and leaders are willing to empower followers more by giving them access to power and influences (Mahsud et al. 2010). For example, research has indicated that as the relationship becomes stronger between leaders and followers, the more creative and secure and the less stressful the workplace becomes. On the other hand, while quantitative studies have mostly been conducted as explanatory to the theory, there might be factors that call for deeper understanding that has not been yet developed well enough (Blom and Alvesson 2014). The vertical dyad linkage model of leadership explains the difference in quality between the "in-group" and the "out-group" in workplaces. One research showed that over 90% of supervisors formed different quality relationships with their employees. Those reporting high-quality relationships with their supervisors assumed greater job responsibility, contributed more, and were rated as higher performers than those reporting low-quality relationships (Liden and Graen 1980). This is what authentic leadership, servant leadership, and transformational leadership are trying to achieve with each follower.

In particular, it is of great importance to measure the actual need that followers have for leadership and the preference for the type of leadership they have as well (Blom and Alvesson 2014; Blom 2016). In theoretical writings there seems to be a paradox in the fact that it is difficult to analyze if these are the leaders or the followers who are ultimately responsible for the relationship between them (Mahsud et al. 2010; Avolio et al. 2009; Blom and Alvesson 2014; Blom 2016).

In sum, the literature on authentic leadership highlights the ability of leaders to be able to gain self-knowledge and other underlying factors, such as the ability to empower and listen to the followers' ideas to increase their capabilities and independence (Mahsud et al. 2010; Walter et al. 2012). Thus, successful leaders are empathetic and have compassion that leads to an understanding and insight into the emotions of others. Leaders who have these capabilities usually have an interest in other people which leads to their ability to build trust among subordinates. They often aim to protect, foster, and nurture others, and this kind of behavior and thinking process empowers others (Pavlovich and Krahnke 2012; Mahsud et al. 2010; Marques 2013; Holt and Marques 2012). Leaders who have compassion and tend to be caring are confirmed to promote organizational resilience (Lilius et al. 2011). The social exchange theory is well fitted where people are giving and trust each other (Grant 2012), and the leaders have the capabilities to foster the well-being of teams and followers (Cameron et al. 2003; Sinclair 2007; Csikszentmihalyi 2003). Kernis (2003), another scholar who has contributed to the body of work around authentic leadership, has shown that those that have greater insight into themselves and strong self-confidence are more likely to know and work to improve their weaknesses. Dweck (2006) has shown that leaders who allow themselves and others to make mistakes are more likely to have high self-esteem as they have learned from experience. It seems that humility seems to be the key in authentic leadership.

Nevertheless, it has been noted that in the business environment, it is often the "takers" who grab resources and opportunities for themselves and are at times unethical in their work even though they are deemed "successful" (Holt and Marques 2012). Leadership studies are analyzing a complex concept and are restricted in the sense of reliability and transferability (Sinclair 2007; Korzynski 2014; Blom and Alvesson 2014). There seems to be a gap in the literature on the interplay between the environment and situations in which followers operate. Thus, the following case presented in the next sections contributes to the evidential inventory of authentic leadership and the limited body of qualitative studies aiming to develop a deeper understanding of this phenomenon while taking both leaders and followers into account.

13.3   Jón Gnarr: The Personality Traits of an Authentic Leader

Up to the point of his high-scale leadership appointment, the life of Jón Gnarr (born 2 January 1967 in Reykjavik, his full name is Jón Gunnar Kristinsson) did not include a traditional leadership path, even though there is likely no single road to take toward any leadership role. In his autobiographical books, Jón Gnarr describes his complicated childhood, even referring to himself as "a case" when he was growing up, especially when his education and experience with learning difficulties were discussed. As a youth, his self-image was poor, and self-confidence was very low. It was only through his hard work and willingness to overcome his weaknesses and challenges that eventually enabled him to develop a strong persona. He believes that eventually his life experience had been applied in all of his endeavors. Those who have worked with him are aware that he was diagnosed with attention deficit hyperactivity disorder (ADHD) and that he "needed to be cared for and that is what his supportive wife Joga still does today." Jón Gnarr said that he was not afraid to reveal his weaknesses and to be vulnerable, stating, "I borrowed others' judgments when some assignments came to my table that I did not understand, no matter how I tried to focus," he recalls.

People need to know themselves well to understand their limitations and have the self-confidence to reveal them to others and thus become heavily exposed. This specific type of behavior, including openness about individual weaknesses and allowing one self to be vulnerable, is highly pronounced in the interviews with both Jón Gnarr and his followers. The theory of authentic leadership involves an assumption that one of the keys of being authentic is to have and employ one's life story for reaching followers (Walumbwa et al. 2008; Kernis 2003; Blom 2016). In line with research by Shamir and Eilam (2005), this life story of a leader eventually was transferred into work, and the "broken" life story of Jón Gnarr enabled him to connect with people, paving the way for his success and that of the Best Party. The critical values that he expressed as a leader with human rights at the forefront and compassion toward marginalized groups were explicit in his communication style that became the next key to leadership once he was appointed the mayor of Reykjavik, discussed in the next section.

13.4   Jón Gnarr and the Best Party: Appointment of a Leader

Jón Gnarr was a comedian, an actor, a writer, and a media professional for a long time, who also at one point worked in an advertising agency. Like many of his countrymen, he lost his work in the aftermath of the financial crisis of 2008. In the following year, he together with his wife Jóhanna Jóhannsdóttir most often referred to as Jóga and their friends, mainly artists, founded a party to run for the city council. The campaign of the party—titled the Best Party—was highly unusual from what was seen as conventional behavior within the political arena. For example, the party released a music video, featuring the song "Simply the best" as a satire on traditional political behavior, including promises on an array of issues and, among them, a hint that they would do "anything for losers." One of the party's core underlying messages was that the politics of Iceland were unethical and in great need of "cleaning up."

The party was reaching voters, and based on the polls, it already gained 12.7% by the beginning of April 2010, according to Visir.is (2010), a leading news agency in Iceland, and 24% by the end of the same month, according to Gallup (Ruv.is 2010). The party was successful in conveying its message as on 29 May 2010, the Best Party won the election and earned 6 out of 15 mandates into the council. They joined forces with the socio-democratic Samfylkingin party, thereby establishing the majority. Eventually, Jón Gnarr was appointed the mayor of Reykjavik, a position that he was not expecting in the beginning. "Why do I always get myself in trouble?" he wondered to himself on the night of the victory (Brockes 2014).

The political landscape was highly unusual in the years before Jón Gnarr became the mayor of Reykjavik. The financial crisis and the breakdown of the Icelandic banks in 2008 completely changed the economic and political contexts in the country. It seemed that the banks had collapsed overnight, and many companies, as well as individuals, went bankrupt, while unemployment skyrocketed, and taxes increased (Guðmundsdóttir and Guðjónsson 2013). This shock led to changes in politics, with distrust and anger as part of the political agenda, and chaos, accompanied by riots in Reykjavik. From 2006 to 2010, four individuals had served as mayors for Reykjavik (Reykjavikurborg 2015), with Jón Gnarr undertaking the position during the time that was overshadowed by great turbulence and uncertainty.

In a poll that was published just after a year after Jón Gnarr was elected, it became evident that he was the public leader who people thought had the most charisma (Mbl 2011). This finding is in line with extant research findings, suggesting that authentic leadership behavior is embraced by followers often during chaotic times. Followers often put more faith into leaders who appear to be authentic and have stronger faith that these leaders will produce better solutions (Williams et al. 2012).

To gain a more in-depth understanding of the period of Jón Gnarr's leadership following his appointment and the effect that it had on both the political environment and the city officials, six in-depth interviews were conducted with his co-workers and one with Jón Gnarr himself. Those that were interviewed were both from the political arena and the highest-ranking officials of the city. These interviews were then transcribed and coded using standard qualitative research methods. Three central themes were identified in the analyses of these accounts: firstly, the influence of the unusual circumstances of his life, the impact of his life story, and his political intuition.

13.5   The Manifestation of Authenticity: An Unusual Leader for an Unusual Situation

All of the interviewees emphasized the unusual circumstances that Jón Gnarr faced when he became the mayor, including not only the financial crisis but also the turbulent times in the city and its surrounding environment. The interviewees also recalled that they did not hold high expectations before he came into the office and that the recent changes in leadership before his arrival had made them tired and wary of politics partly because of internal political struggles both within and between the old parties. The officials in the city and the citizens of Reykjavík were becoming dissatisfied with uncertainty, little or no foresight in policy-making, and no strong vision for Reykjavík's future. One interviewee noted that it had been "liberating" to meet a mayor who had no prior connections to the old political party system. A particular degree of stagnation in their working environment was apparent according to the interviewees. When the Best Party came, it "shook things up," and one of the main contributing factors is considered to be its way of communicating to the people.

As the interviewees recalled, the newly appointed colleagues were more "caring" and "warm" and, as one interviewee said, were always "hugging" each other. Many members of the Best Party were artists who had previously attained great success in their former careers but had since experienced problems and had needed to go through the 12 steps of the Alcoholics Anonymous program. One of the pillars of the program is the idea that people should look to build close relationships and be truthful and sincere in their behaviors toward them. The members of the Best Party who joined the Reykjavik council were both more trusting toward each other and others than people were used to. Another emerging factor was that, while their communication transmitted trust, they also focused on people's well-being and would often ask others how they felt about matters of interest to them. While this form of behavior had previously been unheard in the political environment, the party members successfully met one of the tenets of authentic leadership which states that, in order to increase trust between followers and leaders, the leaders need to be aware of how they physically come across toward their followers (Sinclair 2005; Ladkin and Taylor 2010). How leaders come across is partly made up by the body language and how they speak, not only what they say but how they say it.

After a while, when members of the organization became comfortable with a more open style of communication, they started to open themselves up, too. Jón Gnarr himself said that it had taken some time to "break down the barriers of pointless and wrong communication and build up trust." The extreme economic and political context shaped the leader that followers needed, or, in the words of one interviewee, "what Jón Gnarr was doing, was being an outlet for the anger that prevailed in the society, tried to turn it around and build something positive in the system." Thus, what Jón Gnarr firstly achieved as a leader together with the Best Party was a substantial shift in the communication style of the city council—an essential first step as it must build on communication and the Icelandic cultural context for effective leadership and people needed a change.

Interviewees agreed that Jón Gnarr "had some intuition" in the meaning to have a feeling or insight for both people and situations that came in good use in the campaign before the elections. He was adept at leveraging and applying his experience as a stand-up comedian to capture the audience and surprise his opponents. After he became the mayor of Reykjavik, he behaved in a very different manner compared to his predecessors. For example, he tattooed the symbol of Reykjavik on his arm and sometimes dressed in drag in public. With this he got people's attention and broke the mold of stuffy politicians and showed that he was one of the people. His colleagues mentioned that it could be "fun to work with a leader who is inspirational." One of the explanatory factors was that he had the courage to be authentic and, in that way, with time people came to admire that. When he met the highest-ranking officials for the first time, he suggested that they sit in a circle and have an "emotional meeting, where they would only discuss emotions" as one interview described it. Where deemed appropriate he would express his position on critical matters by relating them to popular culture, such as by dressing as a character from the Star Wars or as one of Pussy Riot members, but they were a controversial all women's band, when they were in custody in Russia. He dressed differently and often would come with nail polish applied to meetings or frequently be the odd one out in other settings. He both behaved and thought out-of-the-box, changing the way the city council operated as well as becoming well-known outside the country by gaining international recognition. As one of the interviewees who had been working over 20 years of experience for the city council said: "the atmosphere in the workplace was just turned around." The case of Jón Gnarr shows that he had a feeling for what people wanted and was able to deliver that. This is in accordance with the definition of authentic leadership style as he was able to relate to people in a way that gained their attention and followership in accordance to who he is and what is his values and purpose.

Another prominent factor in Jón Gnarr's leadership was his emphasis on empowerment. Gnarr would rely on his insight to evaluate when to step in and when to pull back, which shows unbiased processing as is stated in the theory of authentic leadership. For example, he was never intimidated to admit in the public eye that he did not know exactly what to do in all situations and that sometimes other officials were more knowledgeable than him when certain topics were discussed. Such an honest approach was new in the Icelandic political context, did not follow the norms, and gained respect for Jón Gnarr and his co-workers. He had the ability to be humble enough to admit that he needed help and thus sought the input of others which is a critical element in authentic leadership. At the same time, his employees became empowered and more committed toward serving Reykjavík and its people, and thus he cultivated a sense of servant leadership in his people. They would use expressions such as "he became my friend," and many mentioned that they were very "fond" of him and that they thought he was a "good man, who listened to them." Thus, the leader showed appreciation and kindness, and in turn, people felt that they mattered in the big picture. One interviewee described him as a "magician" who could charm people to make them "love" him. However, he did not do this alone, but build a quality relationship by involving others as the model of authentic leadership describes essential. His party members were both genuinely loyal to him and the party's values. Thus, it can be argued that Jón Gnarr was a leader, at the time that took a disillusioned city in the midst of turmoil to a new place where people were hopeful. He did it through being authentic and connecting with people on an authentic level. Being authentic can produce tremendous, even magical results. He created a legacy and a new model of leadership that is in alignment with the nation's values.

13.6   Concluding Remarks

It is no question that some of the extreme factors that led to Jón Gnarr being elected as a leader for both the Best Party and as the mayor of Reykjavik were, historically speaking, unique in the Icelandic context. The anger and mistrust that people felt before his becoming mayor were overwhelming, and as such, they were ready to even vote for somebody who they thought was making a joke of the entire political process. However, by stepping up as truly authentic leader who modelled and championed the change and who undertook responsibility for the situation he found himself in, Jón Gnarr made a difference. Though building trusting relationships, he moved and inspired his followers, both within the system and outside the system. As a professional actor and comedian, he was able to become the type of a leader that was required both in terms of physical and emotional presence. His experience as a scriptwriter for television and the theater came in handy, as he was able to tell a story and connect with people's needs and emotions, and in this way, he is a typical authentic leader who employs his life story and experience to reach his followers, as

Avolio and Gardner (2005) have stated in their theory. Gnarr's way of communicating led to the changes in the system that still can be felt to this day. His compassion increased the well-being of his followers and strengthened the commitment toward him and the organization, similarly to the authentic leadership trend observed in other organizations. Indeed, Gnarr's leadership was not flawless, and one of the factors that many claimed that he could be prone to is attention seeking. Thus, the person serving as a leader became more important than his co-workers in the eyes of the people even though people within the system saw that differently. The general public was not always sure if he was authentic or if he was playing a role. These precautions put aside, this case study documents the story of authentic leadership, exercised by Jón Gnarr while he served as the mayor of Reykjavik, and how he did make a transformational difference and changed the leadership landscape.

References

Avolio BJ, Gardner WL (2005) Authentic leadership development: getting to the root of positive forms of leadership. Leadersh Q 16(3):315–338

Avolio BJ, Walumbwa FO, Weber TJ (2009) Leadership: current theories, research, and future directions. Annu Rev Psychol 60:421–449

Bass BM (1985) Leadership and performance beyond expectations. Collier Macmillan, London

Bass BM (1998) Transformational leadership: industrial, military and educational. Lawrence Erlbaum Associates, Mahwah, NJ

Bass BM (1999) Two decades of research and development in transformational leadership. Eur J Work Org Psy 8(1):9–32

Besti flokkurinn fengi fjóra men kjörna (2010) www.ruv.is/frett/besti-flokkurinn-fengi-fjora-kjorna. Accessed 27 Apr 2018

Blom M (2016) Leadership studies—a Scandinavian inspired way forward? Scand J Manag 32 (2):106–111

Blom M, Alvesson M (2014) Leadership on demand: followers as initiators and inhibitors of managerial leadership. Scand J Manag 30(3):344–357

Borgarstjórar í Reykjavik frá upphafi (2015) http://eldri.reykjavik.is/desktopdefault.aspx/tabid-2784/4398_view-852/

Brockes E (2014) The joker: Jón Gnarr, the comedian who became mayor. The Guardian

Bryman A (2004) Qualitative research on leadership: a critical but appreciative review. Leadersh Q 15(6):729–769

Burns JM (1978) Leadership. Harper and Row, New York

Cameron KS, Dutton JE, Quinn RE (2003) Positive organizational scholarship: foundations of a new discipline. Berrett-Koehler, San Francisco

Csikszentmihalyi M (2003) Good business. Leadership, flow and the making of meaning. Holder and Stoughton, London

Danielsson J, Zoega G (2009) The collapse of a country. Institute of Economic Studies, Reykjavik

Diddams M, Chang GC (2012) Only human: exploring the nature of weakness in authentic leadership. Leadersh Q 23(3):593–603

Dweck CS (2006) Mindset: the new psychology of success. Ballantine books, New York

Fredrickson BL (2001) The role of positive emotions in positive psychology: the broaden-and-build theory of positive emotions. Am Psychol 56(3):218

Grant AM (2012) Leading with meaning: beneficiary contact, prosocial impact, and the performance effects of transformational leadership. Acad Manag J 55(2):458–476

Guðjónsson GI, Gunnarsdóttir S (2014) Þjónandi forysta og starfsánægja í Háskóla Íslands. Icel Rev Polit Adm 10(2):499–521

Guðmundsdóttir ÁE (2011) Af hverju er sjálfsþekking nauðsynleg til að ná árangri sem leiðtogi? Viðskiptastofnun

Guðmundsdóttir ÁE, Guðjónsson J (2013) Skapandi sveigjanleiki. Retrieved from https://skemman.is/bitstream/1946/16764/1/AreliaJon_VID.pdf

Gunnarsdóttir S (2011) Þjónandi forysta. Glíman 8:245–262

Holt S, Marques J (2012) Empathy in leadership: appropriate or misplaced? An empirical study on a topic that is asking for attention. J Bus Ethics 105(1):95–105

Ilies R, Morgeson FP, Nahrgang JD (2005) Authentic leadership and eudaemonic well-being: understanding leader–follower outcomes. Leadersh Q 16(3):373–394

Jónsdóttir BG, Gunnarsdóttir S, Ólafsdóttir ÓÁ (2011) Childbirth and foreign women in Iceland: organization of services, cultural competence and servant leadership. Stjórnmál og Stjórnsýsla 7 (2):369

Kernis MH (2003) Toward a conceptualization of optimal self-esteem. Psychol Inq 14(1):1–26

Korzynski P (2014) Overcoming leadership limitations: a theoretical study of leadership behaviors and methods. Manag Bus Adm Cent Eur 22(4):26–38

Kotter JP (1985) Power and influence. Free Press, New York

Ladkin D, Taylor SS (2010) Enacting the 'true self': towards a theory of embodied authentic leadership. Leadersh Q 21(1):64–74

Liden RC, Graen G (1980) Generalizability of the vertical dyad linkage model of leadership. Acad Manag J 23(3):451–465

Lilius JM, Worline MC, Dutton JE, Kanov JM, Maitlis S (2011) Understanding compassion capability. Human Relat 64(7):873–899

Mahsud R, Yukl G, Prussia G (2010) Leader empathy, ethical leadership, and relations-oriented behaviors as antecedents of leader-member exchange quality. J Manag Psychol 25(6):561–577

Marques J (2013) Understanding the strength of gentleness: soft-skilled leadership on the rise. J Bus Ethics 116(1):163–171

Maslow A (1954) Motivation and personality. Harper and Row, New York

Meindl JR (1995) The romance of leadership as a follower-centric theory: a social constructionist approach. Leadersh Q 6(3):329–341

Michie S, Gooty J (2005) Values, emotions, and authenticity: will the real leader please stand up? Leadersh Q 16(3):441–457

Pavlovich K, Krahnke K (2012) Empathy, connectedness and organisation. J Bus Ethics 105 (1):131–137

Quinn RE, Spreitzer GM, Brown MV (2000) Changing others through changing ourselves: the transformation of human systems. J Manag Inq 9(2):147–164

Rogers CR (1957) The necessary and sufficient conditions of therapeutic personality change. J Consult Psychol 21(2):95

Shamir B, Eilam G (2005) "What's your story?" A life-stories approach to authentic leadership development. Leadersh Q 16(3):395–417

Sinclair A (2005) Body possibilities in leadership. Leadership 1(4):387–406

Sinclair A (2007) Leadership for the Disillusioned. Melb Rev 3(1):65

Steingrímur álitin ákveðinn of Jón Gnarr heiðarlegur (2011) http://www.mbl.is/frettir/innlent/2011/03/10/steingrimur_alitinn_akvedinn_og_jon_gnarr_heidarleg/

Visir.is (2010) Besti flokkurinn bætir gríðarlega við sig í fylgi. http://www.visir.is/g/201049204270. Accessed 29 Apr 2018

Walter F, Cole MS, van der Vegt GS, Rubin RS, Bommer WH (2012) Emotion recognition and emergent leadership: unraveling mediating mechanisms and boundary conditions. Leadersh Q 23(5):977–991

Walumbwa FO, Avolio BJ, Gardner WL, Wernsing TS, Peterson SJ (2008) Authentic leadership: development and validation of a theory-based measure. J Manag 34(1):89–126

Williams EA, Pillai R, Deptula B, Lowe KB (2012) The effects of crisis, cynicism about change, and value congruence on perceptions of authentic leadership and attributed charisma in the 2008 presidential election. Leadersh Q 23(3):324–341

Chapter 14
Navigating Leadership in the Fishing Industry: The Case of Iceland

Ill it is to abandon honor and integrity in exchange for injustice and greed.
Bandamanna Saga, c. 10

Abstract Agust Einarsson, one of the pioneers in the research on Icelandic fishing industry, contends that Icelanders are a small nation that stands among the world's largest fishermen. At a time when international scholars' and practitioners' attention is focused on identifying optimal practices related to the management of fisheries, Iceland serves as a model for excellent performance in this industry. In a country where traditional fishing and processing have declined over the decades, the value has doubled, despite that fishing as an industry in Iceland really only began in the nineteenth century. In light of the broader discourse that emphasizes leadership in fisheries management as one of the keys, yet largely unexplored concepts in the industry, this chapter offers two contributory points. Firstly, it presents a conceptual framework of leadership components in the fishing industry, and secondly, it illustrates a unique interplay of components in the case of Iceland.

Keywords Fisheries management · Fishing industry · Leadership · Iceland

14.1 The Bigger Picture

As Branch et al. (2006) point out, "a fishery consists of two essential elements, populations of fish in their ecosystems and humans capturing the fish" (p. 1647). While the populations of fish are unquestionably, continuously, and substantially decreasing (FAO 2004), the more questionable factor in this equation is the human. Thus, the notion of economic development in the fishing industry is subjected to the shift toward "the ability of the community to initiate action for the sustainable management of natural resources in light of overfishing and resource depletion" (Bodin and Crona 2008, p. 2). At the same time, the behavior of the fishing fleets

© Springer International Publishing AG, part of Springer Nature 2018
I. Minelgaite et al., *Demystifying Leadership in Iceland*, Contributions to
Management Science, https://doi.org/10.1007/978-3-319-96044-9_14

emerges as an equally important topic along with fish population dynamics and has proliferated over the last several decades (Branch et al. 2006). Taken, however, that the fleet dynamics and performance can become a derivative of leadership, the old saying "the fish rots from the head" is, perhaps, most directly applicable in the fishing industry.

In a marine industry landscape, where a third of fish stocks is overharvested or depleted globally (FAO 2004), and which is often characterized by a downfall, the goals that are set for the fisheries concern achieving the optimal equilibrium between the healthy fish stocks and sustainable fisheries in relation to their economic and societal role in providing a valued food source and jobs (Pew Oceans Commission 2003). As leaders of fisheries strategize as to how to best contend with the complex challenges that their industry faces, they might consider the power of having multiple people and perspectives involved. Such an approach of participatory management is not a new idea and actually one that has been recently called for by many (Jentoft 1989; Pinkerton 2003; Berkes 2007; Al Mamun and Brook 2015). In support of these approaches, more recently, Gutiérrez et al. (2011) argue that community-based co-management, which relies on cooperation among fishers, managers, and scientists, arises as the single best realistic solution to address global fishery problems and attain sustainability. Yet, more nuanced aspects and goals related to fishery performance often remain in direct opposition to each other, such as the trade-off between employment and economic efficiency or between the preservation of more critical species (maximization of harvest) and economic profit (Branch et al. 2006).

Fisheries (or fishery) management primarily concerns the management of people involved in a wide array of functions and roles in fisheries, including managers, harvesters, processors, scientists, and other various actors in the structures established by governance systems (Branch et al. 2006). Over time, more and more fisheries will fall under the class of mature (FAO 2004; Branch et al. 2006). When fisheries mature, their management tends to be more intrusive, and stock assessments become critical along with limited entry, eventually leading to large fleets that are too large, decreasing populations of fish, and senescent fisheries (Branch et al. 2006). According to Branch et al. (2006), in these cases fisheries management often entails fleet reduction and rationalization. As such, it is essential to understand the behavior of fishing fleets in order to attain reasonable long-term biological and economic management. While careful "biological and economic management are crucial for the successful development of fisheries" (Branch et al. 2006), leadership manifests as one of its key, albeit, much unexplored and undefined, industry components. As effective leadership has consistently proven to be a critical resource in addressing challenges across the myriad of other business sectors, it would behoove scholars and practitioners alike to more carefully examine leadership in the context of fisheries management today.

14.2   Leadership as a Basis for Fisheries Management

In their large-scale, global study of 130 co-managed fisheries, Gutiérrez et al. (2011) have demonstrated that strong leadership is the key attribute of successful co-management, followed by strong social cohesion between the stakeholders, individual or community quotas, and community-based protected areas as the most critical conditions. Currently, however, there is a lack of empirical findings on the leadership significance and leadership development process with regard to co-management in fisheries (Al Mamun and Brook 2015). As such, there is a sharp need for "long-term ecological, economic and social data from a variety of fisheries in a multidisciplinary context in order to compare empirically different degrees of users' involvement in management decisions and to better understand and improve fisheries co-management" (Gutiérrez et al. 2011, p. 388).

While the relationships among the social capital, leadership, and sustainable outcomes have been documented in the study by Gutiérrez et al. (2011), further studies are required to more deeply understand the subtler relationships among these constructs (Crona et al. 2017). For example, active and engaged leadership can be the means for activation of social capital as a latent asset toward positive outcomes or "common good" (Crona et al. 2017, p. 71). Building on the work by Bodin and Crona (2008), authors such as Krishna (2002), and Crona et al. (2017) apply the framework for distilling and examining the interrelationships among social capital, leadership, and outcomes in the fishing industry. Just like social capital in natural resource governance (including fisheries management), which may need to be addressed differently from social capital required for civic engagement (Crona et al. 2017), leadership in fisheries management similarly calls for a focused revisiting while regarding leadership as a contextual phenomenon. As Branch et al. (2006) note, culture and hierarchy do matter.

The extended theoretical framework of social capital, leadership, and outcomes by Crona et al. (2017) is grounded in the previous works by Krishna (2002) and Bodin and Crona (2008) and identifies three fundamental concepts, namely:

1. Outcomes, which refer to economically important fish species, territorial use rights for fishing (TURF), program management satisfaction, and TURF internal collaboration
2. Social capital, which refers to network closure, sanctioning, and compliance
3. Leadership, which refers to the key individuals in decision-making roles and their characteristics and the legitimacy of their leadership

The framework highlights the interrelationship between social capital and leadership that relates to outcomes. Crona et al. (2017) refer to leadership engagement as the "active engagement of the leader in resource management" and to leadership legitimacy as the "high correspondence between decision-making power and ecological knowledge, as measured by high in-degree in the ecological knowledge network" (p. 74). Here, leadership legitimacy is considered as fairness, correctness, or rightfulness of power relations (Beetham 1991) and more specifically considers through the lens of perceived knowledge and capabilities of influential actors "the degree to which decision-making power and perceived ecological knowledge of the resource to be managed coincide among actors involved in the management of TURFs" (Crona et al. 2017, p. 72).

Upon empirical analysis, Crona et al. (2017) have found only two variables to be associated with TURF performance, namely, the presence of engaged leadership and the agreement among members around the sanctions. In this study, leadership engagement was based on long-term interactions, including participation in meetings, complying with reports, and informing co-management stakeholders regarding fishing operations (Crona et al. 2017).

Building on the works by Bodin and Crona (2008), Krishna (2002), and Crona et al. (2017), it is evident that active and engaged leadership in turn activates and reinforces the social capital and interacts with its particular aspects. In sum, the need is recognized to build an understanding of leadership and its interplay with other constructs, and with social capital in particular, as a basis for sustainable social-ecological outcomes.

While Crona et al. (2017) have included formal leadership in their study (TURF area presidents in six syndicates in Central Chile were identified as the leaders), the relevance of a focus on different types and forms of leadership, for example, distributed leadership, in other settings, has been acknowledged.

14.3 Toward a Framework of Leadership in the Fishing Industry

Leadership in the fisheries management and the fishing industry overall is a complex, multilayer phenomenon that requires careful analysis to fully understand the involved dynamics. Given the multitude of involved actors and their roles, and components of effective co-management, a framework that would disentangle the leadership in the fishing industry is firstly necessary.

With regard to co-management in fisheries, strong leadership calls for the involvement of prominent community leaders who are not only highly motivated but also possess entrepreneurial skills, have the respect of the local community and demonstrate commitment to its collective interest, and, when required, are committed to the co-management implementation process (Gutiérrez et al. 2011). While co-management assumes cooperation among different partners, including harvesters, managers, and scientists, having too large proportion of non-fishing actors in leadership positions can have a negative influence on the effectiveness of co-management programs (Al Mamun and Brook 2015).

In this section, we attempt to achieve the first step and propose a framework for analyzing the leadership in this context. The structure of leadership studies in organizational settings can traditionally be grouped into at least three central strands: leadership emergence and behavior, leadership performance and effectiveness, and leadership development. The academic and practical discourse related to fisheries management continuously points at the significance of leadership development, in line with organizations across a multitude of industries and contexts, driven by the need to adapt their strategies, structures, and practices in order to be able to be resilient and responsive to the dynamic environments they face (DeRue and Myers 2014). When referring to leadership development, researchers traditionally distinguish between two forms: individual capacity and collective capacities to engage in the leadership process (Day 2000). The underlying idea of leadership development is the capacity enhancement of an individual in order to attain higher leadership performance and the collective capacity and interpersonal dynamics enhancement in order to develop social capital (Day 2000). Thus, before the research can move on to the topic of leadership development in the fishing industry, leadership emergence and leadership performance have to be first addressed as the building blocks. Only after questions such as who emerges as a leader, what potential and individual capabilities and characteristics are required, and what is considered to be effective leadership performance are answered, can we consider how leadership could and should be developed. Therefore, our framework of leadership components in the fishing industry will be organized and nested within leadership emergence and performance. Particularly with its emphasis on co-management, leadership in the fisheries is a multifactor and multi-actor phenomenon. In our following discussion, we will highlight one of the essential actor groups—the first-line professionals who are directly involved in the fishing industry processes, such as harvesting and processing.

14.4 The Conceptual Framework of Leadership in the Fishing Industry (GEAR)

In our effort to conceptualize leadership, we consider leadership as primarily a social interaction process where multiple individuals engage in the reciprocal exchange of behaviors as leaders and followers and how these interactions lead toward the accomplishment of a collective goal (Derue et al. 2011; Yukl and Mahsud 2010; Bass and Bass 2009). Stemming from this concept as a basis, we conceptualize the leadership in the fishing industry specifically through the interplay of four essential proposed components; these elements are summarized in the acronym GEAR (Fig. 14.1). This term is coined in an allusion to leadership as a crucial prerequisite of effective fisheries management, just as the proper fishing gear is an essential element of productive fishing. Each of these four components is marked by a duality of sorts, in that each must balance competing demands. This poses additional challenges for effective leadership in the fishing industry, which will be discussed in more details later. The specific configuration of these components and their interplay in different industrial and national contexts along with resulting leadership practices can eventually point to success or failure cases in the fisheries management

Fig. 14.1 The conceptual framework of the dynamic interplay of leadership components in the fishing industry (GEAR)

and allow comparison and development of the most effective leadership models. In order to illustrate our framework in action, we will further introduce the context of Iceland's fishing industry that includes fisheries and offers a context that is rich in the manifestation of some prominent components.

14.4.1   Goals

The GEAR component "Goals" is key to the leadership process, as ultimately, effective leadership requires that some goal is met. To many, the primary purpose of fisheries management is to maximize wealth and profit of the businesses in the fishing industry. However, unbridled pursuit of financial outcomes can lead to negative consequences for the broader society or the tragedy of commons (Hardin 1968). The reality that the natural tendency for some people to act in ways that maximize only their own well-being calls for certain controls to be put in place (Branch et al. 2006). As Ludwig (1993) rather straightforwardly puts it, human greed is frequently an underlying cause of overexploitation and collapse of fisheries. Hence a primary principle of fisheries management is to implement governance systems in incentives to eliminate the race for fish in turn and to control and restrict the greed in favor of sustainable, socially desired outcomes via appropriate governance system (Branch et al. 2006). Since leaders act as key actors and influencers in ensuring such governance and can even serve as role models and inspirational figures for the success of the industry and even Iceland's economy, they should be among the first actors in the fisheries management process to embrace these higher goals.

Yet, however, the definition of leadership performance is subject to duality, just as the goals set for the fisheries management. For example, the dedicated access privilege systems both provide harvesters with a degree of flexibility in choosing the fishing methods and promote economic efficiency, reduce overcapitalization, and increase the quality of products and profitability (Branch et al. 2006). However, definition of the balance or equilibrium between these diverging goals remains a challenging task for researchers and practitioners alike. As Branch et al. (2006) point out, there are only several formal, albeit necessary, discussions that would incorporate the goals. For example, what does the concept of social welfare entail in particular—is it the number of jobs created or the economic efficiency? Alternatively, in light of social welfare, should the economic efficiency with regard to harvest focus on the profit from commercially important species or instead on the economically less important species and thus maximize the harvest? Leadership performance can only be evaluated with regard to the goals set, and thus, leadership goals stand at the forefront of the whole leadership process. Hence, leadership goals are highly context dependent and will remain associated with definition or ambiguity of the goals in the whole fishing industry.

14.4.2   Engagement

Engagement has been marked as an essential component of leadership in the fisheries management (e.g., Crona et al. 2017). Previous studies confirm that engaged and active leadership is required in order to secure the leadership functions and deliverables outlined in the previous sections (Gutiérrez et al. 2011; Bodin and Crona 2008; Newman and Dale 2005). The fisheries practice often calls the leaders for different forms of engagement with an emphasis, for example, on resource management (Crona et al. 2017) or active presence and "engaged" representation of the followers and stakeholder groups and vulnerable member groups, such as women in particular countries (Al Mamun and Brook 2015).

14.4.3   Accountability

Given that the fisheries management is driven by the aims of sustainability for the industry and accountability of all stakeholders (FAO 2015), Accountability arises as a twofold, critical component of leadership. On the one hand, it covers sustainable leadership practices toward the immediate followers, communities, and societies, including sustainable economy, job creation, and employment preservation. On the other hand, it entails accountability for the practice in light of ecologically sustainable practices, including regulated catch or integrity and transparency in cooperation with partner institutions and professionals (e.g., researchers and governing system representative), communities, and societies.

14.4.4   Roles

The component labeled "Roles" considers two aspects of leadership: the emergence of leaders and the roles that are ascribed and enacted by the leaders in the fishing industry. Both of these aspects are closely related to the idea by Katz and Kahn (1978) that social systems rely on roles which are expected and enacted in accordance with norms that prescribe specific behavior and the underlying values behind these norms. In the studies that to some degree capture leadership in the fishing industry, leaders often emerge as the most influential individuals in the broader community, yet as Bodin and Crona (2008) denote, leadership encompasses more attributes than just influence. Still, in this vein, the key individuals are prominent with regard to their structural position in the social network of the community, as illustrated even by the case studies in more rural Kenyan communities (Bodin and Crona 2008). At the same time, existing literature suggests that the emergence of a leader in the fishing industry can to a considerable extent depend on the individual characteristics vis-à-vis societal norms and attitudes. Gender is one of the most prominent examples. In the seafood industry worldwide, women represent 47% of the working population that earns income from fishing and processing fish; the number reaches up to 70% in the aquaculture (FAO 2015). At the same time, only a fraction of these women hold top management or leadership positions (WWF UK Briefings 2012). Particularly in developing countries, women's typical role as the primary family caregiver limits their opportunities to attain higher fishing performance due to time constraints (arising from the primary duty of caregiving and looking after the family). They also face significant financial constraints (limited resources to invest in more advanced fishing equipment, partly related with unbalanced economic remuneration for the work). Finally, societal constraints (limited access aboard larger fishing boats related to fishing primarily perceived as a male activity) add up, though women must simultaneously enact the role of the earner and food provider for the whole family (WWF 2012). Furthermore, women often do have influence over financial matters or activities of the fishery and are not permitted to managerial positions with decision-making power (WWF 2012). At times, however, they have to engage in a rivalry with men over the scarce resources, when male migrants move into the same fishing territories (WWF UK Briefings 2012). According to FAO (2015), partial and local observations indicate that women's participation in the high management positions is low or very rare across all key positions that are attributed to strong leadership and in turn, sustainable fisheries management (Gutiérrez et al. 2011), such as industrial fishing (high capital intensive), industrial aquaculture (high capital intensive), professional organizations, fisheries management, and leadership level.

With regard to role enactment, leadership functions include organizing and representing the social groups on a larger scale, exercising resilience to changes in governance, contributing to conflict resolution in quota allocations, influencing the users' compliance with the regulations, and playing an inspiring role in supporting fisheries co-management (Gutiérrez et al. 2011; Al Mamun and Brook 2015; Olsson et al. 2004). This leadership mission is closely related with another essential condition identified by Gutiérrez et al. (2011)—namely, community cohesion, embeddedness in norms, trust, communication, and connectedness in networks and groups that altogether relate to robust social capital. Although the capabilities and characteristics of critical individuals may influence the outcomes of collective action, the relevance of certain individual characteristics is still likely to depend on a particular context (Crona et al. 2017; Bodin and Crona 2008; Krishna 2002). In relation to context, for example, in developing countries, factors such as social positioning, gender, or education may play an often negative influence on leadership processes and in turn, the co-management success, as illustrated in the study conducted in Bangladesh by Al Mamun and Brook (2015).

In sum, the interplay of specific leadership components can result in leadership practices that are associated with varying degrees of effectiveness and sustainability in leadership management.

14.5 The Framework in Action: The Case of Iceland

Despite Iceland's geographic location and the long fishing traditions by its neighbors, Iceland discovered fishing industry only in the nineteenth century. According to Agust Einarsson, the establishment of fishing as an industry was a turning point for the Icelandic society. While the fishing industry is still a prominent industry today, it has been joined by other activities such as extended production (particularly in pharmaceutics), machine production, fishing gear, and marketing and together with related sectors contributes to more than 20% of GDP and becomes the most critical industry in Iceland.

All four components identified in the GEAR framework are tightly knit in Iceland's fishing industry. This case unfolds as a story of the fishing industry management that took place over several decades and stemmed from the search for economically, socially, and biologically sustainable performance but was disrupted by asymmetric power allocation related to ambiguity around the concept of engagement and, eventually, balanced out by significant accountability and role equality.

The performance of the fishing industry in Iceland, although not characterized by outstandingly high productivity, is well-balanced in comparison to other countries (Einarsson 2011). Even in the face of the crisis of 2008 that had heavy ramifications for Iceland, the situation in the fisheries as part of commodity export sector was comparatively better. Higher employment rates were kept for some time in comparison to other sectors; however, a series of disagreements had also arisen (Benediktsson and Karlsdóttir 2011). In line with the global search for sustainable fisheries management and resource rationalization, the quota management system was introduced in Iceland in 1984 and was followed by the individual transferable quota system (ITQ) establishment in 1990 (Mathiasson 2003). As a result, vessel owners with 3-year previous activity in fishing obtained the quotas, the quota transfers became limited or restricted, and the resource pool that was common for decades became privatized (Benediktsson and Karlsdóttir 2011). Finally, nearly 300 mergers took place in 2003–2007 eventually resulting in about a half of the individual transferable quotas controlled by ten largest quota holders (Benediktsson and Karlsdóttir 2011; Jónsdóttir and Knútsson 2009). In 2007, the United Nations Human Rights Committee delivered a ruling indicating that Icelandic fisheries management system was in violation of basic principles of human rights (Einarsson 2011). While there is an array of underlying reasons leading to this outcome, we would like to highlight one potentially underestimated point behind it—the cultural aspect. In Iceland, low catches have been perceived as humiliating (Branch et al. 2006). This observation can certainly be firstly attributed to the willingness to maximize individuals' gains, or "greed," emphasized by Ludwig (1993) and Branch et al. (2006). However, the findings by Thorlindsson (1988) show that leadership attributes by different captains that could account for 35–49% of the variation in performance can suggest otherwise. The scope of the harvest can be associated with economic and social performance as a derivative of leadership performance and, more specifically, performance of a particular leader. Therefore, the quotas can be perceived as a limitation on leadership performance, and while these measures cannot be avoided, alternative ways of coping with this situation can occur, such as maximizing the power of the company through mergers and acquisitions.

The concentration of power among a number of companies resulted in complicated links between locality and resource and negative effects on coastal communities (Benediktsson and Karlsdóttir 2011). Drawing from a case of a fishing community in a village, Skaptadottir (2000) contended that the inhabitants of the village could not take advantage of the new system, taken over by fewer and larger companies and faced process of increased marginalization. The situation thus reflected the insights by Branch et al. (2006) that the allocation of fishing privileges can result in a specific class of individuals holding control over the access in fisheries. Fortunately, the development of the Iceland's case further also echoes the belief by Branch et al. (2006) that when designed carefully, dedicated access privilege systems can secure proper incentives for the harvesters and offset the balance resource stewardship, economic efficiency, and social welfare.

In response to the heated debate concerning the social justice concerns that reached the public level, and strengthened by the ruling of United Nations Human Rights Committee on the current system's violation of basic principles of human rights, the Accountability component of leadership eventually was activated, and the regulation of the fisheries management system was revisited. The coastal small-scale fishery was reintroduced in 2009, supporting the small-scale actors in the fishing industry who soon expressed their appreciation toward this regulation (Vestfjarda Haskolasetur 2010).

In searching for the rationale that did specifically drive the decisions on the allocation of rights that were eventually questioned on a country level, the Engagement component of leadership manifests itself as an important aspect. The privileged rights for fishing were allocated to the fishermen that, at that time, had been engaged in the industry for 3 years. However, when considering genuinely engaging leaders, a more complex approach involving more characteristics is necessary, such as strong links with the community. Here, Iceland again offers an interesting setting, related to the fourth leadership component presented in the framework—the Roles.

In the context of leader emergence and gender diversity and equality as an instance, Iceland serves as an exemplary case that the cultural perceptions can be shifted even for very traditional, often stereotype driven professions, such as in the fishing industry. Although examples of the fishing industry occupation as exclusively male can still be traced in the middle of the twentieth century (e.g., Kristgeirsson 1947), today, women, engaged in the fishing industry in Iceland, are in a different position than in the developing countries. When looking at employment, it appears that companies in fishing and processing have a higher proportion of women in permanent employment and also more women in full-time employment than others (Gallup and RHA 2017). The study by Gallup and RHA (2017) among senior executives in the fishing industry revealed that in general, women are perceived as equal to men on a number of items, including proficiency (53% disagreed that men are more proficient, while 5% agreed) and knowledge (42% disagreed that women are less knowledgeable than men, especially those with university education, although 20% agreed), supported by the belief that gender equality is emphasized (held by 69% of respondents). When asked if there should be more women in the fisheries industry and whether they should be more influential, the majority (70%) agreed. It is also believed that women and men are given the same opportunities within the organization (73%) and some organizations (according to 38% of respondents) have registered a gender equality policy. Furthermore, a third of respondents believed that efforts were being made to promote women's knowledge and skills within the fisheries sector. An overarching agreement is that women and men earn comparable pay in their workplace (95%), although this observation is still not without ambiguity when considered in the light of Skaptadottir's study (1996). In this study, a female respondent from a freezing plant noted that equal pay and conditions can be observed among the male and female workers employed in positions requiring less education, however, while women often play a critical role in undertaking functions that require cutting and packing fish. This is supported by respondents considering that men and women hold different types of jobs (61%), with only a small proportion of women holding the positions of senior executives and only 14% women holding the majority ownership rights of the company or serving on the company's board. Moreover, these particular instances of female power most often occurred in family-owned and small companies (Gallup and RHA 2017). Migration has also played a role as it relates to the GEAR framework. Iceland experienced an influx in female migrant workers in 1990s, when Icelandic women were leaving the fishing industry as greater education and employment opportunities opened up (Juliusdottir et al. 2013). Even in spite of the crisis of 2008, women's work in the fishing industries was less affected by the crisis in comparison to, for example, construction-related works, where male guest workers were primarily employed (Juliusdottir et al. 2013).

The interplay between leadership engagement and roles in the context of Iceland yields a proposition of equality promotion and social inclusion as an answer for sustainable leadership. Interestingly, the first migration wave in Iceland, which occurred in 1990s, took place when Icelandic women left their less-skilled jobs in pursuit of higher education and employment opportunities (Juliusdottir et al. 2013). As noted, today most Icelandic women holding executive leadership positions and major ownership rights in the fishing industry are often found in small and family-owned companies. At the same time, in line with role theory and role expectations toward genders, women can be more expected to pursue leadership than men. Thus, partly due to role expectations and the business goals with lesser burden to achieve high catches, female leaders can represent a yet underexplored group to be studied as a likely contributor to effective co-management practices and balance between economic, social, and biological goals. This is also supported by the findings in a study Skaptadottir (2000) from a fishing community in an Icelandic village: when confronting the challenges associated with marginalization, men respond on an individual level, while the mechanisms adopted by women rely on community and cooperation, At the same time, leaders would benefit from adopting a more co-management type of style that fosters quality relationships.

However, the duality with regard to roles is also present. Both in developing countries and in Iceland, women are facing the duality of roles as family caregivers (Gilligan 1982) and earners. The differentiating point, however, is that while women in developing countries are often externally limited in their development as earners, the women in Iceland, given access to positions in leadership, may have to enact their leadership roles at the cost of their traditional roles as caretakers. As one of the first exploratory attempts to study the fishing industry in Iceland, in the domain of management (Óladóttir and Pétursdóttir 2018), it illustrates women who act as board members for Icelandic seafood companies are in general content with their positions within the profession, even though the seafood industry is considered to be a very male-oriented environment. Yet, in order to effectively perform their roles which traditionally are designated to men, women may require to adopt masculine behavior models in a professional context. While holding dual roles as earners and caretakers, women will still need to achieve role congruity with regard to both roles. Failure to do so can result in role conflict with an additional set of negative outcomes, which further illuminates the topic as requiring more detailed investigation.

14.6   Concluding Remarks

As suggested by Branch et al. (2006), case studies of fisheries management successes and failures in international contexts, in particular the ones that explore the incentives of the management system and responses by individuals and fishing fleets, are highlighted as essential. The purpose of our proposed framework is to facilitate the structured discourse and analysis of leadership specifically in the fishing industry sector. The presented framework is therefore grounded in the significant findings specific to the fishing industry and the theoretical basis and empirical findings in the broader organizational leadership literature. Application of this framework in different cultural contexts and countries could increase our understanding how different configurations of leadership components and practices are related with success and failure in the fisheries management, thereby providing the basis for the identification of efficient models and giving direction for leadership development. As this framework remains to be among the first to address the leadership in the fishing industry, taking into account the fisheries management, further development and crystallization of the underlying components are anticipated in the future studies. Hopefully, the framework can serve as a preliminary tool of a systematic approach for both researchers and practitioners—actors involved in the process of leadership, including fisheries managers, scientists, harvesters, processors, policy-makers, and other stakeholders.

References

Al Mamun A, Brook RK (2015) Evaluating local rules and practices for avoiding tragedies in small-scale fisheries of oxbow lakes, Southern Bangladesh. Int J Commons 9(2):772–807

Bass BM, Bass R (2009) The Bass handbook of leadership: theory, research, and managerial applications. Simon and Schuster, New York

Beetham D (1991) The legitimation of power. Macmillan, Basingstoke

Benediktsson K, Karlsdóttir A (2011) Iceland: crisis and regional development–thanks for all the fish? European Urban and Regional Studies 18(2):228–235

Berkes F (2007) Community-based conservation in a globalized world. Proc Natl Acad Sci 104 (39):15188–15193

Bodin Ö, Crona BI (2008) Management of natural resources at the community level: exploring the role of social capital and leadership in a rural fishing community. World Dev 36(12):2763–2779

Branch TA, Hilborn R, Haynie AC, Fay G, Flynn L, Griffiths J, Marshall K, Randall J, Scheuerell J, Ward E, Young M (2006) Fleet dynamics and fishermen behavior: lessons for fisheries managers. Can J Fish Aquat Sci 63(7):1647–1668

Crona B, Gelcich S, Bodin Ö (2017) The importance of interplay between leadership and social capital in shaping outcomes of rights-based fisheries governance. World Dev 91:70–83

Day DV (2000) Leadership development: a review in context. Leadersh Q 11(4):581–613

DeRue DS, Myers CG (2014) Leadership development: a review and agenda for future research. In: Day DV (ed) Oxford handbook of leadership and organizations. Oxford University Press, New York, NY, pp 832–855

Derue DS, Nahrgang JD, Wellman N, Humphrey SE (2011) Trait and behavioral theories of leadership: an integration and meta-analytic test of their relative validity. Pers Psychol 64 (1):7–52

Einarsson N (2011) Culture, conflict and crises in the Icelandic fisheries: an anthropological study of people, policy and marine resources in the North Atlantic Arctic. Acta Universitatis Upsaliensis, Uppsala

FAO (2004) Fisheries and aquaculture statistics 2004

FAO (2015) Fisheries and aquaculture statistics 2015

Gallup, RHA (2017) Staða kvenna í sjávarútvegi frá sjónarhorni fyrirtækja og stofnana

Gilligan C (1982) In a different voice. Harvard University Press, Cambridge, MA

Gutiérrez NL, Hilborn R, Defeo O (2011) Leadership, social capital and incentives promote successful fisheries. Nature 470(7334):386

Hardin G (1968) The tragedy of the commons. Science (162):1243–1248

Jentoft S (1989) Fisheries co-management: delegating government responsibility to fishermen's organizations. Mar Policy 13(2):137–154

Jónsdóttir FB, Knútsson Ö (2009) Samrunar á Íslandi 2003–2007. In: Hannibalsson I (ed) Rannsóknir í félagsvísindum X – Hagfræðideild og viðskiptafræðideild. Reykjavík, Félagsvísindastofnun Háskóla Íslands, pp 127–140

Júlíusdóttir M, Skaptadóttir UD, Karlsdóttir A (2013) Gendered migration in turbulent times in Iceland Norsk Geografisk Tidsskrift-Norwegian. J Geogr 67(5):266–275

Katz D, Kahn RL (1978) The social psychology of organizations, vol 2. Wiley, New York

Krishna A (2002) Active social capital: tracing the roots of development and democracy. Columbia University Press, New York

Kristgeirsson J (1947) Hvar á sjóðbaðsstaður Reykjavíkur að vera? Menntamál 20(3):62–67

Ludwig D (1993) Environmental sustainability: magic, science, and religion in natural resource management. Ecol Appl 3(4):555–558

Matthíasson T (2003) Closing the open sea: development of fishery management in four Icelandic fisheries. Nat Res Forum 1:1–18

Newman L, Dale A (2005) Network structure, diversity, and proactive resilience building: a response to Tompkins and Adger. Ecol Soc 10(1):r2

Óladóttir ÁD, Pétursdóttir G (2018) Sjávarútvegur, karllæg atvinnugrein: „þeir hefðu ekki gúdderað einhverja stelpugálu – nema að því að ég hafði tengsl" (Forthcoming)

Olsson P, Folke C, Hahn T (2004) Social-ecological transformation for ecosystem management: the development of adaptive co-management of a wetland landscape in southern Sweden. Ecol Soc 9(4):2

Pew Oceans Commission (2003) America's living oceans: charting a course for sea change

Pinkerton E (2003) Toward specificity in complexity. In: The fisheries co-management experience. Springer, Deordrecht, pp 61–77

Skaptadóttir UD (1996) Gender construction and diversity in Icelandic fishing communities. Anthropologica 38:271–287

Skaptadóttir UD (2000) Women coping with change in an Icelandic fishing community: a case study. Women's Stud Int Forum 23(3):311–321

Thorlindsson T (1988) The skipper effect in the Icelandic herring fishery. Hum Organ 47 (3):199–212

Vestfjarða Háskólasetur (2010) Háskólasetur Vestfjarða 2005–2010 University Centre of the Westfjords

WWF (2012) WWF UK Briefings

Yukl G, Mahsud R (2010) Why flexible and adaptive leadership is essential. Consult Psychol J Pract Res 62(2):81

Chapter 15
Sports Leadership and the Biggest Small Nation in the World

It is all about love, when these boys get together, they feel at home.
Þorgrímur Þráinsson

Abstract In August 2008, Iceland's male handball team stood on the podium at the Olympic Games in Beijing, having just been awarded their silver medals. The team's journey toward this tremendous accomplishment was closely and passionately followed by all Icelanders regardless of age, gender, or station in life. The broadcast of the games was a sacred time for the nation's people, who excitedly but nervously watched "their boys" progress to the finals in the name of the whole nation. This journey was a crusade to the top of Olympus uplifting the identity for Icelanders and empowered them to be truly the "biggest small nation" in the world, a title that was created by the First Lady at the time. However, what later really moved the sports world was not the otherwise obvious leadership and life lesson that "small can be great." It was the return of the heroes back home, who were welcomed by thousands of people in the streets anxiously waiting to greet them. The atmosphere felt like a genuine celebratory carnival (Kjarninn.is 2015).

Keywords Sports leadership · Team leadership · Iceland

15.1 The Bigger Picture

Eight years later, on 28 June 2016, Iceland beat England 2–1 in the pre-quarter finals of the largest sporting competition in the world, the European Men's Football Championship. Icelanders had qualified for the UEFA European Championship finals in 2015 and reached the quarter-finals stage (Halldorsson 2017). Again, almost the entire nation of people was watching the game on television, and 8% of the population physically traveled to France to cheer their team (Halldorsson 2017). Upon their return home on 4 July 2016, there was a carnival in the streets all over

© Springer International Publishing AG, part of Springer Nature 2018
I. Minelgaite et al., *Demystifying Leadership in Iceland*, Contributions to Management Science, https://doi.org/10.1007/978-3-319-96044-9_15

again, and the team was driven through the center of town, while thousands of loyal fans wildly cheered them. The peak of this national celebration was when the crowd and the team started singing together, creating a lasting memory no Icelander will forget. Even though it was late in the evening, the midnight sun in June cast its light on the team and thousands of people who lived their moment of victory together with the team (Ruv.is 2016).

What broad these teams to this moment was a different kind of leadership that created a willingness to excel. Arguably, however, the unique moment of this leadership success story is not the victory itself, but its antecedents and outcomes are further discussed in this chapter. The chapter starts with an introduction to Iceland's development in recent sports history. Next, leadership theories are introduced and then results of a focus group discussion that took place among leading figures in Icelandic team sports. The nation's success in team sports is not only an example of inspirational leadership with great leaders/coaches but on public policy that took the initiative to bring sports to every child that wants to develop its skills with professional coaches and an opportunity to practice, for example, football, in 1 of the 111 fields that are all around the country.

In between these major sports events in the life of a nation, there were big moments in the history of the sports of the country. The women's football team qualified for the European Championship finals in 2008, just weeks after the handball team won their silver. The Icelandic national women's handball team also qualified for the European Championship and the men's basketball team later as well. Continuing this trend of success, in 2010 and 2013, the women's gymnastics team won the European Championship. In sum, Icelandic national teams have managed to qualify 44 times for major international tournaments, and almost half of these occasions have been in the period since 2008 (Halldorsson 2017). As these achievements have been impressive, they also represent more than just significant victories for a small nation. More importantly, they portray a trend of the Icelandic national teams succeeding at the international level in all country's major team sports—football, handball, basketball, and team gymnastics. A legitimate question, then, is what elements contributed to these accomplishments. Like with any other organization that is working to achieve a goal, sports teams, and governing bodies, must rely on leadership as a means to achieve it. Whether leadership is exhibited by certain individuals in formal or informal roles who influence other members, or through a collective, shared team leadership, some form of leadership is at play. Thus, this trend points to a case study of specific leadership development which can be learned from in a broader perspective.

This chapter will explore the contextually unique leadership development practices in Icelanders as they apply to sports and how they enable the rise and flourishing of athletes or "Vikings" as they are often labeled in the sporting world. As a means to explain this phenomenon, the chapter builds on both extant literature and the commentary of experts. A focus group was conducted to gain insights and perspectives from participants who have reached the highest ranks of sports leadership in Iceland: the main coach of the Icelandic men's football team, the coach for the women's gymnastics team, the former captain of the men's handball team, and the coach who has served on the national basketball men's team. They had shared themes of leadership being a part of a cultural context where success is made possible by hard work and a willingness of the members of the team to sacrifice themselves on behalf of the team. Many leaders within the team make that possible, but to inspire such a culture, the leadership within the country's sports world has gained enormously by becoming more strategic in the last decade.

15.2 Teams and Leadership

Research on a vast range of teams begun in the 1930s as the human relations movement started to investigate cooperation in the workplace (McGrath et al. 2000). The human relations movement began to investigate the socio-emotional elements and their impact on organizations, and this had not been considered in early organizations theories. As research into teams and their function progressed, sports teams and military teams were initially the teams most often analyzed. However, as companies such as Ford, General Motors, Toyota, Volvo, and Saab began using teams in order to increase their performance, more research on functions in teams was initiated (Sundstrom et al. 2000; Zaccaro et al. 2001). Sports teams have benefited from these research.

Research into successful teams has identified some common factors such as clear vision, support, access to the right resources, decisive leadership, and a general success mentality within the team. Cooperation and the way members and leaders handle disagreements can make or break a team as such. Even though communication, aligning people around a goal, collaboration, resource sharing and providing feedback are all of the importance as well. Research has indicated that a spirit of hard work and a culture of learning within the team are an underlying theme with successful teams (Zaccaro et al. 2001; Hackman 2002; Larson and LaFasto 1989; Day et al. 2004; Maack 2011). Thus, leaders of the team that provide the structure and strategy are of profound importance in the team's development.

Thus, the list of successful team characteristics indicates that in all fields, be it business or sports, the leader is the one who sets the tempo, chooses and mobilizes members, and assumes the responsibility for the creating synergy in the team. According to Zaccaro et al. (2001), the essence of leadership within teams is to ensure that every member of the team understands what needs to be accomplished and how they fit into that picture. Successful team leaders motivate team members with challenging goals and work ethic and help them to cope with the associated pressures of the work. The leader organizes the work by taking into account the specific skill set of every member and then assigning roles based on the best match between these skills and tasks. As the team begins to work toward its objectives, the leader provides regular feedback, both to individual team members and the team as a collective whole, and assists in helping them adapt to changes in the internal and external environments. In sports this is essential.

However, one of the leader's main responsibilities is ensuring that members feel secure as well as keeping the morale up and providing encouragement. The underlying rationale for the importance of members feeling secure is that, in order to learn, they must feel emotionally secure in order to take risks and engage in new activities. According to Edmondson (1999), a leader who demonstrates these capabilities is both accessible and open to the team's opinions and actively listens to what the team members have to say. An essential component of this process is the leader's ability to acknowledge his own shortcomings and learn from their mistakes like authentic leaders are able to do as has been demonstrated elsewhere in this book. Building an esprit de corps and cultivating an environment of comraderies are essential and are achieved by the leader investing time with their team to foster quality relationships that lead to cooperation and collaboration.

Thus, the primary mission of a leader of a team is not to make the team work together but to properly facilitate how the team members can best work together collectively. Teams rise and fall by the way their members communicate with each other, which is something that the members often feel even though it cannot be seen (Rousseau et al. 2006). Thus it is crucial for leaders to address these socio-emotional aspects of their work.

The leader is also responsible for bringing out positive emotions that enable people to perform at their best (Fredrickson and Losada 2005). When a leader increases members' self-efficacy, members become more optimistic about their ability to reach their goal, more creative, and more helpful. In sum, the climate, i.e., how people feel about belonging to the working environment, can account for a significant part of their performance. Thus, how members of the group perceive the working climate can be traced back directly to the actions of their leader. This is evident in the case of Icelandic sports team.

When leadership is inspirational, followers become positive and enthusiastic and resonate with the leaders. Resonance amplifies the emotional impact of leadership. When leadership is dissonant, people have a sense of being continually out of sync. According to Goleman (2000), dissonant leaders lack empathy and tend to transmit emotional tones that resound most often in a negative register. A dissonant leader is described as the "abusive tyrant, who bawls out and humiliates people, to the manipulative sociopath" (p. 2). Some dissonant leaders are subtler. They use a surface charm or social polish to mislead and manipulate their followers. Gifted leadership involves a combination of many factors. In many situations, especially during stress or emergency, the emotional centers command the rest of the brain, but stressful situations are a part of sports. Goleman (2000), who was a pioneer and leading contributor to the research on emotional intelligence, identifies four components of the construct. The first component is *self-awareness*, which refers to having a deep understanding of one's strengths, limitations, values, and motives. People with high self-awareness are honest with themselves and about themselves. They have realistic insights into themselves, which is a product of frequent and thoughtful self-control. Such individuals usually think about things deeply and do not react impulsively. The second component is *self-management*, which includes such attributes as emotional self-control, transparency, adaptability, achievement, initiative, and optimism. Self-management is needed to appropriately control personal feelings and emotions, facilitate mental clarity, and provide focus. The third component encompasses *social awareness*, which includes empathy, organizational awareness, and ability to serve the needs of the teams. By being attuned to how others feel, a leader can say and do what is appropriate, to calm fears and control anger. Empathy includes easy approachability, ability to listen, and responding suitably. Finally, the fourth component is *relationship management*, which can be observed in influencing, developing others, change management, conflict management, building bonds, and teamwork. Handling relationships is about moving members of a team or organization toward future goals. For sports, coach self-awareness might be demonstrated to be being nervous before a match but knowing that he or she has to maintain composure. Self-management could be demonstrated by resisting the temptation to yell at a judge. Social awareness might be demonstrated by cheering the team and calming their fears before a game. Relationship management which focuses on proactively taking steps to create and preserve quality relationships is demonstrated by having the ability to calm waters and handle disagreements before they get out of hand.

Successful leaders who possess emotional intelligence leverage these skills by adapting their leadership styles to fit the needs of the situation at hand, which is crucial in sports (Goleman et al. 2002). These leaders understand that effective leadership is a function of their ability to assess their surroundings. The necessity identifies the best behavioral options to contend with it and then successfully engage in those appropriate leadership behaviors to match.

According to (Goleman et al. 2002), the more of these styles a leader can deploy, the better. Leaders who have mastered to be adaptable tend to be the most effective. Effective leaders scan the environment and people, individually and as a group, and adjust their style suitably. To be able to switch between leadership styles and focus on others, leaders that are humble seem to get better results (Collins 2001). Viðar Halldórsson's (2017) research on the culture of Icelandic sports teams concludes that "all athletes need a tradition, which consists of values, motivation, social support and knowledge and a window of opportunity. A successful athlete needs a community that prepares him for the world of sports" (p. 17). This result is in line to Goleman's and others' remark within the business, i.e., that leaders need to adapt to their team member and adjust their leadership style based on the team's values and culture; this is the same in the world of sports.

15.3   The Case of Iceland: "You Do Not Need Miracles, Just Hard Work"

Headlines of the international sports press in 2016 heralded the Icelandic football team's success. In Goal Euro, a premier football magazine, Joshua Kloke exclaimed: "HOW DID A NATION OF 330.000 PEOPLE QUALIFY FOR THE EURO 2016

KNOCKOUT STAGES? THE SECRET BEHIND THE ICELAND MIRACLE"
(Kloke 2016). Another article was published in The Guardian: "A football moment
to remember. Iceland lights up Euro 2016." CNN Sports asked: "Euro 2016: how
tiny Iceland reached Europe's pinnacle?" (CNN 2016).

The international sports community, commentators, sponsors, and those interested in the field became fascinated as to how it was possible that such a small nation
achieved such a huge success. However, the Icelandic men's football team, as has
been said before, was just one example of Iceland's national teams that had gained
international recognition in the decade before this moment. The men's handball team
had on several occasions come close to winning a medal at major championships,
but it took 50 years until it won the silver at the Olympic Games in 2008
(Halldorsson 2017). They continued their success in Austria in 2010 and won the
bronze. The rise of the men's football team has been swift. In 2010 they were 133rd
in the FIFA ranking but by 2016 had risen to 21st and by 2017 to 18th. The women's
football team has also been recognized as a national force, as demonstrated by its
rank of 20th in the world (FIFA 2017). Moreover, it has been argued that Iceland is
one of the top eight European football nations (Halldorsson 2017).

Before 2008, however, aside from the men's handball team, Icelandic national
teams were generally unorganized and lacked discipline. Despite some occasional
impressive results and progress, they were marked by low self-confidence among
players and an unprofessional overall culture relative to those of elite global teams.
When analyzing how the culture of the national teams changed, several factors
explain the success of the last decade; one of the crucial factors could be the change
in leadership toward more professional or strategic coaching in accordance with
theories on effective teamwork and effective leadership. As Heimir Hallgrímsson,
the main coach of the men's football team, said: "We read the same leadership books
as business leaders do."

This chapter aims to explore how leadership can affect team's results and sports
are a great way of analyzing that as the goals are rather clear or that of winning.
Studying Icelandic sports teams is a great example of that as the country is very
homogeneous in its structure regarding sports.

Looking at other factors, direct leadership contributes to the understanding of this
rising of Icelandic sports teams. It is noteworthy that Icelandic sports is fundamentally based on the ethos of amateur sport. The foundation of the Icelandic sports
system is built on national sentiments, associated with the time when the first sports
clubs were established as a movement for independence from Denmark at the turn of
the twentieth century. Sports clubs are community-based, and participation begins
when Icelanders are still quite young: up to 90% of 10-year-olds already belong to a
club (Halldorsson 2017).

Thus, the Icelandic sports system is grounded in the idea that sport is for
everybody regardless of age, gender, or ability. In the focus group, the top coaches
in Iceland agreed that even though coaches spot children that have the potential to be
the best early on, they still are obliged to train everybody well. This is different in
many other European countries as talents that are spotted early on are often taken
apart to be trained with the top athletes. Until the age of 20, all children and teenagers

are able to join a sports club and expect to be trained alongside those that are elite athletes in their age group. The clubs operate on the efforts of parents and volunteers who give their time and energy to the sports community, and often the team members have had to "Work very hard both in training and for the operation of the club, such as looking for ways to finance traveling etc.," as Heimir Hallgrímsson, the main coach of the men's football national team, noted. Even when they reach the top levels of competition, they still have to "chip in. Belonging to a club is more than just a competition; it requires full engagement even in non-sports ways. Team members are personally invested in their teams, not just through competition and training but also by being actively engaged in the actual operation of the club. It requires some sacrifice and deep commitment in comparison to playing for fun.

In 2000, an extended youth research program titled *Youth in Iceland* was conducted and involved a cross-sectional sample of adolescents in Iceland. One of the main conclusions of this research was that adolescents who are active in sports fair better in both academic outcomes as well as manifest greater self-esteem (Kristjánsson et al. 2010). These results have gained attention from a broad audience and eventually have led to Icelandic schools becoming formally linked to the organized sports clubs. The municipalities subsidize club participation fees for children and teenagers. There are 111 football fields around the country (Þráinsson 2018). Everyone has the chance to be coached by appropriately credentialed professional coaches from an early age, and this is different than, for example, in countries where parents are used to training their children when they are young (Þráinsson 2018).

One of the reasons that Icelandic sports steam far well is that professionalism in the sense of how sports people are trained and a new commitment to excel. Ólafur Stéfansson, who is one of the best handball players in Iceland and served as a captain for the national team that won the silver, describes this well: "I had trained and had a passion for the game since I was a small boy and was at the top in Iceland. Then, when I went abroad, I suddenly realized that I was not that good in comparison to others and I thought to myself, 'What have I been doing wrong all this time?'." In terms of technique and tactics, world-class professionalism in Iceland was lacking. This issue was specifically addressed by inviting internationally successful coaches from abroad, and by the 1990s, the best East-European coaches were leading the Icelandic handball team. They brought and quickly instilled a new professional attitude and "dragged the Icelandic amateurs out of their comfort zone" (Halldorsson 2017, p. 45). A similar case was observed with the men's national team when the Swede Lars Lagerback took the team over in 2011. Heimir Hallgrímsson recalls that this approach completely changed the team and the training culture: "If I had started coaching the team without Lars, I would have just continued to coach as I did with my club. The difference is in setting the strategy and installing discipline at a new level." According to Heimir, the main difference was the level of knowledge that Lars brought to the team, stating "One does not need a miracle to make dreams come true; it takes hard work" (Þráinsson 2018, p. 13). Another factor for the heightened sense of professionalism was that many national team members played professionally elsewhere and brought the knowledge and attitude back to their home country (Halldorsson 2017).

Winning the silver medal seems to have had a profound effect on increasing the self-confidence of all the other Icelandic teams. In the focus group, all participants agreed that it had been a watershed moment in the history of Icelandic sports. "We just thought if they can do it, so can we," said Íris Mist, who led and coached the women's gymnastics team in 2010. Somehow, the atmosphere changed in sports in general, and the members of the national teams started believing that they could indeed beat the best in the world. One of the participants said that they went from a "tiny nation's mentality" to be a player in the field. Halldorsson (2017) explains that the "younger brother" psychological barrier was broken leading to a more general and collective belief in the Icelandic athletes and teams.

The core characteristic of Icelandic teams according to the members of the focus group is playing with their "heart and soul." This was entirely harnessed by leadership and by a camaraderie in the teams and the thrill of playing for their nation, with a new type of motivation and dedicating themselves to working together to represent Iceland. This is a new sort of passion; rather than just playing to win, they are playing to represent their country. They are not just playing as friends for a club but as professionals aligned with accomplishing a goal that is built on the national pride. They are fiercely loyal to the team and the cause.

When asked what explained the teams' newly found success and recognition, Þorgrímur Þráinsson, a former football player and later the motivating coach for the Icelandic men's football team player, commented, "It is all about love, when these boys get together, they feel at home." The Icelandic teams have a spirit of fun and giving their best. "You give it all it takes," says Íris Mist. They are used to hard work, and they continue to do it with "love" when they play. Ólafur Stéfansson explained: "You cannot explain what happens when you put on the national attire, it is something bigger than you."

Finally, what helps to explain the recent success of the Icelandic national teams is their general mindset which embraces the spirit of not giving up, building up character, leveraging the strengths of the team members, and presenting themselves professionally. In the context of leadership, this has come about with a new emphasis on both strategies and on building up both the right environment such as football fields and better equipment but different leadership styles of coaches. One of the factors that contribute to this concept is the small population, where people mainly enact more than one occupational role. This means that the common approach is usually reflected in a "we-can-do-it" attitude, followed by actions. "I hope that we do not lose this attitude within the team's spirit," says Heimir Hallgrímsson, as this gives them more flexibility. Pálmi who is a professional coach stresses that "we have gone up a level in the way we approach coaching as nobody can coach, not even very small children without having the formal training." On top of being educated in the field, Icelandic coaches have demonstrated emotional intelligence and are not afraid to express their emotions and read into the emotions of others. They have overall been very flexible in their leadership style, "winning together and losing together" (Þráinsson 2018).

15.4 Concluding Remarks

The case on the sports leadership in Iceland illustrates how communities with strong social identification, closely knit relations, and multilevel talent development can enable the individuals on the whole and how small nations sports team have reinvented themselves built on different leadership. Once again, it confirms how effective individual's leadership, in this case, exercised by coaches, precedes the blooming potential of talents. Such leadership teases out the cultural uniqueness, harnesses the strengths of the organizational members, and encourages a hard-working adaptive workforce by creating a growth mindset and a desire to excel. In contrast to common conceptions of leadership, these stories highlight how success in the homeland of "Vikings" does not necessarily require the heroic leadership often glorified in the western cultures. Instead, it admires and celebrates leaders who are often characterized as humble and able to foster emotional security and positive emotions in their followers and, at the same time, practice and promote discipline and professionalism among their followers. Icelandic leadership development culture strongly emphasizes the room for multi-talent education within the society, encouraging multiple occupational roles and providing equal talent building conditions for every individual. This particular approach to plural leadership development can further open up a new approach that counterbalances the traditional heroic conceptualizations of leadership. Furthermore, this chapter has given a glimpse into how successful teams need vision, support, access to the right resources, decisive leadership, and a general success mentality in order to succeed as the research on teams had indicated.

References

CNN (2016) Euro 2016 how tiny Iceland reached Europes pinnacle? https://edition.cnn.com/2016/06/06/football/iceland-football-euro-2016-gylfi-sigurdsson-eidur-gudjohnsen-island/index.html. Accessed 29 Apr 2018

Collins J (2001) Level 5 leadership: the triumph of humility and fierce resolve. Harv Bus Rev 79 (1):67–77

Day DV, Gronn P, Salas E (2004) Leadership capacity in teams. Leadersh Q 15(6):857–880

Edmondson A (1999) Psychological safety and learning behavior in work teams. Adm Sci Q 44 (2):350–383

FIFA (2017) Ranking. http://www.fifa.com/fifa-world-ranking/associations/association=isl/men/index.html. Accessed 29 Apr 2018

Fredrickson BL, Losada MF (2005) Positive affect and the complex dynamics of human flourishing. Am Psychol 60(7):678

Goleman D (2000) Leadership that gets results. Harv Bus Rev 78(2):78–90

Goleman D, Boyatzis RE, McKee A (2002) The new leaders: transforming the art of leadership into the science of results. Little, Brown, London

Hackman JR (2002) Leading teams: setting the stage for great performances. Harvard Business School Press, Boston

Halldorsson V (2017) Sport in iceland: how small nations achieve international success. Routledge, New York, NY

Kjarninn.is (2015) Sjö eftirminnilegustu stórmót í sögu Íslenska handboltalandsliðsins. https:// kjarninn.is/greinasafn/sjo-eftirminnilegustu-stormot-islenska-handboltalandslidsins/. Accessed 29 Apr 2018

Kloke J (2016) How did a nation of 330.000 people qualify for the Euro 2016 knockout stages? The secret behind the Iceland miracle. Goal Euro.

Kristjánsson ÁL, Sigfúsdóttir ID, Allegrante JP (2010) Health behavior and academic achievement among adolescents: the relative contribution of dietary habits, physical activity, body mass index, and self-esteem. Health Educ Behav 37(1):51–64

Larson CE, LaFasto FM (1989) Teamwork: what must go right/what can go wrong. Sage, Newbury Park, CA

Maack KÁ (2011) Einkenni framúrskarandi liða. 13 leiðir til árangurs. Háskóli Íslands, Reykjavik

McGrath JE, Arrow H, Berdahl JL (2000) The study of groups: past, present, and future. Personal Soc Psychol Rev 4(1):95–105

Rousseau V, Aubé C, Savoie A (2006) Teamwork behaviors: a review and an integration of frameworks. Small Group Res 37(5):540–570

Ruv.is (2016) Ekið með landsliðið í opinni rútu. http://www.ruv.is/frett/ekid-med-landslidid-i-opinni-rutu. Accessed 29 Apr 2018

Sundstrom E, McIntyre M, Halfhill T, Richards H (2000) Work groups: from the Hawthorne studies to work teams of the 1990s and beyond. Group Dyn Theory Res Pract 4(1):44

Þráinsson Þ (2018) Íslenska Kraftaverið. In: Á bak við tjöldin. Bjartur, Reykjavik

Zaccaro SJ, Rittman AL, Marks MA (2001) Team leadership. Leadersh Q 12(4):451–483

CPSIA information can be obtained
at www.ICGtesting.com
Printed in the USA
LVHW06*1038081018
592718LV00003BB/22/P